AN INTRODUCTION TO ARAMAIC

SOCIETY OF BIBLICAL LITERATURE

Resources for Biblical Study

Edited by
Steven L. McKenzie

Number 46
AN INTRODUCTION TO ARAMAIC
CORRECTED SECOND EDITION
by
Frederick E. Greenspahn

AN INTRODUCTION TO ARAMAIC

CORRECTED SECOND EDITION

by

Frederick E. Greenspahn

Society of Biblical Literature
Atlanta, Georgia

AN INTRODUCTION TO ARAMAIC

CORRECTED SECOND EDITION

by

Frederick E. Greenspahn

Copyright © 1999, 2003, 2007 by the Society of Biblical Literature
First Edition 1999
Second Edition 2003
Corrected Second Edition 2007

Funerary Inscription of Uzziah, Jerusalem, 1st Century B.C.E.–1st Century C.E. is from the Collection, The Israel Museum, Jerusalem. Photo © The Israel Museum. Used with permission.

Dolerite wall relief from Sinjerli (Sam'al) showing King Barrekib on his throne with a scribe. Aramean c. 750 B.C.E. Vorderasiatisches Museum, Staatliche Museen, Berlin, Germany. Used with permission of Foto Marburg/Art Resource, NY.

Library of Congress Cataloging-in-Publication Data

Greenspahn, Frederick E., 1946–
    An introduction to Aramaic / by Frederick E. Greenspahn.—2nd. ed.
        p. cm. — (Resources for biblical study ; no. 46)
    ISBN 978-1-58983-059-2
1. Aramaic language.   2. Bible. O.T.—Language, style.   I. Title.   II. Series.
PJ5211.G74 2003b
492'.29—dc21

                                                        2003001992

11   10   5   4   3

Printed in the United States of America
on acid-free paper

CONTENTS

PREFACE

This book is intended for students who are just beginning to study Aramaic. Seldom is it the language's inherent value which attracts such individuals; more often, they are motivated (if not always directly) by an interest in the Bible, although some may want to explore early Judaism or Christianity as well. This fact has several fairly obvious corollaries for a book such as this. First, it means that those using it already have some familiarity with Hebrew, typically biblical Hebrew. At the same time, however, that knowledge is probably rudimentary, given the stage at which most students are encouraged, or expected, to learn Aramaic. Finally, it suggests that students are likely to proceed to other Aramaic texts or other Semitic languages, whether they realize it yet or not. In other words, although biblical Aramaic is usually introduced as an end in itself, it most often functions as a bridge between the Hebrew Bible and some other, related area.

This text tries to take these facts seriously. Recognizing students' existing knowledge and motivation, it treats Aramaic as if it were a dialect of Hebrew, without trying to cover all of the language's depth and richness. This is a widespread, if seldom acknowledged, approach with a long pedigree. The fourteenth century grammarian Profiat Duran described Aramaic as "the Holy Tongue corrupted" (לשון הקדש שנשתבש).* That, however, is a patently inaccurate and very unfair way to characterize an independent language that has produced several quite separate bodies of literature, each historically and linguistically important in its own right.

Our only justification for this approach is pedagogic utility. Indeed, pedagogic considerations have governed most of the presentation here, which has been kept as non-technical as possible. Thus verb, noun, and pronoun charts include hypothetical forms (unmarked) on the premise that students will find it easier to learn patterns as a whole without trying to distinguish attested from theoretical forms or to remember where direct evidence is lacking. Where several alternative forms exist, only one is presented. The selection of these preferred forms has frequently been difficult, especially in cases of *ketîv* and *qerê*, where the problem of deciding whether it is pre-Christian or masoretic Aramaic that is being taught had to be con-

---

Ma'aseh Efod, ed. J. Friedländer and J. Kohn (Vienna: Haltswarte, 1865) p. 40.

fronted. Our decisions have been somewhat eclectic. Thus the second person masculine singular pronoun is presented as אַנְתְּ, in conformity with the *qerê*, rather than the presumably earlier *ketîv* אַנְתָּה, while proper names have been presented exactly as they occur in the standard *Biblia Hebraica Stuttgartensia*; thus דָּנִיֵּאל, despite the obvious anomaly in the placement of the vowel. In order to ensure the consistency of what students encounter, the biblical text has occasionally been normalized to fit the regular patterns taught in the grammar. Students may, therefore, wish to read the original exactly as it appears in the Bible after finishing this course.

Pedagogical concerns have also affected terminology. Thus the conjugations are identified as G, D, and H in order to facilitate comparison among Semitic languages, which would be complicated by terms such as *peᶜal*, *paᶜᶜel* and *hafᶜel*, which are appropriate for Aramaic alone.

A word about the terms "conjugation" and "tense" is also in order. The nature of the phenomena which these terms designate is enmeshed in difficult technical issues. We have chosen to use terms that are likely to be familiar from the study of other languages, letting instructors choose whether to describe the problems involved or to leave that for some later stage of study. Similarly, the periodization presented in chapter 2 is only one of several that are possible. Since any such scheme is inherently arbitrary and heuristic, a straightforward one that would facilitate clarity was selected.

It should by now be obvious that this is not intended to be a reference work, although paradigms and a glossary are included at the end. There is already an abundance of advanced and technically proficient resources for those who choose to continue beyond the introductory level. This book is meant to help students take advantage of those tools. It has, therefore, been constructed as a kind of workbook, organized around the Aramaic passages from the Bible. These are at first simplified and abridged, in order to keep the quantity of new vocabulary to within manageable proportions. Daniel 7, the last biblical passage in Aramaic, is read exactly as it occurs in the Bible (chapter 27).

Each chapter introduces a grammatical feature. Vocabulary has been coordinated with the biblical passages and divided into two sections: words that are "To Be Learned" and others that are for "Reference" only. This distinction makes it possible to define all the words that appear in the selected biblical readings without requiring students to learn more than about ten at a time. Definitions of "Reference" words are repeated in any chapter in which they recur. Of course, all vocabulary words are listed in the glossary, which is not a complete lexicon of biblical Aramaic, but contains only words actually used in the passages which appear in this book; for that reason, it also includes the handful of Hebrew terms that occur in some of the late texts presented in the readings. Both grammar and vocabulary are reviewed in practice exercises.

While there is much about this presentation of the material that may appear idiosyncratic, I am deeply aware of my debt to many scholars whose knowledge and experience of Aramaic far exceeds my own. Experienced teachers will likely recognize the influence of Ethelyn Simon, Irene Resnikoff, and Linda Motzkin's *The First Hebrew Primer* (3d edition, Oakland, CA: EKS Publishing Co, 1992), Isaac Jerusalmi's *The Aramaic Sections of Ezra and Daniel* (Cincinnati: Hebrew Union College-Jewish Institute of Religion, 1972), and Ehud ben Zvi, Maxine Hancock, and Richard Beinert's *Readings in Biblical Hebrew, An Intermediate Textbook* (New Haven: Yale University Press, 1993), a debt gratefully acknowledged. The grammar draws heavily on Franz Rosenthal's *A Grammar of Biblical Aramaic* (Wiesbaden: Otto Harrasowitz, 1963) and Hans Bauer and Pontus Leander's *Grammatik des Biblisch-Aramäischen* (Halle/Saale: Max Niemayer Verlag, 1927). Rather than supplanting these valuable tools, this book is intended to prepare students to use them easily and profitably. Like training wheels, the surest sign of its success will be when it is no longer necessary. For students to outgrow it will, therefore, be a source of pleasure rather than evidence of its inadequacy. Indeed, after finishing this course, students should be encouraged to acquire other tools, primarily Rosenthal's *Grammar*, which is in English and in print.*

Several individuals contributed to this project in a variety of ways. Marvin Sweeney and David Petersen had the confidence to propose that I undertake it in the first place. Barbara Beckman helped with technical elements of preparing the manuscript, while Jeanne Abrams and Diane Rutter provided a supportive environment. Paul Kobelski and Maurya Horgan shared their skill and creativity to bring that manuscript to final form. Paul Flesher, Peter Miscall, Gary Rendsburg, and Seth Ward reviewed an earlier draft, rooting out errors and proposing improvements, while David Ackerman, Scott Althof, Susan Brayford, Gary Collier, Brandon Fredenberg, Arlene Lance, Joy Lapp, Gilberto Lozano, Aquiles Martinez, Andrew Tooze, and David Valeta shared students' perspectives. Special gratitude belongs to those who have shared their observations about earlier editions, particularly, the errors and problems they found in it. Steven E. Fassberg, Richard Hess, Joseph L. Malone, Scott Noegel, Ken Penner, Max Rogland, Antoon Schoors, Eileen Schuller, and Eibert Tigchelaar, provided

---

*Other grammars which might be helpful are Alger F. Johns, *A Short Grammar of Biblical Aramaic* (Berrien Springs, MI: Andrews University Press, 1972) and Elisha Qimron, ארמית המקראית (2nd ed.; Jerusalem: Mosad Bialik and Ben Gurion University, 2002).

particular assistance in this regard. For all of these contributions I am deeply grateful. Any other corrections or suggestions readers can share with me would be very much appreciated. In the end, the decision of how to use the information they so generously shared was my own along with responsibility for the finished product, which often, but not always, followed their suggestions. I hope it will provide a straightforward introduction to a subject rarely begun in a simple way and a coherent enough presentation to kindle interest in proceeding further.

ABBREVIATIONS

A   alef (א) stem (*ʾafᶜel*)

c   common (number)

cstr   construct

D   D stem (*piᶜel* or *paᶜᶜel*)

f   feminine

G   G stem (*qal, peᶜal*)

H   H stem (*hifᶜil* or *hafᶜel*)

imf   imperfect

imv   imperative

inf   infinitive

inter.   interrogative

intrans   intransitive

lit.   literally

m   masculine

obj.   object

p   plural

pass   passive

pf   perfect

ptc   participle

s   singular

š   šin (ש) stem (*shafᶜel*)

sf   suffix

t   conjugation with prefixed *t* (as in Hebrew *hitpaᶜel*)

trans   transitive

Chapter 1

INTRODUCTION

What is Aramaic and why should you learn it? Although the Aramaic language is not as familiar as French or Hebrew so that its importance may not appear self-evident, it is as old as the Bible. In fact, the language's name first appears in the Bible (Ezra 4:7, Daniel 2:4, 2 Kings 18:26 = Isaiah 36:11); other ancient sources call it Chaldean or Syrian. The language is named after the ancient Arameans, among whom it originated; they lived in what is today Syria at the same time that the Israelites were establishing themselves in Canaan. Their language spread, eventually becoming *the* language of government and international communication throughout the Near East, from about the time of the Babylonians, who destroyed the Jerusalem temple in the sixth century B.C.E., and continued to be widely used even after the coming of the Greeks until the Arab conquest in the seventh century, long after the Arameans themselves had disappeared.

Strangely, the best known writings in Aramaic were produced by other peoples. According to Jewish tradition it was spoken by Adam (*b. Sanhedrin* 38b), and was probably the native language of Jesus, of numerous talmudic rabbis, and of the third century religious innovator Mani, the founder of what we call Manicheanism. Moreover, a formidable body of literature, including many formative texts of both Judaism and Christianity, were written in or influenced by Aramaic. Aramaic was also used by the Nabateans, an Arab desert people who flourished around the time of Jesus, the later Syrian church, and the Mandeans, a gnostic sect that originated close to two thousand years ago in what is today southern Iraq. It continues to be used as a spoken language to the present day, albeit only in small pockets of Syria, Iraq, and Iran, as well as among Jews and Christians who have migrated to Israel and the United States from these regions.

Today few people study Aramaic because they are interested in the Arameans. Most are motivated by the fact that parts of the Bible are written in Aramaic, specifically major sections of the books of Ezra (4:6–6:18 and 7:12–26) and Daniel (2:4–7:28), as well as one sentence in Jeremiah (10:11) and two words in Genesis (31:47). In order to read the entire "Hebrew" Bible in the original, then, one must know Aramaic.

With only some 200 verses of the Bible in Aramaic, there would be little reason to learn the dialect for that reason alone. However, mastering this limited body of material can open the door to a wide range of possibilities.

1

Because Aramaic was a dominant language among the Jews of first century Palestine, a wealth of important texts are written in it. Although Jesus' teachings survive only in the Greek New Testament, the Gospels provide ample evidence of Aramaic traditions surrounding him, and the language's influence can be felt in several other passages as well. Being familiar with Aramaic can, therefore, deepen your appreciation of the New Testament. Extensive bodies of both Jewish and Christian literature are also written in Aramaic. Among these are several of the Dead Sea Scrolls, many rabbinic texts, including parts of both talmuds and various midrashim, a substantial number of ancient Jewish Bible translations, called targumim, masoretic notes to the biblical text, and legal and mystical works from as late as the eighteenth century. Within Christian tradition, important writings from the Syrian church, including the Peshitta translation of the Bible, are written in a dialect of Aramaic known as Syriac. In order to provide a taste of the riches which await those who have mastered Aramaic, a small selection from some of these has been included in the final chapters of this book.

Learning Aramaic can also be a first step into the Semitic family of languages as a whole, for those who choose to explore some of its other members. Familiarity with these languages can illuminate elements of biblical Hebrew by providing greater perspective than is possible from knowledge of Hebrew alone, much as we can see things better with two eyes than is possible with only one. For example, it can sensitize us to what might otherwise seem ordinary and unremarkable features of Hebrew, ranging from its system of "tenses" to the existence of internal passives and the changing function of the participle. Indeed, because they belong to the same Northwest branch of the Semitic language family, Aramaic can be a relatively easy second language to learn and a particularly useful way to achieve a deeper understanding of Hebrew itself, offering insights into the nuances of individual Hebrew words and alerting us to differing styles within the Bible. It will, for example, make us aware of "Aramaisms" not only in late passages, such as the books of Esther or Chronicles where one would expect them, but also in earlier parts of the Bible, such as the song of Deborah (Judges 5). These characteristics have even led some scholars to speculate that certain books of the Bible were originally written in Aramaic and only later translated into Hebrew. The knowledge you are about to gain will, therefore, open the door to an entirely new world, one which is interesting and rewarding in its own right.

Because most people who undertake the study of Aramaic are motivated by their interest in the Bible, we will presume that you already have a working knowledge of biblical Hebrew. Since Hebrew and Aramaic share many words, this is a substantial advantage, because it means that you already have an extensive Aramaic vocabulary and understand a variety of Aramaic grammatical principles without even knowing it. For example, many of the following Aramaic words are, undoubtedly, already familiar:

fall	נפל	consider	חשׁב	father	אַב
lift up	נשׂא	seal	חתם	stone	אֶבֶן
give	נתן	dew	טל	brother	אָח
end	סוֹף	hand	יָד	after	אַחֲרֵי
until	עַד	know	ידע	eat	אכל
still	עוֹד	day	יוֹם	these	אֵלֶּה
bird	עוֹף	be able	יכל	say	אמר
eye	עַיִן	sea	יַם	four	אַרְבַּע
on	עַל	add	יסף	in	בְּ־
Most High	עֶלְיוֹן	like, as	כְּ־	between	בֵּין
with	עִם	all	כֹּל	house	בַּיִת
people	עַם	thus	כֵּן	build	בנה
answer	ענה	write	כתב	bless	ברך
open	פתח	to	לְ־	reveal	גלה
rise	קוּם	heart	לֵב (לְבָב)	bear	דֹּב
buy	קנה	wear	לבשׁ	judgment	דִּין
call	קרא	scroll	מְגִלָּה	resemble	דמה
draw near	קרב	what	מָה	he	הוּא
battle	קְרָב	be full	מלא	be	הוה
horn	קֶרֶן	word	מִלָּה	she	הִיא
wind	רוּחַ	king	מֶלֶךְ	go	הלך
height	רוֹם	queen	מַלְכָּה	and	וְ־
ask	שׁאל	from	מִן	time	זְמַן
praise	שׁבח	count	מנה	see	חזה
dwell	שׁכן	(D—appoint)		live	חיה
send	שׁלח	meal offering	מִנְחָה	strength	חַיִל
hear	שׁמע	bed	מִשְׁכָּב	wisdom	חָכְמָה
be low	שׁפל	prophesy	נבא	be gracious	חנן
drink	שׁתה	prophecy	נְבוּאָה	magician	חַרְטֹם

You are also already familiar with the outline of Aramaic grammar, whether you have studied it or not. For example, Aramaic verbs are built on 3-letter roots, which can be conjugated in several different patterns, including one in which the middle letter is marked with a *dagesh* (doubled), just like Hebrew's *pi*ᶜ*el*, and another characterized by a prefixed ה, like the *hif*ᶜ*il*.

We will, therefore, take advantage of your Hebrew background, rather than trying to introduce everything you would need to learn if you were studying Aramaic from scratch. Aramaic phenomena will often be explained in terms of their Hebrew counterparts. We will not, for example, describe the alphabet, since biblical Aramaic is written with the same script and follows several of the same principles (e.g., the use of *dagesh lene* in the letters בג"ד כפ"ת) as biblical Hebrew.

However useful it may be to treat Aramaic as a dialect of Hebrew, we need to remember that it is really a separate language. This approach can, therefore, create problems. Chief among these is the fact that the vowels, on which so much of biblical grammar centers, were added by the Masoretes over a thousand years after the biblical books had themselves been written. We should, therefore, at least wonder how reliable a guide they are to ancient Aramaic usage. Of course, that is a problem for the study of biblical Hebrew as well; indeed, since the Masoretes wrote their own notes in Aramaic, they may have been more familiar with Aramaic grammar than with Hebrew and, therefore, imposed some of its principles onto the Hebrew sections of the Bible.

Because of our presumption that your reason for learning Aramaic is based in the Bible, its Aramaic passages will be used as the focus of our study, with sample readings included in each chapter. These have been edited in order to progress from relatively simple to more complex usage, until the last chapter of biblical Aramaic (Daniel 7) will be read exactly as it appears in the Bible. Because our focus will be on grammar and vocabulary, you should turn to the standard commentaries for historical and exegetical questions. The most useful ones on Ezra are those by Loring Batten (International Critical Commentary), Jacob Myers (Anchor Bible), and H. G. M. Williamson (Word Biblical Commentary); and for Daniel, those of James Montgomery (International Critical Commentary), John Collins (Hermeneia), and Louis Hartman and Alexander DiLella (Anchor Bible). Since only part of Ezra and Daniel are in Aramaic,* it would be helpful to read the preceding (Hebrew) sections (Ezra 1:1–4:7), at least in English, before beginning with the Aramaic in chapter 3 of this book.

---

*This strange phenomenon is discussed in many of the standard introductions to the Bible, such as Otto Eissfeldt, *The Old Testament, An Introduction* (New York: Harper and Row, 1965) pp. 516–17, 543, and 551.

Chapter 2

A BRIEF HISTORY OF ARAMAIC

The term "Aram" was used in place names almost four thousand years ago; the book of Genesis mentions places called Paddan-Aram and Aram-Naharaim. However, there are no references to the Aramean people themselves until the eleventh century, when the Assyrian ruler Tiglath Pileser I encountered them on military expeditions along the Euphrates. They had apparently established small, independent kingdoms, primarily in Syria, but extending as far east as the Persian Gulf. One Aramean ruler, named Adad-apla-iddina, even seized the Babylonian throne before coming under attack from other Arameans.

The Bible describes close connections between Israel's patriarchs and Aram, where they "returned" from time to time (Genesis 24:1–10, 28:1–5), usually to find suitable wives. Deuteronomy even refers to the Israelites as being descended from "a wandering Aramean" (26:5) in a passage traditionally linked to Jacob, whose father-in-law Laban is called an Aramean in Genesis 31:20. Although scholars are not certain about the historical reliability of biblical statements about the patriarchs, such passages do demonstrate that the Israelites believed they were related to the Arameans.

During the period of Israel's monarchy, the Aramean kingdoms of Zobah and Damascus jockeyed with Israel for power and preeminence. The Bible reports that David defeated Hadadezer, the ruler of Zobah (2 Samuel 8:3–10), and that Solomon battled with Rezon, who had fled from Zobah and become king in Damascus (1 Kings 11:23–25).

After the Israelite kingdom split near the end of the 10th century, regional control passed back and forth between the now-divided kingdoms of Israel and Judah and the Arameans, depending most often on whether the Israelite kingdoms were united or not. Sometimes they were subordinate to the Aramaeans (1 Kings 15:8–20, 20:34, 2 Kings 10:32, 12:17, 13:7,22); at others, they were dominant (1 Kings 20:34, 2 Kings 13:25). In the ninth century, an alliance linking Damascus and Hamath with the Northern Kingdom as well as nine other countries was able to withstand the powerful Assyrian ruler Shalmaneser III (853 B.C.E.); a decade later, the coalition fell apart and these same nations were defeated (841 B.C.E.).

In the middle of the eighth century, Damascus entered into another alliance with Northern Israel, this time including the Phoenicians of Tyre. They tried to gain Judean support, but the king of Judah turned instead to Assyria, which was more than willing to intervene. As a result, the Aramean states were conquered by Tiglath-Pileser III, who claims to

5

have destroyed "592 towns . . . of the sixteen districts of the country of Damascus."* He put several Aramean kingdoms under direct Assyrian control, including ultimately Damascus itself. The Arameans' political power thus came to an end; however, their language survived, ironically achieving a far wider presence than the people among whom it had originated.

Aramaic is usually divided into several dialects, organized according to chronological and geographic principles. Although several systems have been proposed for doing this, each with its own idiosyncrasies, their general structures are quite similar.

Our earliest evidence of Aramaic comes from the Aramaic kingdoms just described. These are said to be written in "Old" or "Ancient" Aramaic. Among them are several inscriptions from northern Syria (mostly near the town of Aleppo) that were written early in the first millennium B.C.E. (probably between the tenth and the seventh centuries). The language of these texts shares a variety of features with Hebrew, suggesting that the division between the Aramaic and the Canaanite (Hebrew and Phoenician) branches of Northwest Semitic was relatively recent. A sample of an Aramaic text from this period will be read in chapter 28.

The next period of Aramaic is dominated by what is called Official, Imperial, or Standard Literary Aramaic because it served as the official administrative language of the Persian empire from the sixth to the fourth centuries, although it may have begun to spread somewhat earlier, under the Assyrians and Babylonians. This is also the dialect found in the Bible, although some scholars assign the book of Daniel to a later category.

Several ancient sources document the growing prevalence of Aramaic. The Bible reports a request by Judean leaders that the Assyrian army, which was besieging Jerusalem near the end of the eighth century, use Aramaic so that the people would not understand what they were saying (2 Kings 18:26 = Isaiah 36:11), suggesting that the leaders of the time were familiar with it. A century later, when a Philistine ruler sought assistance from the Egyptian Pharaoh, he wrote in Aramaic, demonstrating that the language had already achieved a significant role in international communication.**

After Judah fell to the Babylonian emperor Nebuchadnezzar, the Jews adopted the Aramean form of what had originally been the Phoenician alphabet. (It is important to distinguish between a language and a script; one could, for example, theoretically write English using the Hebrew, Cyrillic or Japanese scripts, or any other alphabet for that matter. Some Aramaic texts were written in Egyptian [demotic] and cuneiform scripts.) Interestingly, derivatives of the older script were still used by Jews from time to time, as in coins produced by the Maccabees and the later rebel leader Bar Kochba as well as some of the Dead Sea Scrolls.

---

*James Pritchard, *Ancient Near Eastern Texts Relating to the Old Testament* (Princeton, NJ: Princeton University Press, 1969) p. 283.

**See Bezalel Porten, "The Identity of King Adon," *Biblical Archaeologist* 44 (1981) 36–52; the role of Aramaic is comparable to that of Akkadian in the fourteenth-century correspondence between Egypt and its Canaanite subordinates from Tell el-Amarna.

The Arab tribe known as the Nabateans also used an alphabet that was based on the older letters, as do the Samaritans to the present day.

When Persia, which defeated Babylonia in 539, adopted Aramaic for official administrative purposes, the language's importance grew dramatically. Eventually, the Persian empire stretched from Egypt to India, ensuring Aramaic's widespread use and prominence. Official sponsorship also created a kind of standardization, something which did not begin to wane until the encroachment of Greek under Alexander the Great and then, many centuries later, Arabic.

Among those who returned from the Babylonian exile, familiarity with Aramaic was no longer limited to the leaders of Judea. In addition to the extensive sections of Daniel and Ezra which are written in Aramaic, its influence can be felt in Hebrew books of the Bible which were composed after the exile. Some scholars have even understood Nehemiah 8:8 to suggest that the Jews of this period needed to have their scriptures translated into Aramaic.

Aramaic continued unchallenged among Jews until the coming of the Greeks. It was particularly prevalent in Palestine during the time of Jesus, a period for which we use the term "Middle" Aramaic. Since the Persian empire, which had been responsible for the language's earlier uniformity, no longer existed, it is not surprising that regional variation begins to be apparent at this time (note the reference to Peter's distinctive accent in Matthew 26:73). These include the dialects attested in the Dead Sea Scrolls (see chapter 30) and the New Testament, as well as that in use among the Arab tribes known as Nabateans. The earliest layers of the targumim to the Pentateuch (Onkelos) and the Prophets (Jonathan) also probably date from this period. Other dialects are known from Palmyra (biblical Tadmor) and Edessa in Syria, and Hatra, which is in Mesopotamia.

The title "Late" Aramaic is used for material written between the second and the ninth (or possibly later) centuries C.E. From Palestine come a wide range of Jewish sources, including the Palestinian Talmud, midrashim, and several targumim (see chapters 31 and 32). Other writings from this region are by Christians (presumably converts from Judaism) and Samaritans. In the east, one finds Babylonian Jewish (for the Babylonian Talmud), Mandaic, and Syriac texts, with the latter divided into eastern and western dialects.

Finally, there is "Modern Aramaic," which is spoken in several villages near Damascus, the largest of which is Ma'lula, as well as among Christians in southeastern Turkey (near Tur ʿAbdin), Mandeans in southern Iran, and Jews and Christians from Iraqi and Iranian Kurdistan, virtually all of whom have now migrated to Israel and the United States.

Thus, the Aramaic language has outlived the people whose name it bears, with a rich and extensive literature created by several different communities. Indeed, the language's very survival is the result of its having been adopted, for various purposes, by several different peoples who created with it a substantial body of documents that have played an important historical role.

Chapter 3

THE ARAMAIC LANGUAGE

Because they are both members of the Northwest branch of the Semitic language family, Aramaic and Hebrew have many words in common, as we saw in Chapter 1. Further evidence of this can be seen by comparing Jesus' words on the cross as presented by the Gospels of Matthew and Mark with the Psalm verse from which they were taken:

ηλι ηλι λεμα σαβαχθανι   (Matthew 27:46)

ελωι ελωι λαμα σαβαχθανι   (Mark 15:34)

אֵלִי אֵלִי לָמָה עֲזַבְתָּנִי   (Psalm 22:1[2])

Although the first three words in these passages are virtually identical,[*] the difference in the last word of the quote demonstrates that the Gospels are not reporting a Hebrew tradition, since there is no Hebrew word which might be represented by σαβαχθανι. Such a word does, however, exist in Aramaic, where שבק means "abandon," just like the Hebrew עזב; indeed, the ancient Aramaic translation (targum) of Psalm 22 uses שבק to translate עזב in this very passage.

The striking similarity between the first three words in both Gospel accounts and their Hebrew equivalent demonstrates how close Hebrew and Aramaic really are. Even the structure of the final verb is essentially the same, once one accounts for their different roots (עזב instead of שבק); that is to say that in each text the verb's root consonants are separated by the vowel *a* and followed by *tha* (the second person masculine singular suffix) and then *ni* (for the first person singular direct object).[**]

The Hebrew Bible contains one Aramaic sentence outside the books of Daniel and Ezra. It is found in Jeremiah 10:11:[***]

---

[*] The transliteration of the New Testament passages is *eli eli lema sabakhthani* (Matthew) and *eloi eloi lama sabakhthani* (Mark).

[**] Vowel differences in the first three words as presented by Matthew and Mark may reflect characteristically Aramaic features — the reduction of originally pretonic short vowels (see chapter 5), hence Hebrew לָמָה = Aramaic לְמָה, and the 3d person masculine singular pronominal suffix ־וֹהִי (see chapter 13).

[***] As one might imagine, the existence of this one Aramaic sentence has raised a host of questions in the minds of biblical scholars, many of whom have theorized that it is a gloss which was introduced into the text by mistake.

כִּדְנָה תֵּאמְרוּן לְהוֹם אֱלָהַיָּא דִּי שְׁמַיָּא וְאַרְקָא לָא עֲבַדוּ
יֵאבַדוּ מֵאַרְעָא וּמִן תְּחוֹת שְׁמַיָּא אֵלֶּה.

A close look at this verse demonstrates many similarities with Hebrew:

כִּדְנָה תֵּאמְרוּן לְהוֹם

דְּנָה — כְּ + דְּנָה is equivalent to Hebrew זֶה.

כְּ — means "like" or "as" in Aramaic, just as it does in Hebrew.

אמר — is a very common verb in biblical Hebrew, where it means "say." The תְּ- pre-fix and ־וּן suffix indicate that the word is imperfect, 2d person, masculine plur-al (plural suffixes often have a final ־ן in Aramaic, as sometimes occurs in bib-lical Hebrew), so that the whole form means "you shall say."

לְהוֹם =Hebrew לָהֶם.

Thus, the phrase כִּדְנָה תֵּאמְרוּן לְהוֹם ("thus shall you say to them") corresponds to the Hebrew כֹּה תֹאמְרוּ לָהֶם.

אֱלָהַיָּא דִּי שְׁמַיָּא וְאַרְקָא לָא עֲבַדוּ

Most of these words are very similar to Hebrew:

$$
\begin{array}{rcl}
\text{אֱלָהַיָּא} & = & \text{אֱלֹהִים} \\
\text{שְׁמַיָּא} & = & \text{שָׁמַיִם} \\
\text{לָא} & = & \text{לֹא}
\end{array}
$$

The root עבד also occurs in Hebrew, although its meaning "serve" is inappropriate here; the meaning is clearly "make" (i.e. עשׂה).

Since דִּי means "which" or "who," this phrase can be recognized as corresponding to the Hebrew: (הָ)אֱלֹהִים אֲשֶׁר לֹא עָשׂוּ (אֶת) הַשָּׁמַיִם וְ . . . .

The context clearly requires that the next word (אַרְקָא) be equivalent to Hebrew הָאָרֶץ.

Notice the Aramaic ending ־ָא on אֱלָהַיָּא, שְׁמַיָּא and אַרְקָא where Hebrew uses a pre-fixed הַ־. Thus the whole phrase means "the gods which did not make the heavens and the earth."

יֵאבַדוּ מֵאַרְעָא וּמִן תְּחוֹת שְׁמַיָּא אֵלֶּה

Every word in this section has an exact Hebrew equivalent, so it is easily translated as:

יֹאבְדוּ מִן הָאָרֶץ וּמִ(ן)תַּחַת הַשָּׁמַיִם (הָ)אֵלֶּה

(shall perish from the earth and from under these heavens)

Notice how this phrase uses אַרְעָא where the earlier part of the verse had אַרְקָא as the equivalent to the Hebrew אֶרֶץ.*

VOCABULARY

You will need the following vocabulary to understand the simplified version of Ezra 4:8-11 that is given below. Before reading that, it would be a good idea to read the preceding sections of Ezra (1:1-4:7) either in the original Hebrew or in English translation.

To Be Learned		*Reference*	
letter	אִגְּרָה	perish	אבד
the letter	אִגַּרְתָּא	these	אֵלֶּה
God	אֱלָהּ (אֱלָהַיָּא)	say	אמר
which, that, of	דִּי	earth	אַרְעָא
this	דְּנָה	earth	אַרְקָא
write	כתב	and	וְ
to	לְ	from	מִן
to them	לְהוֹם	do, make	עבד
king	מֶלֶךְ	heaven	שְׁמַיָּא
the king	מַלְכָּא	under	תְּחוֹת
the scribe	סָפְרָא		
on, to, against, concerning	עַל		
send	שלח		

---

* See page 14 below.

FROM THE BIBLE (Ezra 4:8–11)

רְחוּם וְשִׁמְשַׁי סָפְרָא כְּתַבוּ אִגְּרָה חֲדָה עַל יְרוּשְׁלֶם לְאַרְתַּחְשַׁשְׂתְּא מַלְכָּא.

דְּנָה אִגַּרְתָּא דִּי שְׁלַחוּ עַל אַרְתַּחְשַׁשְׂתְּא מַלְכָּא.

Proper Nouns

> אַרְתַּחְשַׁשְׂתְּא — Artaxerxes, the Persian king (ruled 465–425 B.C.E.), who appointed Nehemiah governor of Jerusalem; either he or Darius' son Artaxerxes II (ruled 404-359 B.C.E.) authorized Ezra's mission to Jerusalem. The Bible also spells the name as אַרְתַּחְשַׁשְׂתְּא and אַרְתַּחְשַׁסְתְּא (e.g., Ezra 4:7 and 7:12).

> יְרוּשְׁלֶם — Jerusalem, where the Judeans who had returned from Babylonian exile had settled. Although the city's name has come to be spelled יְרוּשָׁלַיִם in Hebrew, it appears without a ' in the Bible (see p. 43 below).

> רְחוּם וְשִׁמְשַׁי — Officials in Persia's Trans-Euphrates province.

EXERCISES

The following Aramaic sentences use vocabulary that should be familiar from biblical Hebrew (the vowels may be somewhat different). Read each sentence out loud and translate it into English:

(1) סָפְרָא כְּתַב אִגַּרְתָּא לְהוֹם.

(2) אֱלָהָא עֲבַד שְׁמַיָּא.

(3) אֲמַר מַלְכָּא עַל יְרוּשְׁלֶם. . . .

‫(4) מַלְכָּא שְׁלַח אִגַּרְתָּא לְסָפְרָא.‬

‫(5) אֲמַר אֱלָהָא מִן שְׁמַיָּא . . . .‬

‫(6) אֲבַד סָפְרָא דְּנָה תְּחוֹת אַרְעָא.‬

‫(7) אֱלָהָא אֲמַר דִּי אַרְעָא לְמַלְכָּא.‬

Chapter 4

CONSONANTS

Although some Aramaic dialects, such as Syriac and Nabatean, have their own scripts, the Aramaic sections of the Bible are written with the same alphabet as its Hebrew passages. Therefore, you already know how to read biblical Aramaic. And since Aramaic belongs to the same Northwest group of the Semitic family of languages as does Hebrew, these two languages have a goodly number of words in common, so that your knowledge of Hebrew provides a substantial Aramaic vocabulary as well. However, the number of these words can be easily multiplied.

The consonantal alphabet used for both Hebrew and Aramaic was probably invented by the Phoenicians, but it did not fit either language perfectly, since both originally had more sounds than the number of Phoenician letters. (English has the same problem, since our 26 letter alphabet, which also derives from the Phoenicians, does not have enough symbols to represent all the sounds we use. That is why we have to use pairs of letters, such as *sh* and *th*, for some sounds.) For Hebrew and Aramaic, certain individual letters were used to represent what were originally different sounds; however, the two languages sometimes use different letters for what were originally the same sounds. Words that look different in Hebrew and Aramaic may, therefore, actually be historically related.

An example of this involves the letter שׁ, which Hebrew uses for what were originally two different sounds — *sh* and *th* (as in English "thin"). The first of these quite separate consonants occurs in the word שלח ("send"), while the second was in the Hebrew word ישב ("sit, dwell"). However, Aramaic uses שׁ only for words which originally included *sh*, representing the *th* sound with the letter ת, which it also uses for the sound *t*, as does Hebrew. Thus, שלח and כתב ("write") are found in both languages, whereas Aramaic has יתב for the Hebrew word ישׁב.

13

Semitic	Hebrew	Aramaic	
sh	שָׁלַח שׁ	שְׁלַח שׁ	(send)
th	יָשַׁב שׁ	יְתֵב ת	(dwell)
t	כָּתַב ת	כְּתַב ת	(write)

A similar phenomenon occurs with the letters ד and ז. In Hebrew ז is used both for the sound *z* (as in the word זֶרַע, which means "seed") and for a letter that was once pronounced as *d̲* (like the *th* in "than"), which occurs in the word זֶבַח ("sacrifice"). However, Aramaic uses ז only for the *z* sound, whereas *d̲* is represented with the letter ד, which both languages also use for the sound *d*. Thus, the Hebrew word זֶרַע corresponds to זְרַע in Aramaic, but the Aramaic cognate of the Hebrew word זֶבַח is דְּבַח.

Semitic	Hebrew	Aramaic	
z	זֶרַע ז	זְרַע ז	(seed)
d̲	זֶבַח ז	דְּבַח ד	(sacrifice)
d	ידע ד	ידע ד	(know)

A final example of this phenomenon involves the letter צ, which Hebrew uses for what were originally *three* different sounds: (1) *ṣ*, as in the word צֶלֶם ("image"), (2) *ṭ*, as in קַיִץ ("summer"), and (3) *ḍ*, as in אֶרֶץ ("land"). However, Aramaic represents these with three different consonants — צ, ט, and ע.[*] Therefore, the Hebrew word צֶלֶם is צְלֵם in Aramaic, but קַיִץ occurs as קַיִט, and אֶרֶץ as אֲרַע.

Semitic	Hebrew	Aramaic	
ṣ	צֶלֶם צ	צְלֵם צ	(image)
ṭ	קַיִץ צ	קַיִט ט	(summer)
ḍ	אֶרֶץ צ	אֲרַע ע	(earth, sometimes written אַרְק)

The following chart summarizes these equivalences according to which letter is used in Aramaic. Being familiar with them will make it possible to recognize many Aramaic words that do not look exactly like their Hebrew counterparts.

---

[*] This last consonant is sometimes represented with a ק, as in the form אַרְקָא, which occurs alongside אַרְעָא in Jeremiah 10:11 (see p. 10) and in early inscriptions (see p. 168).

Aramaic	Hebrew	Semitic
ד	ד	*d*
	ז	*ḏ*
ז	ז	*z*
ט	ט	*ṭ*
	צ	*ṯ**
ע	ע	ʿ or *ġ*
ק/ע	צ	*ḍ*
צ	צ	*ṣ*
שׂ	שׂ	*š*
ת	שׁ	*ṯ*
	ת	*t*

Other historical-linguistic processes can help in recognizing more word relationships. For example, many Semitic languages form nouns by adding an initial ("prosthetic") א to a three letter root. Thus the number "four" (אַרְבַּע) has four letters in both Hebrew and Aramaic; however, its root is actually רבע, as can be seen from the ordinal רְבִיעִי ("fourth"). Similarly, the word for "arm" exists in two forms, both in Hebrew (זְרוֹעַ and אֶזְרוֹעַ) and in Aramaic (דְּרָע and אֶדְרָע). This principle accounts for the relationship between the Hebrew word חִדָה and the Aramaic אֲחִידָה, both of which mean "riddle." Conversely, the Aramaic word חַד ("one") corresponds to the Hebrew אֶחָד.

Less certain is the relationship between the word אָע, which means "tree" in biblical Aramaic, and its apparent Hebrew cognate עֵץ. The original root was presumably ʿḍ, which came to be עֵץ in Hebrew and is represented as עק in several fifth century Aramaic documents (see p. 178). It should be עע in biblical Aramaic, but the first ע apparently dissimilated to an א in order to avoid having two identical consonants next to each other.

*This letter is sometimes transliterated as *ḏ* or *ẓ*.

VOCABULARY

To Be Learned		*Reference*	
we	אֲנַחְנָה	there is	אִיתַי
in	בְּ	tax	בְּלוֹ
build	בנה	search	בקר
participle (mp)	בָּנַיִן	*imf 3 ms*	יְבַקַּר
passive imf 3 fs	תִּתְבְּנֵא	if	הֵן
that	דָּךְ	memoranda	דָּכְרָנַיָּא
know	ידע	be	הוה
passive participle	יְדִיעַ	*imf 3 ms*	**לֶהֱוֵא
causal pf (1 p)	הוֹדַעְנָא	portion	חֲלָק
causal ptc (mp)	מְהוֹדְעִין	to you	לָךְ
now	כְּעַן	find	שכח
not	לָא	*causal imf 2 ms*	תְּהַשְׁכַּח
rebellious *(fs)*	מָרָדְתָּא	שלח *perfect 1 p*	שְׁלַחְנָא
give	נתן		
imperfect (3 mp)	*יִנְתְּנוּן		
the city	קִרְיְתָא		

FROM THE BIBLE (Ezra 4:12–16)

יְדִיעַ לֶהֱוֵא לְמַלְכָּא דִּי יְהוּדָיֵא יְרוּשְׁלֶם קִרְיְתָא מָרָדְתָּא בָּנַיִן. כְּעַן יְדִיעַ לֶהֱוֵא
לְמַלְכָּא דִּי הֵן קִרְיְתָא דָךְ תִּתְבְּנֵא בְּלוֹ לָא יִנְתְּנוּן. עַל דְּנָה שְׁלַחְנָא וְהוֹדַעְנָא לְמַלְכָּא
דִּי יְבַקַּר בִּסְפַר דָּכְרָנַיָּא   וּתְהַשְׁכַּח דִּי קִרְיָא דָךְ קִרְיָא מָרָדָא. מְהוֹדְעִין אֲנַחְנָה
לְמַלְכָּא דִּי הֵן קִרְיְתָא דָךְ תִּתְבְּנֵא חֲלָק בַּעֲבַר נַהֲרָא לָא אִיתַי לָךְ:

Note: תָא- is a feminine suffix; thus both קִרְיָא מָרָדָא and קִרְיְתָא מָרָדְתָּא mean "rebellious city."

* Note that the initial נ does not assimilate in this form as it does in the Hebrew equivalent.
** See p. 79.

Proper Nouns

יְהוּדָיֵא‎ — (the) Judeans.

עֲבַר־נַהֲרָא‎ — Trans-Euphrates, one of the Persian Empire's several major provinces (satrapies); it stretched along the Mediterranean coast, west (and south) of the Euphrates River, and included the land of Judah (יְהוּד).

EXERCISES

Write the following Aramaic words next to their Hebrew cognates:

שֵׁת (six)	חֲדַת (new)	אֶדְרָע (arm)
תוּב (return)	יְעַט (advise)	אֲחִידָה (riddle)
תּוֹר (ox)	יְתִב (sit, dwell)	אִיתַי (there is)
תְּלַג (snow)	כִּדְבָה (lie)	אֲרַע (land)
תְּלָת (three)	נְטַר (guard)	דְּבַח (sacrifice)
תְּקֵל (unit of weight)	קַיְט (summer)	דְּהַב (gold)
		דִּכְרָן (memorandum)

_____ נְצַר		_____ יֵשׁ	
_____ שָׁלוֹשׁ		_____ שֶׁלֶג	
_____ כָּזָב		_____ קַיִץ	
_____ יָעַץ		_____ שֶׁקֶל	
_____ אֶזְרֹעַ		_____ זִכָּרוֹן	
_____ יָשַׁב		_____ שׁוֹר	
_____ זָהָב		_____ חִדָה	
_____ אֶרֶץ		_____ חָדָשׁ	
_____ זֶבַח		_____ שׁוּב	
		_____ שֵׁשׁ	

Translate into English:

(1) אֲנַחְנָה בָּנַיִן קִרְיְתָא.

(2) סָפְרָא שְׁלַח אִגַּרְתָּא דָךְ.

(3) תְּהַשְׁכַּח אֱלָהָא בִּירוּשְׁלֶם מָרָדְתָּא.

(4) לָא אִיתַי חֲלָק לְהוֹם בַּעֲבַר־נַהֲרָה.

(5) כְּעַן יְדִיעַ דִּי יִנְתְּנוּן יְהוּדָיֵא בְּלוֹ לְמַלְכָּא.

(6) רְחוּם כְּתַב דָּכְרָן דְּנָה.

Chapter 5

VOWELS

The Hebrew Bible was originally written with only consonants. The Masoretes, who added the vowels, used essentially the same system for both the Hebrew and the Aramaic sections; however, the vowel systems are not completely identical. For example, the composite *sh'va* is not limited to guttural letters as it is in Hebrew, but also appears before and after the letters ק and ג and before ל, נ, and ר, as can be seen in the following words:

גְּלִי		מַדְּקָה	
בְּנַיְתַהּ		קֳדָם	
צִפְּרֵי		סְגַר	

Other differences between Hebrew and Aramaic involve the way each of them treats certain vowels:

(1) The Canaanite Shift (*ā > ō*) — long *a* usually became long *o* (*ō*) in some Northwest Semitic languages, including Hebrew. However, Aramaic belongs to a non-Canaanite group of languages, in which the original vowel (*ā*) is retained. A familiar example is the Hebrew word שָׁלוֹם. Both vowels in this word were once pronounced *a*, but the second one was long (the Arabic word is *salām*). In the Canaanite branch that vowel became *ō,* but not in Aramaic where the word is, therefore, pronounced שְׁלָם. The following words provide several other examples:

Aramaic		*Hebrew*
אֱנָשׁ	(man)	אֱנוֹשׁ
דָּר	(generation)	דּוֹר
טָב	(good)	טוֹב
לָא	(not)	לֹא
עָלַם	(eternity)	עוֹלָם
קָל	(sound)	קוֹל

(2) Reduction of Short Vowels — short vowels that occur in syllables immediately prior to the accent become long in Hebrew but are reduced in Aramaic. That is why the first syllable of שָׁלוֹם has a *qameṣ* (*ā*) in Hebrew, but a *sh'va* (שְׁלָם) in Aramaic. Other Aramaic words reflect this same principle:

Aramaic		*Hebrew*
מְאָה	(hundred)	מֵאָה
נְבִיא	(prophet)	נָבִיא
עֲתִיד	(ready)	עָתִיד

Both of these principles can be seen by comparing the Aramaic word for "three" (תְּלָת) with its Hebrew equivalent (שָׁלוֹשׁ), in which the first vowel, which was originally a short *a* preceding the accent, has become a *sh'va* in Aramaic but a long *a* in Hebrew while the second vowel, which was originally a long *a,* has shifted to *ō*. Notice also the equivalence of Hebrew שׁ and Aramaic ת.

(3) Segolate nouns — Many Hebrew nouns with the accent on their first syllable and a *segol* in the second (e.g., מֶלֶךְ, סֵפֶר, and קֹדֶשׁ) developed out of words that were originally mono-syllabic (i.e. מַלְךְ, סִפְר, קֻדְשׁ). In Aramaic these usually have only one full vowel, but it is found under the *second* consonant. (As in Hebrew, it often shifts to *a* when there is a guttural or ר nearby.)

Aramaic		*Hebrew*
לְחֶם	(meal)	לֶחֶם
צְלֵם	(statue)	צֶלֶם
תְּקֵל	(unit of weight)	שֶׁקֶל
כְּסַף	(silver)	כֶּסֶף
פְּשַׁר	(interpretation)	פֵּשֶׁר
נְשַׁר	(eagle)	נֶשֶׁר
עֲמַר	(wool)	צֶמֶר
תְּלַג	(snow)	שֶׁלֶג
סְפַר	(book)	סֵפֶר
שְׁבַט	(tribe)	שֵׁבֶט
רְגַז	(anger)	רֹגֶז
זְרַע	(seed)	זֶרַע
בְּעֵל *	(master)	בַּעַל

---

* For the vocalization of this form, compare its Akkadian cognate *bēlu,* in contrast to the Hebrew בַּעַל.

In Aramaic, as in Hebrew, the original vowel often returns when a suffix is added:

e.g., כַּסְפָּא — the silver

סִפְרִין — documents

פִּשְׁרֵהּ — its interpretation

VOCABULARY

To Be Learned		*Reference*	
then	אֱדַיִן	go (G)	אזל
stop	בטל	*pf 3 mp*	אֲזַלוּ
G *(intrans) pf 3 fs*	בְּטֵלַת	be	הוה
D *(trans) pf 3 p*	בַּטִּלוּ	G *pf 3 mp*	הֲווֹ
D *(trans) inf*	לְבַטָּלָה	days *(p cstr)*	יוֹמָת
house	בַּיִת	dwell (G)	יתב
master	בְּעֵל	G *ptc mp*	יָתְבִין
them	הִמּוֹ	G *inf of* בנה	מִבְנֵא
decree	טְעֵם	kings	מַלְכִין
official	בְּעֵל טְעֵם	after	מִן דִּי
do	עבד	rebellion	מְרַד
Gt *(passive) participle*	מִתְעֲבֵד	letter	נִשְׁתְּוָנָא
work, service	עֲבִידָה	message	פִּתְגָמָא
eternity	עָלְמָא	is read	קְרִי
before	קֳדָם	issue	שִׂים
before me	קָדָמַי	*imv mp*	שִׂימוּ
peace	שְׁלָם	remnant	שְׁאָר
strong	תַּקִּיף	G *pf 2 mp of* שלח	שְׁלַחְתּוּן
mp	תַּקִּיפִין		

FROM THE BIBLE (Ezra 4:17–24)

פִּתְגָמָא שְׁלַח מַלְכָּא עַל רְחוּם בְּעֵל טְעֵם וְשִׁמְשַׁי סָפְרָא דִּי יָתְבִין בְּשָׁמְרָיִן וּשְׁאָר עֲבַר־

נַהֲרָה: שְׁלָם. וּכְעֶנֶת. נִשְׁתְּוָנָא דִּי שְׁלַחְתּוּן קֳרִי קֳדָמָי. מְרַד מִתְעֲבֶד בְּקִרְיְתָא דָךְ מִן יוֹמָת

עָלְמָא וּמַלְכִין תַּקִּיפִין הֲווֹ עַל יְרוּשְׁלֶם. כְּעַן שִׂימוּ טְעֵם לְבַטָּלָה מִבְּנֵא קִרְיְתָא דָךְ.

אֱדַיִן מִן דִּי נִשְׁתְּוָנָא דִּי אַרְתַּחְשַׁשְׂתְּא מַלְכָּא קֱרִי קֳדָם רְחוּם וְשִׁמְשַׁי סָפְרָא אֲזַלוּ

לִירוּשְׁלֶם עַל יְהוּדָיֵא וּבַטִּלוּ הִמּוֹ. בֵּאדַיִן בְּטֵלַת עֲבִידַת בֵּית אֱלָהָא דִּי בִּירוּשְׁלֶם.

Proper Nouns

שָׁמְרָיִן — Persian province in the central hill country; named after the capital of Israel's Northern Kingdom when it was conquered by the Assyrians in 721 B.C.E.

EXERCISES

Explain the *differences* between the following pairs of Hebrew and Aramaic cognates:

Aramaic	Hebrew		Difference
לָא	לֹא	(not)	_____
עֲמַר	צֶמֶר	(wool)	_____
דָּא	זוֹ	(this)	_____
אֶדְרָע	אֶזְרֹעַ	(arm)	_____
תְּלַג	שֶׁלֶג	(snow)	_____
שָׁפְטִין	שׁוֹפְטִים	(judges)	_____
נְהַר	נָהָר	(river)	_____
תּוּב	שׁוּב	(return)	_____

Aramaic	**Hebrew**		**Difference**
שֵׁת	שֵׁשׁ	(six)	_____
סָפַר	סוֹפֵר	(scribe)	_____
נְשִׁין	נָשִׁים	(women)	_____
חֲדַת	חָדָשׁ	(new)	_____
שְׂעַר	שֵׂעָר	(hair)	_____
חֲבַר	חָבֵר	(companion)	_____
דְּהַב	זָהָב	(gold)	_____
עֲשַׂר	עֶשֶׂר	(ten)	_____
אָת	אוֹת	(sign)	_____
תבר	שבר	(break)	_____
עָלַם	עוֹלָם	(eternity)	_____

Translate into English:

(1) כְּתַב בְּעֵל עָלְמָא אִגְּרָה לְמַלְכִין תַּקִּיפִין.

(2) אֲנַחְנָא בָּנַיִן בַּיִת בְּקִרְיְתָא מָרָדְתָּא.

(3) אֱדַיִן הִמּוֹ בַּטִּלוּ מִבְנֵה בִּירוּשְׁלֶם.

(4) שִׂימוּ טְעֵם קֳדָם סָפְרָא מִן דִּי נִשְׁתְּוָנָא קֱרִי.

(5) כְּעַן לָא יִנְתְּנוּן עֲבִידָה עַל יְהוּדָיֵא.

(6) מַלְכַיָּא תַּקִּיפַיָּא אֲזַלוּ עַל קִרְיְתָא.

(7) טְעֵם אֱלָהָא קֱרִי קֳדָם בְּעֵל.

(8) אֱדַיִן אֲמַר שִׁמְשַׁי לְבַטָּלָה מִבְנֵה בַּיְתָא דְּנָה.

(9) הִמּוֹ עֲבַדוּ מְרַד בִּירוּשְׁלֶם.

(10) שִׂימוּ שְׁלָם לְהוֹם מִן עָלְמָא.

(11) אֲנַחְנָא מְהוֹדְעִין לְסָפְרָא דִּי בְּטֵלַת עֲבִידַת בַּיְתָא דִּי מַלְכָּא.

Chapter 6

Nouns, Definite Article

Nouns behave much the same way in Aramaic as they do in Hebrew: They can be masculine or feminine, absolute or construct, singular or plural (or dual). However, Aramaic nouns are unique in two, nearly ubiquitous features.

(1) Alongside the absolute and construct, Aramaic has a third "state," called "determined." This form typically ends with אָ-, although it is occasionally spelled with the letter ה. It functions much like the definite article in Hebrew (-הַ); that is to say, words with the determinative ending אָ- can be translated "the . . ." (In some later dialects of Aramaic this determined form of the noun became the normal one and thereby lost its connotation of definiteness.)

Although there is nothing *formally* comparable to the determined suffix אָ- in biblical Hebrew, it does exist in a word which occurs several times in the New Testament and has become standard in modern Hebrew. In Mark 14:36, Jesus refers to God as αββα.* This is obviously the determined form of the noun אָב ("father"), which has survived into modern Hebrew, where it and its feminine counterpart אִמָּא serve as familiar forms, equivalent to the English "Daddy" and "Mommy."

(2) Masculine plural forms usually end with ן-, rather than the ם- that is familiar in Hebrew. In fact, the Hebrew Bible contains many masculine forms that end with ן. Before either Aramaic or Hebrew had reached the stage with which we are familiar, masculine plural forms were apparently marked with י-. Later, Hebrew and Aramaic added different consonants to this original suffix. As a result, masculine plural nouns usually end with ין- rather than ים- as they do in Hebrew.

Aramaic's added ן can also be found on verbs, most notably in the imperfect:

---

* Contrast the parallel passages Matthew 26:39 and Luke 22:42; but see Romans 8:15 and Galatians 4:6. This is the source of our own English term "Abbot."

25

	Aramaic	**Hebrew**
2d feminine singular	תִּכְתְּבִין	תִּכְתְּבִי
2d masculine plural	תִּכְתְּבוּן	תִּכְתְּבוּ
2d feminine plural	תִּכְתְּבָן	תִּכְתֹּבְנָה
3d masculine plural	יִכְתְּבוּן	יִכְתְּבוּ
3d feminine plural	יִכְתְּבָן	תִּכְתֹּבְנָה

The resulting noun patterns are:

		masculine	*feminine*
singular	absolute	מֶלֶךְ	מַלְכָּה *
	construct	מֶלֶךְ	מַלְכַּת
	determined	מַלְכָּא	מַלְכְּתָא
plural	absolute	מַלְכִין	מַלְכָן
	construct	מַלְכֵי	מַלְכָת
	determined	מַלְכַיָּא	מַלְכָתָא

Notice the ־ָת - ending on the construct and determined forms of the feminine plural. This corresponds to Hebrew's feminine plural suffix וֹת-. (Remember that long *ā* becomes long *ō* in Hebrew.)

Not all nouns fit these patterns perfectly. As in any language, Aramaic has some irregular forms. These include plurals which do not seem to match their singulars, whether in form or in gender:

נְשִׁין "women" (The Bible does not include a singular form, but compare Hebrew אִשָּׁה, for which the plural is נָשִׁים.)

אֲבָהָן "fathers" (This form is inferred from the construct אֲבָהָת, which can be compared to the Hebrew plural אָבוֹת.)

שְׁמָהָן "names," judging from the construct שְׁמָהָת (cf. Hebrew שֵׁמוֹת).

Similarly, the plural for "great" (רַבְרְבִין) is an expanded form of רַב (cf. רַבְרְבָנִים, "chiefs").

---

* In the Bible, the feminine suffix ה־ is sometimes spelled with an א, just as the determined suffix א־ is sometimes spelled with a ה. Notice the inconsistent use of *dagesh*, which occurs in the כ of singular but not the plural forms of both masculine and feminine.

Like Hebrew, Aramaic also has dual forms, although there are not many examples in the Bible. Perhaps some dual forms are indistinguishable from the plural so that we cannot identify them. However, those that can be recognized resemble their Hebrew equivalents, except for the no-longer surprising presence of ן- where Hebrew has ם-:

e.g.,   יְדַיִן   (2 hands)

מָאתַיִן   (200)

VOCABULARY

To Be Learned		*Reference*	
say	אמר	god	אֱלָה
participle (m p)	אָמְרִין	their gods	אֱלָהֲהֹם
he came	אֲתָא	was (*G pf 3 fs of* הוה)	הֲוָת
son	בַּר	thus	כֵּן
man (*plural* גֻּבְרִין)	גְּבַר	to you (*m p*)	לְכֹם
and	וְ/וּ	build (*G infinitive*)	מִבְנֵא
who	מַן *	prophesy (Dt הִתְנַבִּי)	נבא
governor	פֶּחָה	prophet	נְבִיא
arise (G)	קוּם	eye	עַיִן
perfect 3 mp	קָמוּ	on them	עֲלֵיהֹון
issue (an order)	שִׂים		
G pf 3 ms	שָׂם		
name (*plural* שְׁמָהָת)	שֵׁם		

FROM THE BIBLE (Ezra 5:1–5)

וְהִתְנַבִּי חַגַּי וּזְכַרְיָה בַר עִדּוֹא נְבִיַּאָּ עַל יְהוּדָיֵא דִּי בִיהוּד וּבִירוּשְׁלֶם בְּשֻׁם אֱלָהּ
יִשְׂרָאֵל עֲלֵיהֹון. בֵּאדַיִן קָמוּ זְרֻבָּבֶל בַּר שְׁאַלְתִּיאֵל וְיֵשׁוּעַ בַּר יוֹצָדָק לְמִבְנֵא בֵּית
אֱלָהָא דִּי בִירוּשְׁלֶם. אֲתָא עֲלֵיהֹון תַּתְּנַי פַּחַת עֲבַר נַהֲרָה וּשְׁתַר־בּוֹזְנַי וְכֵן אָמְרִין
לְהֹם: מַן שָׂם טְעֵם בַּיְתָא דְנָה לְמִבְנֵא? מַן שְׁמָהָת גֻּבְרַיָּא דִּי דְנָא בָנַיִן?
וְעֵין אֱלָהֲהֹם הֲוָת עַל יְהוּדָיֵא וְלָא בַטִּלוּ הִמּוֹ.

---

* In Exodus 16:15 this word is the basis for a pun with the Hebrew word מָן, meaning "manna."

Proper Nouns

זְכַרְיָה בַּר עִדּוֹא — A Judean prophet of priestly descent during the reign of Darius I (521–486 B.C.E.), who encouraged the reestablishment of the kingdom.

זְרֻבָּבֶל בַּר שְׁאַלְתִּיאֵל — Grandson of Judah's king Jehoiachin, who was appointed governor by the Persians and led a group of exiles back to Judah, where he was viewed by some Judeans with messianic fervor.

חַגַּי — Prophesied to those who had returned to Judah in 520 on the importance of rebuilding the Temple.

יְהוּד — Province of Persian empire, centered in Jerusalem.

יִשְׂרָאֵל — Still used after the exile to refer to the ethnicity of the people chosen by God.

יֵשׁוּעַ בַּר יוֹצָדָק (called יְהוֹשֻׁעַ in Haggai and Zechariah) — Descendant of Seriah, a leading priest who was killed when the Babylonians conquered Jerusalem and whose son Jozadak was taken into exile; he returned to Judah in 520 with Zerubbabel, alongside of whom he played a major role in the reestablishment of sacrifice.

שְׁתַר־בּוֹזְנַי — Persian official.

תַּתְּנַי — Persian governor of Trans-Euphrates under Darius I.

EXERCISES

Fill in the blank with the Aramaic translation of the parenthesized words:

(1) יְהָדְיֵא בָּנַיִן בֵּית _____ (of a king).

(2) _____ (scribe) דְּנָה כְּתַב אִגַּרְתָּה.

(3) _____ (the names of) גֻּבְרַיָּא.

Fill in the following charts with the noun forms given below:

רֵאשַׁי, רֵאשָׁא, רֵאשׁ, רֵאשַׁיָּא, רֵאשִׁין

	absolute	construct	determined
Singular			
Plural			

נְבִיאֵי, נְבִיא, נְבִיאַיָּא, נְבִיאִין, נְבִיאָא

	absolute	construct	determined
Singular			
Plural			

סִפְרִין, סִפְרֵי, סִפְרַיָּא, סִפְרָא, סְפַר

	absolute	construct	determined
Singular			
Plural			

עֲבִידַת, עֲבִידָת, עֲבִידָן, עֲבִידְתָא, עֲבִידָה, עֲבִידָתָא

	absolute	construct	determined
Singular			
Plural			

קִרְיַת, קִרְיָתָא, קִרְיָן, קִרְיָה, קִרְיָתָא, קִרְיָת

	absolute	construct	determined
Singular			
Plural			

אֱלָהִי, אֱלָהַיָּא, אֱלָהָא, אֱלָהִין, אֱלָה

	absolute	construct	determined
Singular			
Plural			

סָפְרָא, סָפַר, סָפְרִין, סָפְרַיָּא, סָפְרֵי

	absolute	construct	determined
Singular			
Plural			

Translate into Aramaic:

(1) The scribe wrote the names of the men.

(2) The prophets of Israel arose before the kings.

(3) They sent the letter to Trans-Euphrates.

(4) God came to Israel.

(5) They are building the city of Jerusalem

(6) A master issued a decree.

(7) We informed the men of the city.

(8) Who are the governors of Judah and Samaria?

Chapter 7

THE VERB SYSTEM

Verbal systems are a prominent feature of most languages and provide a particularly useful way to classify them. Semitic verbs are based on three-letter roots, which can be conjugated in several different ways. Hebrew is usually said to have 7 of these conjugations (בִּנְיָנִם)—*qal, nifꜥal, piꜥel, hifꜥil, puꜥal, hofꜥal,* and *hitpaꜥel.* In order to facilitate comparisons with other languages, these are identified here with single letters, which reflect their characteristic features: *Qal* is called G for the German *Grundstamm,* which means "basic conjugation," as does the Hebrew term *qal. Piꜥel* is designated D for its doubled middle letter. The *hifꜥil* will be called H, and the *nifꜥal* (which does not exist in Aramaic) N in recognition of the letter which is prefixed to each.

This scheme of 7 separate conjugations is somewhat artificial. In the first place, several of these conjugations are actually related to each other. These include the *puꜥal* and the *hofꜥal,* which are patently variations (sometimes called internal passives) of the *piꜥel* and *hifꜥil,* with which they are identical except for their *u-a* vowel pattern, which shifts the meaning from active to passive.* (Significantly, Hebrew's *qal* passive participle, e.g., כָּתוּב, also uses *a* and *u* vowels.)

The *hitpaꜥel* (here designated Dt) is built on the *piꜥel,* as can be seen from the fact that its middle root letter is doubled. The prefix -הִת conveyed a reflexive meaning and was not necessarily limited to a *piꜥel* base, as can be seen from other Semitic languages.** The Bible preserves a handful of Hebrew words in which this prefix was added to *qal* forms (הִתְפָּקֵד in Judges 20:15,17, 21:9; note the passive forms beginning with with -הָת in Numbers 1:47 and 2:33).

At the same time that several of these seven standard conjugations appear to be related to one another, there are conjugations that this list does not include. Thus Gesenius' Hebrew grammar lists *pôꜥēl, paꜥlēl, pěꜥalꜥal, pilpēl, tifꜥēl,* and *šafꜥēl.****

---

*The Hebrew *qal* probably had an internal passive, too; for the evidence, see *A Grammar of Biblical Hebrew* by Paul Joüon and T. Muraoka (Rome: Pontifical Biblical Institute, 1991) §58, pp. 166–68.

** Although Aramaic is the only Semitic language in which a *t* can be added to the H conjugation, several languages which form their causatives with שׁ have it (including Hebrew הִשְׁתַּחֲוָה); see Sabatino Moscati, *An Introduction to the Comparative Grammar of the Semitic Languages* (Wiesbaden: Otto Harrassowitz, 1969) §16.17–23, pp. 127–30.

*** A. E. Cowley, *Gesenius' Hebrew Grammar* as edited and enlarged by the late E. Kautzsch (2d English edition, Oxford: Clarendon Press, 1910) §55, pp. 151–54.

Because Aramaic belongs to the same Northwest group of the Semitic language family as does Hebrew, its verbal system is essentially the same and can be characterized with the following pattern:

		Passive	Prefixed t
G	*pᵉᶜal*	*pᵉᶜil*	Gt—*hitpᵉᶜel*
D	*paᶜᶜel*	*puᶜᶜal*	Dt—*hitpaᶜᶜal*
H	*hafᶜel*	*hofᶜal*	Ht—*hitafᶜal* (not in biblical Aramaic)
N	not in Aramaic		

As in Hebrew, each Aramaic conjugation comprises two major tenses, one of which generates its various forms with a series of suffixes (the perfect), while the other uses primarily prefixes (the imperfect). Each also has imperative, infinitive, and participial forms.

VOCABULARY

To Be Learned		*Reference*	
go	אזל	we said	אֲמַרְנָא
G pf 1 p	אֲזַלְנָא	also	אַף
those	אִלֵּךְ	everything	כֹּלָּא
interior	גֹּו	write (G)	כתב
3 ms (him, his) *suffix*	ـֵהּ	*passive participle*	כְּתִיב
3 mp (they, them) *suffix*	ـהֹם	*imf 1 p*	נִכְתֻּב
2 mp (you, your) *suffix*	ـכֹם	let it be *(imf 3 ms)*	לֶהֱוֵה
colleague (*plural* כְּנָוָת)	כְּנָת	elder	שָׂב
province	מְדִינָה	ask	שאל
head	רֵאשׁ		
great	רַב		

FROM THE BIBLE (Ezra 5:6–10)

אִגַּרְתָּא דִּי שְׁלַח תַּתְּנַי פַּחַת עֲבַר־נַהֲרָה וּשְׁתַר־בּוֹזְנַי וּכְנָוָתֵהּ דִּי בַּעֲבַר־נַהֲרָה עַל
דָּרְיָוֶשׁ מַלְכָּא וְכִדְנָה כְּתִיב בְּגַוֵּהּ: לְדָרְיָוֶשׁ מַלְכָּא שְׁלָמָא כֹלָּא. יְדִיעַ לֶהֱוֵא לְמַלְכָּא
דִּי אֲזַלְנָא לִיהוּד מְדִינְתָּא לְבֵית אֱלָהָא רַבָּא. אֱדַיִן שְׁאֵלְנָא לְשָׂבַיָּא אִלֵּךְ אֲמַרְנָא
לְהֹם: מַן שָׂם לְכֹם טְעֵם בַּיְתָא דְנָה לְמִבְנְיָה. וְאַף שְׁמָהָתְהֹם שְׁאֵלְנָא לְהֹם
דִּי נִכְתֻּב שֻׁם גֻּבְרַיָּא דִּי בְרָאשֵׁיהֹם.

Proper Names

דָּרְיָוֶשׁ — Darius I conquered Persia after the death of Cambyses II and reigned from 522 to 486 B.C.E.

EXERCISES

Identify the base conjugation (G, D, or H) to which the following Aramaic verbs belong. Note that some of these forms are passive and reflexive, so that their vowel patterns may differ from those of the active form or they may have a prefixed -הִת (or -אֶת), much like the Hebrew *hitpaᶜᶜel*.

הִתְקְטִלָה _____	נְחַוֵּא _____	אָכְלָה _____
מְהֵימַן _____	סָגְדִין _____	הַדְּרֵת _____
מִתְכַּנְּשִׁין _____	בְּנַס _____	הוּבַד _____
מִתְנַשְּׂאָה _____	הִתְרְגִזוּ _____	הָחָרְבַת _____
יְבַקַּר _____	הֶעְלוּ _____	יִשְׁאֲלֶנְכוֹן _____
תִּקְנֵא _____	הַשְׁכַּחַת _____	בְּטֵלַת _____
רְשִׁמְתְּ _____	תִּתְרְמוֹן _____	הֻשְׁפֵּלַת _____
הִתְרְחִצוּ _____	נְפַלוּ _____	מַלִּל _____
מְהַלְּכִין _____	הִתְנַבִּי _____	שַׁבַּחֵת _____
אֶתְעַקַּרוּ _____	בְּטִלוּ _____	חֲשִׁיבִין _____
מְצַבְּעִין _____	מְהַעְדֵּה _____	אֶבְעֵה _____
	הִתְגְּזֶרֶת _____	

Translate into Aramaic:

(1) We went to the great province.

(2) They sent a letter to the house and to the men inside it.

(3) Now Darius is the head of those elders.

(4) The elders say that the decree is known to them.

(5) Let peace be over Jerusalem.

(6) Everything is written.

Chapter 8

G Perfect

Not only are the Aramaic verb conjugations (G, D, and H) and tenses (perfect, imperfect, etc.) analogous to those of Hebrew, but the individual forms are also similar, once the various principles that have already been discussed are taken into account. For example, the perfect tense, which describes completed action, uses pronominal suffixes attached at the end of the verbal root. Moreover, although these suffixes are somewhat different from those in Hebrew (but not unrecognizably so), the pattern itself is built on the same (3d person, masculine singular) base—כְּתַב, with the accent on the final syllable as is usual in these languages. Because the short vowel in the first syllable precedes the accent, it is lengthened in Hebrew, resulting in the form כָּתַב, but reduced in Aramaic, yielding כְּתַב.

All the various perfect forms are built on this base. In a few cases the first two letters could both have *sh'va*s (i.e., -כְּתְ); since Aramaic will not tolerate two vocal *sh'va*s in a row any more than Hebrew, the first of these shifts to *ḥiriq* (i.e., -כִּתְ).*

Overall, the G perfect conjugation looks like this:

		Singular	*Plural*
1		כִּתְבֵת	כְּתַבְנָא
2	masculine	כְּתַבְתְּ (or כְּתַבְתָּ)	כְּתַבְתּוּן
	feminine	כְּתַבְתִּי	כְּתַבְתֵּן**
3	masculine	כְּתַב	כְּתַבוּ
	feminine	כִּתְבַת	כְּתַבָה***

---

* The same process is responsible for the Hebrew plural imperative שִׁמְרוּ, which results when the imperfect prefix is dropped from יִשְׁמְרוּ, and for the vocalization of prepositional prefixes attached to words beginning with *sh'va*, such as בִּסְפָרִים.

** Note that Aramaic uses different vowels for masculine and feminine plural forms of verbs in the second person perfect (-תֵּן/תוּן-) and for pronominal suffixes in the second (-כֹ/כֵן-), and third (-הֹם/הֵן-) persons (see chapter 13), unlike Hebrew, which uses the same vowels in the second person (e.g., כְּתַבְתֶּם/תֶּן and סְפַרְכֶם/כֶן).

*** Sometimes the masculine form is used as a common plural.

The vowel under the second root letter (e.g., the *pataḥ* under the ת in many of the forms above) is called the "theme vowel" and is particular to specific roots. Examples of verbs with different theme vowels in the perfect include:

בְּטֵלַת   she stopped

שְׁאֵלְנָא   we asked

סְגֵד   he bowed down

VOCABULARY

To Be Learned		*Reference*	
earth	אַרְעָא	father	אַב
be	הוה / הוא	our ancestors	אֲבָהָתַנָא
palace, temple	הֵיכַל	these	אֵלֶּה
one	חַד	build	בנה
give	יהב	*passive participle*	בְּנֵה
G pf passive 3 p	יְהִיבוּ	*infinitive*	לְבְנֵא
vessel	מָאן	*Gt (passive) imf 3 ms*	יִתְבְּנֵא
go out	נפק	exile	גלה
H (causal) pf 3 ms	הַנְפֵּק	*H (causal) pf 3 ms*	הַגְלִי
many, large	שַׂגִּיא	descend	נחת
heaven	שְׁמַיָּא	*H ("deposit") imv*	אֲחֵת
year	שְׁנָה	tear down (G)	סתר
		servant	עֲבֵד
		his servants	עַבְדּוֹהִי
		people, nation	עַם
		former time	קַדְמָה
		anger (H)	רגז
		perfect 3 p	הַרְגִּזוּ
		reply (H)	תוב
		they replied	הֲתִיבוּ

FROM THE BIBLE (Ezra 5:11–15)

הֲתִיבוּ: אֲנַחְנָא עַבְדוֹהִי דִּי אֱלָהּ שְׁמַיָּא וְאַרְעָא וּבָנַיִן בַּיְתָא דִּי הֲוָא בְנֵה מִקַּדְמַת דְּנָה

שְׁנִין שַׂגִּיאָן. הַרְגִּזוּ אֲבָהֳתַנָא לֶאֱלָהּ שְׁמַיָּא וִיהַב הִמּוֹ לִנְבוּכַדְנֶצַּר מֶלֶךְ בָּבֶל כַּסְדָּיָא

וּבַיְתָה דְנָה סְתַר וְעַמָּה הַגְלִי לְבָבֶל. בִּשְׁנַת חֲדָה לְכוֹרֶשׁ מַלְכָּא דִּי בָבֶל כּוֹרֶשׁ מַלְכָּא

שָׂם טְעֵם בֵּית אֱלָהָא דְנָה לִבְּנֵא וּמָאנַיָּא דִי בֵית אֱלָהָא דִּי נְבוּכַדְנֶצַּר הַנְפֵּק מִן הֵיכְלָא

דִּי בִירוּשְׁלֶם לְהֵיכְלָא דִּי בָבֶל הַנְפֵּק הִמּוֹ כּוֹרֶשׁ מַלְכָּא מִן הֵיכְלָא דִּי בָבֶל וִיהִיבוּ

לְשֵׁשְׁבַּצַּר וַאֲמַר: אֵלֶּה מָאנַיָּא אֲחֵת הִמּוֹ בְּהֵיכְלָא דִּי בִירוּשְׁלֶם וּבֵית אֱלָהָא יִתְבְּנֵא.

Proper Names

בָּבֶל — A central Mesopotamian city on the Euphrates, which established an empire in
the sixth century that conquered Judah and destroyed Jerusalem, taking its
leading citizens into exile.

כּוֹרֶשׁ — Founder of Persian empire, which he ruled from 559–30 B.C.E.; he conquered
Media, Lydia, and Babylonia (in 539 B.C.E.), granted the various nations under
his control cultural autonomy, and, according to Herodotus, believed himself
"more than a man" (1:204).

כַּסְדָּי — Member of a tribe in southern part of Mesopotamia, where the Babylonian
empire was centered in the seventh and sixth centuries (for the spelling, see p.
70).

נְבוּכַדְנֶצַּר — Chaldean ruler of Babylonian empire (605–562 B.C.E.), who conquered
Jerusalem in 587.

שֵׁשְׁבַּצַּר — Babylonian-born Judean who was appointed governor by Cyrus in 538
B.C.E. and returned to Jerusalem with the temple vessels.

EXERCISES

Conjugate the following verbs, all of which have a *pataḥ* theme vowel, in the G perfect:

עבד   נטל

singular 1

2 m

2 f

3 m

3 f

plural 1

2 m

2 f

3 m

3 f

רשם   שלח

singular 1

2 m

2 f

3 m

3 f

plural 1

2 m

2 f

3 m

3 f

Identify the form of the following G perfect verbs:

	Root	Person	Gender	Number
יְדַעְתָּ				
יִדְעֵת				
יְהַב				
כְּתַבְנָא				
כְּתַבוּ				
מְלַחְנָא				
נְטֶרֶת				
נְפַל				
סְלִקֵת				
עֲבַד				

Translate from Aramaic into English:

(1) אֲזַל מַלְכָּא קֳדָם קִרְיְתָא.

(2) אֲנַחְנָה יְדַעְנָא דִי בְּעֵל עָלְמָא בִּירוּשְׁלֶם.

(3) כִּתְבֵת אִגְּרָה עַל בֵּית מַלְכָּא.

(4) אֱדַיִן שְׁלַח אֱלָהָא טְעֵם עַל מְדִינְתָּא דָךְ.

(5) יְהַבְתְּ עַבְדִּין שַׂגִּיאִין לְפַחַת יְהוּדָיֵא.

(6) אֲבָהָתַנָא יְהַבוּ מָאנַיָּא אִלֵּךְ לְכוֹרֶשׁ.

(7) רֵאשׁ הֵיכְלָא הֲוָא בִשְׁמַיָּא.

(8) נְבוּכַדְנֶצַּר לָא הַנְפֵּק גֻּבְרַיָּא לְאַרְעָא.

(9) בַּיְתָא רַבָּא דֵּךְ יִתְבְּנֵה בִּשְׁנָה חֲדָה.

Chapter 9

G PARTICIPLE

Like the G perfect, Aramaic participles are morphologically and functionally similar to their Hebrew counterparts. In both languages they act like nouns. Moreover, they look very much alike, with Aramaic's active participle even vocalized like its Hebrew equivalent (כּוֹתֵב), except that the Hebrew *ō*, of course, appears as *ā* in Aramaic. Thus:

		Masculine	*Feminine*
singular	absolute	כָּתֵב	כָּתְבָה
	construct	כָּתֵב	כָּתְבַת
	determined	כָּתְבָא	כָּתְבְתָא
plural	absolute	כָּתְבִין	כָּתְבָן
	construct	כָּתְבֵי	כָּתְבָת
	determined	כָּתְבַיָּא	כָּתְבָתָא

This vowel pattern is affected by the letters ח, ע, and ר, particularly when they come at the end of the root. Thus אָמַר and יָדַע are participles, derived from the theoretical forms אָמֵר and יָדֵעַ. (Do not confuse these with the Hebrew 3d person masculine singular perfect, which looks identical.)

Aramaic also has a passive participle. As in Hebrew, this form is characterized by its theme vowel. In Hebrew that is *ū* (e.g., בָּרוּךְ, כָּתוּב); in Aramaic, it is *ī*:

		Masculine	*Feminine*
singular	absolute	כְּתִיב	כְּתִיבָה
	construct	כְּתִיב	כְּתִיבַת
	determined	כְּתִיבָא	כְּתִיבְתָא
plural	absolute	כְּתִיבִין	כְּתִיבָן
	construct	כְּתִיבֵי	כְּתִיבָת
	determined	כְּתִיבַיָּא	כְּתִיבָתָא

42

If you have studied the text of the Hebrew Bible, you may recognize the term כְּתִיב, which was used by the Masoretes to indicate places where the "written" text (כְּתִיב) differs from what is to be "read" (קְרֵי). In such passages, many editions of the Bible print the consonants of the כְּתִיב and the vowels of the קְרֵי. For example, the name Jerusalem is often printed יְרוּשָׁלֵם, with an extra vowel between the last two consonants. The name was apparently pronounced יְרוּשָׁלֵם when these texts were written (כְּתִיב), just as it is in the Aramaic sections of the Bible (compare the English "Jerusalem"); however, by the time the vowels were added, the final *segol* had shifted to the diphthong *a-i*, yielding the reading יְרוּשָׁלַיִם (קְרֵי).

VOCABULARY

To Be Learned

there is	אִיתַי
search	בְּקַר
D perfect 3 mp	בַּקַּרוּ
Dt (passive) imf 3 ms	יִתְבַּקַּר
treasure	גְּנַז
gold	דְּהַב
if	הֵן
good	טָב
silver	כְּסַף
from	מִן
we/our	‑נָא
there	תַּמָּה

Reference

foundations	אֻשִּׁין
build	בְּנָה
G infinitive	לְמִבְנֵה
Gt (pass) participle	מִתְבְּנֵא
Gt (pass) imf 3 ms	יִתְבְּנֵא
give	יְהַב
Gt imf 3 fs	תִּתְיְהִב
scroll	מְגִלָּה
expenses	נִפְקָה
wish (*noun*)	רְעוּ
give (*G pass participle*)	שִׂים
find	שְׁכַח
be found	הִשְׁתְּכַח
finished	שְׁלֵם
return	תּוּב
H (trans imf 3 mp)	יַהֲתִיבוּן

FROM THE BIBLE (Ezra 5:16–6:5)

אֱדַיִן שֵׁשְׁבַּצַּר אֲתָא יְהַב אֻשַּׁיָּא דִּי בֵית אֱלָהָא דִּי בִירוּשְׁלֶם וּמִן אֱדַיִן וְעַד כְּעַן מִתְבְּנֵא וְלָא שְׁלִם. וּכְעַן הֵן עַל מַלְכָּא טָב יִתְבַּקַּר בְּבֵית גִּנְזַיָּא דִּי מַלְכָּא תַמָּה דִּי בְּבָבֶל הֵן אִיתַי דִּי מִן כּוֹרֶשׁ מַלְכָּא שִׂים טְעֵם לְמִבְנֵא בֵּית אֱלָהָא בִירוּשְׁלֶם וּרְעוּת מַלְכָּא עַל דְּנָה יִשְׁלַח עֲלֶינָא. בֵּאדַיִן דָּרְיָוֶשׁ מַלְכָּא שָׂם טְעֵם וּבַקַּרוּ תַמָּה בְּבָבֶל וְהִשְׁתְּכַח מְגִלָּה חֲדָה וְכֵן כְּתִיב בְּגַוַּהּ: בִּשְׁנַת חֲדָה לְכוֹרֶשׁ מַלְכָּא כּוֹרֶשׁ מַלְכָּא שָׂם טְעֵם בֵּית אֱלָהָא בִירוּשְׁלֶם יִתְבְּנֵא וְנִפְקְתָא מִן בֵּית מַלְכָּא תִּתְיְהִב וּמָאנֵי בֵית אֱלָהָא דִּי דַהֲבָה וְכַסְפָּא דִּי נְבוּכַדְנֶצַּר הַנְפֵּק מִן הֵיכְלָא דִּי בִירוּשְׁלֶם יַהֲתִיבוּן.

EXERCISES

List the participle forms of the following verbs:

Active		נטל	רשם	טרד	קטל
Singular m	absolute				
	construct				
	determined				
Singular f	absolute				
	construct				
	determined				
Plural m	absolute				
	construct				
	determined				
Plural f	absolute				
	construct				
	determined				

Passive		נטל	רשם	טרד	קטל
Singular m	absolute				
	construct				
	determined				
Singular f	absolute				
	construct				
	determined				
Plural m	absolute				
	construct				
	determined				
Plural f	absolute				
	construct				
	determined				

Translate the following sentences into English:

(1) נְבוּכַדְנֶצַּר אָמַר דִּי קִרְיְתָא תִּתְיְהִב לִיהוּדָאיִן.

(2) מְגִלָּה רַבָּה שְׁלִיחָה לְפַחַת מְדִנְתָּא.

(3) מַלְכָּא יְדַע דִּי עֲבִידָה בָּטְלָה.

(4) אֲנַחְנָה יָדְעִין לְמִבְנֵה בַּיְתָא דְּנָה.

(5) אִיתַי דְּהַב בְּבֵית גִּנְזַיָּא תַּמָּה בְּבָבֶל.

(6) גֻּבְרַיָּא בַּקָּרוּ הֵן כְּסַף טָב יְהִיב לְסָפְרָא.

Translate into Aramaic:

(1) The men rose up against them.

(2) Who sent the silver and the gold from Trans-Euphrates?

(3) There is a governor inside Jerusalem.

(4) We gave the house to them.

(5) The scribe went to the city.

Chapter 10

VOCABULARY

Although it is helpful to know Hebrew when learning Aramaic, their similarities can also be a trap for the unwary Hebraist engaged in the study of an Aramaic text. For the two languages are not the same, and one must avoid unintentionally reading an Aramaic passage as if it were Hebrew when they actually diverge. An example of this is the forms אֲמַר and יָדַע, which would be G (*qal*) perfect verbs in Hebrew, but are participles in Aramaic.

Likewise, the languages' vocabulary, though often similar, are not identical. This was demonstrated in chapter 3 by the Gospel accounts of Jesus' words on the cross, which are taken from the beginning of Psalm 22. Although the Gospel versions are virtually identical with the original, the Hebrew word עזב (abandon) has been rendered with its Aramaic equivalent— שׁבק.

Vocabulary differences are evident in the very first Aramaic words in the Bible, which occur in the story of Jacob's flight from his father-in-law (Genesis 31:47). After Laban caught up with Jacob, they made an agreement, and Jacob erected a pile of stones, which he called גַּלְעֵד but which Laban identified as יְגַר שָׂהֲדוּתָא. Although both phrases mean "pile-witness" —Jacob's in Hebrew and Laban's in Aramaic—they, too, bear no resemblance whatsoever.

An especially common idea that is expressed differently in the two languages is "son," which is בַּר in Aramaic but בֵּן in Hebrew. Interestingly, this is not the only case where Hebrew and Aramaic words with the same meaning differ only in the latter's having a ר where Hebrew has a נ. The Aramaic word for "two" (תְּרֵין) correlates with the Hebrew שְׁנָיִם (remember that Aramaic ת can correspond to Hebrew שׁ).

On the other hand, the two languages sometimes use altogether different roots. Several of these are very common words having to do with motion:

	Hebrew	*Aramaic*
"come"	בּוֹא	אתא
"go"	הלך	אזל
"go up"	עלה	סלק
"go down"	ירד	נחת
"go in"	בּוֹא	עלל
"go out"	יצא	נפק

Complicating matters are words (or roots) which exist in both languages but are used differently. For example, רַב can mean either "many" or "great" in Hebrew, but in Aramaic it always means "great"—a concept which Hebrew usually expresses with גָּדוֹל. How, then, does Aramaic say "many"? With a totally different word—שַׂגִּיא (which sometimes also means "great").

	Hebrew	*Aramaic*
"big"	גָּדוֹל	רַב
"many"	רַב	שַׂגִּיא

Similarly, the verb עבד occurs in both languages; however, it means "to serve" or "work" in Hebrew, but "to make" or "do" in Aramaic. Thus it has the same meaning in Aramaic that עשׂה has in Hebrew. As if to compensate, Aramaic also uses another verb—פלח, which means "to serve."

	Hebrew	*Aramaic*
"do, make"	עשׂה	עבד
"work, serve, worship"	עבד	פלח

Translating Aramaic עבד as if it were Hebrew could, therefore, lead to serious misunderstanding.

The very common Hebrew verbs נתן and שׂים also occur in Aramaic, where שׂים has a far broader semantic range than its Hebrew cognate, which means "put." In Aramaic it can mean "issue (a decree)," "appoint," or "give (a name)"; it also occurs in several idioms, including "have regard for" (שִׂים טְעֵם עַל) and "set the mind on" (שִׂים בַּל לְ).

In biblical Aramaic נְתַן appears only in the imperfect and infinitive; perfect and participle forms of "give" are expressed with the more characteristically Aramaic verb יהב. This root also occurs in Hebrew parts of the Bible, where its imperative (הָבָה and הָבוּ) is used both literally ("give") and with the connotation "let us." Thus Rachel implores Jacob הָבָה לִּי בָנִים ("Give me sons," Genesis 30:1), whereas the inhabitants of Babel say: הָבָה נִבְנֶה לָּנוּ עִיר ("Let's build a city for ourselves," Genesis 11:4).

VOCABULARY

To Be Learned		*Reference*	
I	אֲנָה	build	בנה
man	אֱנָשׁ	*G inf*	מִבְנֵא
destroy (D)	חֲבַל	be	הוה
infinitive	חַבָּלָה	*G imv mp*	הֱוֹו
all	כֹּל	*G imf 3 ms*	לֶהֱוֵא
what	מָה	*G imf 3 fs*	תֶּהֱוֵא
dunghill	נְוָלוּ	*G imf 3 mp*	לֶהֱוֹן
message, word	פִּתְגָם	life	חַיִּין
pray (D)	צלה	needed thing	חַשְׁחָה
participle mp	מְצַלִּין	hand	יַד
distant	רַחִיק	give	יהב
leave (alone)	שׁבק	*Gt (passive) participle*	
G imv mp	שְׁבֻקוּ	*ms*	מִתְיְהֵב
		fs	מִתְיַהֲבָא
		overthrow (D)	מגר
		D imf 3 ms	יְמַגַּר
		property	נְכַס
		expenses	נִפְקָה
		do	עבד
		Gt (passive) imf 3 ms	יִתְעֲבֵד
		people	עַם
		sacrifice (H)	קרב
		H participle mp	מְהַקְרְבִין
		change (D, H)	שׁנה
		H (trans) imf 3 ms	יְהַשְׁנֵא

FROM THE BIBLE (Ezra 6:6–12)

כְּעַן תַּתְּנַי פַּחַת עֲבַר־נַהֲרָה שְׁתַר־בּוֹזְנַי וּכְנָוָתְהוֹן רַחִיקִין הֲווֹ מִן תַּמָּה.

שְׁבֻקוּ לַעֲבִידַת בֵּית־אֱלָהָא דֵךְ וּמִנִּי שִׂים טְעֵם לִיהוּדָיֵא לְמִבְנֵא בֵּית־אֱלָהָא וּמִנִּכְסֵי

מַלְכָּא נִפְקְתָא תֶּהֱוֵא מִתְיַהֲבָא לְגֻבְרַיָּא אִלֵּךְ דִּי־לָא לְבַטָּלָא. וּמָה חַשְׁחָן וּבְנֵי

שְׁמַיָּא לֶהֱוֵא מִתְיְהֵב לְהֹם דִּי־לֶהֱוֹן מְהַקְרְבִין לֶאֱלָהּ שְׁמַיָּא וּמְצַלַּיִן לְחַיֵּי מַלְכָּא.

וּמִנִּי שִׂים טְעֵם דִּי כָל־אֱנָשׁ דִּי יְהַשְׁנֵא פִּתְגָמָא דְנָה וּבַיְתֵהּ נְוָלוּ יִתְעֲבֵד עַל־דְּנָה.

וֵאלָהָא יְמַגַּר כָּל־מֶלֶךְ וְעַם דִּי יִשְׁלַח יְדֵהּ לְהַשְׁנָיָה לְחַבָּלָה בֵּית־אֱלָהָא דֵךְ דִּי בִירוּשְׁלֶם.

אֲנָה דָרְיָוֶשׁ שָׂמֶת טְעֵם.

The phrase דִּי־לָא לְבַטָּלָא (v. 8) literally means "in order not to stop (the work),"
i.e., "not to stop."

EXERCISES

Find the Hebrew and English words that mean the same as each of the following Aramaic
words. (Be careful—not all the Hebrew-Aramaic pairs are cognates.)

English translations: arm, big, come, do, document, dwell, give, go, god, go down,
gold, go out, go up, heaven, it will be, known, land, lie (*noun*), many, memorandum, one, ox, peace, return, sacrifice, scribe, six, snow, son, summer, there
is, this, to them, three, tree, two, weight, we, work

Hebrew equivalents: אֶחָד, אֱלֹהִים, אֲנַחְנוּ, אֶרֶץ, בֵּן, בּוֹא, גָּדוֹל, הָלַךְ, הַסּוֹפֵר, זֶבַח, זֶה,
זָהָב, זִכָּרוֹן, זְרוֹעַ, יָדוּעַ, יִהְיֶה, יָצָא, יָרַד, יֵשׁ, יָשַׁב, כָּזָב, לֶחֶם, נָתַן, סֵפֶר, עָבַד, עָלָה,
עֵץ, עָשָׂה, קַיִץ, רַב, שׁוּב, שׁוֹר, שֶׁלֶג, שָׁלוֹם, שָׁלוֹשׁ, שָׁמַיִם, שְׁנַיִם, שֶׁקֶל, שֵׁשׁ

	Hebrew equivalent	English translation
אֲזַל		
אִיתַי		
אֱלָהַיָּא		
אֲנַחְנָה		

	Hebrew equivalent	English translation
אָע		
אַרְעָא		
אתה		
בַּר		
דְּבַח		
דְּהַב		
דָּכְרָן		
דְּנָה		
דְּרָע		
חַד		
יְדִיעַ		
יהב		
יתב		
כִּדְבָה		
לֶהֱוֵא		
לְהֹם		
נחת		
נפק		
סלק		
סְפַר		
סָפְרָא		

	Hebrew equivalent	*English translation*
עֲבַד		
פְּלַח		
קַיִט		
רַב		
שַׂגִּיא		
שְׁלָם		
שְׁמַיָּא		
שֵׁת		
תּוּב		
תּוֹר		
תְּלַג		
תְּלָת		
תְּקֵל		
תְּרֵי		

Translate into Aramaic:

(1) The treasures are far from the dunghill.

(2) I wrote a letter to the scribes.

(3) He sent God's message to the city.

(4) The head of the province is a man.

(5) Leave everything there!

(6) They are praying to God to destroy the earth.

Chapter 11

INDEPENDENT PRONOUNS, אִיתַי

In the Semitic languages, pronouns exist in several different forms. Some of these stand alone, while others are suffixes which can be attached to the end of words, including verbs, where they serve as direct objects, nouns, indicating possession, or prepositions, of which they are the object.

Aramaic's pronominal suffixes will be described in chapter 13. The independent forms look very much like their Hebrew equivalents, especially if one allows for the sound changes already described as characteristic of each language.

		Singular	*Plural*
1		אֲנָה	אֲנַחְנָה
2	masculine	אַנְתְּ (or אַנְתָּה)*	אַנְתּוּן (or אַנְתֹּם)
	feminine	אַנְתִּי	אַנְתֵּן
3	masculine	הוּא	הִמּוֹ (or אִנּוּן or הִמּוֹן)
	feminine	הִיא	אִנִּין

Although 2d person Hebrew pronouns do not have a נ where their Aramaic equivalents do, the *dagesh* in the ת indicates that there was once a נ which has now assimilated to the ת. (The *dagesh* in the Aramaic forms is *lene*, since these letters follow a now closed syllable.) Although the 2d person feminine singular pronoun (אַנְתִּי) may appear unfamiliar, its Hebrew equivalent (אַתִּי) can be found several places in the Hebrew Bible, albeit only as the כְּתִיב.** The יִ- ending is also used to mark feminine forms of the Hebrew imperfect (תִּכְתְּבִי) and imperative (כִּתְבִי).

One of the differences between Hebrew and Aramaic has to do with the verb "to be." Although the root היה exists in both languages, neither one uses it in the present tense. For that, Hebrew uses noun sentences, in which there simply is no verb:

---

*Most Bibles show a mixed form אַנְתָּה, which has the consonants (כְּתִיב) for אַנְתָּה and the vowels (קְרִי) for אַנְתְּ.

**Cf. Judges 17:2, 1 Kings 14:2, 2 Kings 4:16,23, 8:1, Jeremiah 4:30, and Ezekiel 36:13.

דָּוִד מֶלֶךְ.	David is king.
דָּוִד הַמֶּלֶךְ.	David is the king.

Aramaic accomplishes this by using the 3d person pronouns as a copula:

כּוֹרֶשׁ הוּא מֶלֶךְ.	Cyrus is king.
כּוֹרֶשׁ הוּא מַלְכָּא.	Cyrus is the king.

The subject of such sentences need not be in the 3d person:

אֲנַחְנָא הִמּוֹ עַבְדוֹהִי.	We are his servants. (Ezra 5:11)
אַנְתְּ הוּא רֵאשָׁה דִּי דַהֲבָא.	You are the head of gold. (Daniel 2:38)

This same construction also occurs in biblical Hebrew; for example:

אַתָּה הוּא מַלְכִּי.	You are my king. (Psalm 44:5)

Sometimes Aramaic uses the particle אִיתַי to express the present tense of "to be." Like the Hebrew word יֵשׁ, to which it may be related,* אִיתַי normally means "there is":

אִיתַי אֱלָהּ בִּשְׁמַיָּא.	There is a god in heaven. (Daniel 2:28)
לָא אִיתַי אֱלָהּ אָחֳרָן.	There is no other god. (Daniel 3:29)

Also like יֵשׁ, אִיתַי is used with the preposition -לְ to indicate possession:

חֲלָק בַּעֲבַר־נַהֲרָא לָא אִיתַי לָךְ.
You (will) have no portion in Trans-Euphrates. (Ezra 4:16)

Notice that Aramaic uses לָא (= Hebrew לֹא) to negate אִיתַי, whereas in Hebrew an entirely separate word (אֵין) functions as the negative of יֵשׁ. Centuries after the Bible was written, לָא and אִיתַי merged into a single word—לֵית. Thus Targum Onkelos, an Aramaic translation of the Pentateuch, renders the Hebrew phrase וְלֶחֶם אֵין בְּכָל הָאָרֶץ (Genesis 47:13) as וְלַחְמָא לֵית בְּכָל אַרְעָא. The Masoretes used this same word, abbreviated as ל, to identify forms which occur only once in the Hebrew Bible. Examples can be seen in the marginal notes on almost any page of the *Biblia Hebraica* or in many editions of the rabbinic Bible (מִקְרָאוֹת גְּדוֹלוֹת).

---

* Note 2 Samuel 14:19 and Micah 6:10, where the word אֵשׁ may have the same meaning (and perhaps אִישׁ in Proverbs 18:24).

In addition to those functions, אִיתַי can also serve as a copula (present tense of "to be," i.e. "am, are, is"). This is clearest in those passages where it has a pronominal suffix (see chapter 13) and cannot, therefore, easily be rendered "there is/are":*

לֵאלָהָיךְ לָא אִיתַנָא פָלְחִין.   We do not worship your god. (Daniel 3:18)

VOCABULARY

To Be Learned		*Reference*	
exactly, diligently	אָסְפַּרְנָא	*plural construct of* בַּר	בְּנֵי
priest	כָּהֵן	exile	גָּלוּ
thus	כְּנֵמָא	joy	חֶדְוָה
writing	כְּתָב	dedication	חֲנֻכָּה
reign	מַלְכוּ	day	יוֹם
book	סְפַר	month	יְרַח
just as	(לְ)קֳבֵל	prophecy	נְבוּאָה
rest	שְׁאָר	succeed (H)	צלח
they completed	שַׁכְלִלוּ	*H participle mp*	מַצְלְחִין
six	שֵׁת	establish (H)	קוּם
		H pf 3 mp	הֲקִימוּ
		he finished	שֵׁיצִיא

FROM THE BIBLE (Ezra 6:13–18)

אֱדַיִן תַּתְּנַי פַּחַת עֲבַר־נַהֲרָה שְׁתַר־בּוֹזְנַי וּכְנָוָתְהוֹן לָקֳבֵל דִּי שְׁלַח דָּרְיָוֶשׁ מַלְכָּא כְּנֵמָא

אָסְפַּרְנָא עֲבַדוּ. וִיהוּדָיֵא בָּנַיִן וּמַצְלְחִין בִּנְבוּאַת חַגַּי וּזְכַרְיָה בַּר עִדּוֹא וְשַׁכְלִלוּ מִן

טַעַם אֱלָהּ יִשְׂרָאֵל וּמִטְּעֵם כּוֹרֶשׁ וְדָרְיָוֶשׁ וְאַרְתַּחְשַׁשְׂתְּא מֶלֶךְ פָּרָס וְשֵׁיצִיא בַּיְתָה דְנָה

עַד יוֹם תְּלָתָה לִירַח אֲדָר דִּי הִיא שְׁנַת שֵׁת לְמַלְכוּת דָּרְיָוֶשׁ מַלְכָּא. וַעֲבַדוּ בְנֵי

יִשְׂרָאֵל כָּהֲנַיָּא וְלֵוָיֵא וּשְׁאָר בְּנֵי גָלוּתָא חֲנֻכַּת בֵּית אֱלָהָא דְנָה בְּחֶדְוָה. וַהֲקִימוּ

כָהֲנַיָּא וְלֵוָיֵא עַל עֲבִידַת אֱלָהָא דִּי בִירוּשְׁלֶם כִּכְתָב סְפַר מֹשֶׁה.

---

* Compare the Hebrew אִם יֶשְׁךָ מוֹשִׁיעַ — "if you will save" (Judges 6:36; cf. Genesis 24:42 and 49).

Proper Names

אֲדָר — Last month of the Hebrew calendar (late winter).

לֵוָיֵא — Ritual officials whose ancestry was traced back to Jacob's son Levi.

פָּרַס — Sixth-century empire founded by Cyrus II when he conquered Media, Lydia, and Babylon.

EXERCISES

Fill in the correct pronoun and translate into English:

(1) _____ דְּבַחְתְּ תּוֹר לֵאלָהָא.

(2) _____ יְדַע דִּי שָׁבַיָּא בִּמְדִינְתָּא.

(3) _____ יְהַבְתֵּן סִפְרָא לְפֶחָה.

(4) _____ כְּתַבְתּוּן אִגְּרָה.

(5) _____ נְפַלוּ לְאַרְעָא.

(6) _____ נְפַקְנָא מִבַּיְתָא.

(7) _____ פְּלַחַת בִּירוּשְׁלֶם.

(8) _____ שָׂם טְעֵם.

(9) _____ שְׁלַחִתִּי פִּתְגָם לְבָבֶל.

(10) _____ יְדָעֵת לְמִבְנָא בַּיִת.

(11) _____ סְלִקוּ לִשְׁמַיָּא.

(12) _____ שְׁלַחְנָא מְגִלָּה לְבֵית גִּנְזַיָּא.

Translate the following sentences into English:

(1) אִיתַי הֵיכַל בְּקִרְיְתָא רַבְּתָא.

(2) אַנְתּוּן הִמּוֹ כָּהֲנֵי אֱלָהָא דִּי שְׁמַיָּא.

(3) בֵּית אֱלָהָא אִיתַי בִּירוּשְׁלֶם.

(4) לְגַבְרָא לָא אִיתַי רֵאשׁ.

(5) זְרֻבָּבֶל הוּא פֶּחָה דִּי יְהוּדָיֵא.

(6) כְּנֵמָא כְּתִיב בִּסְפַר דָּרְיָוֶשׁ: אֲנַחְנָא מְצַלַּיִן לְאַרְעָא.

(7) אַנְתְּ הוּא מֶלֶךְ שְׁלָם.

(8) אֱדַיִן שַׁכְלִלוּ עֲבִידַת בַּיִת תַּקִּיף.

Translate into Aramaic:

(1) The six men did exactly as the king said.

(2) We gave the rest of the kingdom to Darius.

(3) The decree is in writing.

(4) There is no palace in Judah.

(5) She is sending a book to the priest there.

Chapter 12

PREPOSITIONS

Some Aramaic prepositions are prefixed to an object; others can stand on their own:

Prefixed		*Independent*	
in	-בְּ	after	אַחֲרֵי
like, as	-כְּ	between	בֵּין
to, for	-לְ	from	מִן
from	-מִ	until	עַד
		on, concerning,	
		to, against	עַל
		with	עִם
		under	תְּחוֹת

Prefixed prepositions are vocalized according to the same patterns that are used in Hebrew. -בְּ, -כְּ, and -לְ normally have a *sh'va*, which shifts to a *ḥiriq* (e.g., -בִּ) when the next consonant has a *sh'va*.

לְהֵיכְלָא   to the palace
לִמְדִינְתָּא   to the province

When מִן is attached to its object, the נ assimilates, where possible, to the first consonant of the following noun (e.g., מִטְּעֵם).

Several other prepositions are unique to Aramaic. Some of these obviously originated from nouns (like the Hebrew לִפְנֵי and בְּתוֹך):

61

בָּאתַר — From the noun אֲתַר ("place"), the preposition means "after" (i.e. "in place of"). Because the א has no vowel, it can drop out, leaving בָּתַר (e.g., Daniel 2:39 on p. 87; for a later development of this form, see p. 153).

גַּו (when standing alone, it is spelled גּוֹא)—"Midst"; can be combined with other prepositions, such as -בְּ and -לְ to mean "inside (i.e. in the midst) of" or "into."

לָקֳבֵל (notice the composite *sh'va* under the ק, as explained on p. 19)—"Just as, opposite, corresponding to"; this preposition often occurs in the expanded form -כָּל קֳבֵל דְּ ("because").

קֳדָם — "In front of"; though literally spatial, it can also be used temporally (e.g., קַדְמָה, "former time"; cf. Hebrew לִפְנֵי, "to the face of").

Aramaic has a direct object marker just like the Hebrew אֵת. Its form is יָת. (The Phoenician equivalent is spelled אית.) Although it is common in later texts (see the synagogue inscription on p. 173 and the Targum Pseudo-Jonathan to Genesis 22:1–2 on pp. 198–200) as well as in Syriac and Nabatean, it occurs only once in the Bible (Daniel 3:12), where direct objects are more often indicated by the preposition -לְ:

e.g., הַרְגִּזוּ אֲבָהֳתַנָא לֶאֱלָהּ שְׁמַיָּא
Our ancestors angered the God of heaven. (Ezra 5:12)*

VOCABULARY

To Be Learned		*Reference*	
judgment	דִּין	tax	בְּלוֹ
judge	דַּיָּן	search	בקר
law	דָּת	*D inf*	בַּקָּרָה
be	הוה/הוא	ram	דְּכַר
G imperfect 3 ms	לֶהֱוֵא	him/his	־הּ
go	הלך	*1s suffix*	־י
G infinitive	מְהָךְ	bring	יבל
G imperfect 3 ms	יְהָךְ	*H inf*	הֵיבָלָה

---

* This same usage occurs occasionally in biblical Hebrew, e.g., זְכֹר לְאַבְרָהָם וּלְיִצְחָק וּלְיִשְׂרָאֵל ("Remember Abraham, Isaac, and Israel"—Exodus 32:13).

To Be Learned		*Reference*	
know	יְדַע	give	יְהַב
H (inform) *ptc mp*	מְהוֹדְעִין	*Gt ptc mp*	מִתְיַהֲבִין
H imf 2 mp	תְּהוֹדְעוּן	be pleasing	יְטַב
be willing (D)	נְדַב	*G imf 3 ms*	יֵיטַב
Dt ptc ms	מִתְנַדַּב	you	ךְ
people	עַם	appoint (D)	מַנָּה
ask	שְׁאַל	*imperative*	מֶנִּי
G imf 3 ms + 2 mp	יִשְׁאֶלְנְכוֹן	do	עֲבַד
(the נ is energic and need not		*G inf*	מֶעְבַּד
be translated)		*Gt imf 3 ms*	יִתְעֲבֵד
authorized	שַׁלִּיט	*G imf 2 mp*	תַּעַבְדוּן
		buy	קְנָה
		G imf 2 ms	תִּקְנֵה
		sacrifice (D)	קְרַב
		D imf 2 ms	תְּקָרֵב
		impose (lit. throw)	רְמָה
		G inf	לְמִרְמֵא
		wish	רְעוּ
		deliver (H)	שְׁלֵם
		imperative	הַשְׁלֵם

FROM THE BIBLE (Ezra 7:12–26)

Ezra 6:19–7:11 is in Hebrew. After describing the celebration of the Passover by those who had returned from the exile and those "who had separated themselves from the impurity of the nations of the land," it announces the return of more exiles. Among them was Ezra, a priest and "scribe, expert in the Teaching of Moses," who presented a letter he had received from Artaxerxes, the text of which is given in Aramaic:

אַרְתַּחְשַׁסְתְּא מֶלֶךְ מַלְכַיָּא לְעֶזְרָא כָהֲנָא סָפַר דָּתָא דִּי אֱלָהּ שְׁמַיָּא: מִנִּי שִׂים טְעֵם דִּי
כָל מִתְנַדַּב בְּמַלְכוּתִי מִן עַמָּא יִשְׂרָאֵל וְכָהֲנוֹהִי וְלֵוָיֵא לִמְהָךְ לִירוּשְׁלֶם עִמָּךְ יְהָךְ.
מִן קֳדָם מַלְכָּא שְׁלִיחַ לְבַקָּרָה עַל יְהוּד וְלִירוּשְׁלֶם בְּדָת אֱלָהָךְ וּלְהֵיבָלָה כְּסַף וּדְהַב
דִּי מַלְכָּא לֶאֱלָהּ יִשְׂרָאֵל דִּי בִירוּשְׁלֶם וְכֹל כְּסַף וּדְהַב בְּכֹל מְדִינַת בָּבֶל
לְבֵית אֱלָהֲהֹם דִּי בִירוּשְׁלֶם. אָסְפַּרְנָא תִקְנֵא בְּכַסְפָּא דְּנָה דִכְרִין וּתְקָרֵב הִמּוֹ
בִירוּשְׁלֶם. וּמָה דִּי עֲלָךְ יֵיטַב בִּשְׁאָר כַּסְפָּא וְדַהֲבָה לְמֶעְבַּד כִּרְעוּת אֱלָהֲכֹם
תַּעַבְדוּן. וּמָאנַיָּא דִּי מִתְיַהֲבִין לָךְ לְבֵית אֱלָהָךְ הַשְׁלֵם קֳדָם אֱלָהּ יְרוּשְׁלֶם. וּמִנִּי אֲנָה
אַרְתַּחְשַׁסְתְּא מַלְכָּא שִׂים טְעֵם דִּי כָל דִּי יִשְׁאֲלֶנְכוֹן עֶזְרָא כָהֲנָא סָפַר דָּתָא דִּי אֱלָהּ
שְׁמַיָּא אָסְפַּרְנָא יִתְעֲבִד. כָּל דִּי מִן טַעַם אֱלָהּ שְׁמַיָּא יִתְעֲבֵד לְבֵית אֱלָהּ
שְׁמַיָּא. וּלְכֹם מְהוֹדְעִין דִּי כָל כָּהֲנַיָּא וְלֵוָיֵא בְּלוֹ לָא שַׁלִּיט לְמִרְמֵא עֲלֵיהֹם.
וְאַנְתְּ עֶזְרָא כְּחָכְמַת אֱלָהָךְ דִּי בִידָךְ מֶנִּי דַיָּנִין לְכָל עַמָּא דִּי בַּעֲבַר־נַהֲרָה לְכָל יָדְעֵי דָּתֵי
אֱלָהָךְ וְדִי לָא יָדַע תְּהוֹדְעוּן. וְכָל דִּי לָא לֶהֱוֵא עָבֵד דָּתָא דִּי אֱלָהָךְ וְדָתָא
דִּי מַלְכָּא אָסְפַּרְנָא דִּינָה לֶהֱוֵא מִתְעֲבֵד מִנֵּהּ.

This concludes the Aramaic section of Ezra. You may wish to read the rest of the book either in Hebrew or in English translation.

EXERCISES

Translate the following sentences into English:

(1) הוּא שְׁאֵל עַל דַּת מַלְכָּא.

(2) עַמָּא דְּנָה שַׁלִּיט לְהֵיבָלָה מָאנַיָּא מִן הֵיכְלָא.

(3) נְבוּכַדְנֶצַּר הֲוָה מֶלֶךְ בָּבֶל מִן עָלְמָא.

(4) מַן מִתְנַדַּב לְמֶעְבַּד נְוָלוּ עַל אַרְעָא.

(5) אַנְתּוּן תְּהוֹדְעוּן לְדַיָּנָא דִּי לֶהֱוֵא מְרַד בִּמְדִינְתָּא.

Translate into Aramaic:

(1) We will go to Jerusalem with Ezra.

(2) The city will be built after they give tax to the king.

(3) The judgment was between the king and the people.

(4) They said: Leave the book in Babylon.

(5) The head was in the sky.

Chapter 13

PRONOMINAL SUFFIXES

Besides independent pronouns, Aramaic also has pronominal suffixes, which can be attached to verbs (direct object), to nouns (possession), and to prepositions (object). Although the actual suffixes can vary, depending on the nature of the word to which they are attached, the various possibilities are all similar to each other and to the independent forms of the pronouns.

singular	1 common	אֲנָה	־ִי	(on verbs ־ַנִי)
	2 masculine	אַנְתְּ	־ָךְ	
	2 feminine	אַנְתִּי	־כִי	
	3 masculine	הוּא	־ֵהּ	(־ִהִי, ־וֹהִי)
	3 feminine	הִיא	־ַהּ	
plural	1 common	אֲנַחְנָה	־נָא	
	2 masculine	(אַנְתֹּם) אַנְתּוּן	־כֹם	(־כוֹן)
	2 feminine	אַנְתֵּן	־כֵן	
	3 masculine	(אִנּוּן) הִמּוֹ	־הֹם	(־הוֹן)
	3 feminine	אִנִּין	־הֵן	

Notice the resemblance between these suffixes and their Hebrew counterparts, which extends to the use of ת as a base for the 2d person independent pronouns while the suffixes have a כ (thus Hebrew אַתָּה and ־ךָ). The exact form of the suffixes depends on the number and gender of the noun to which they are attached.

SUFFIX	SINGULAR NOUNS *Masculine*	SINGULAR NOUNS *Feminine*	PLURAL NOUNS *Masculine*	PLURAL NOUNS *Feminine*
singular 1c	פִּשְׁרִי	מַלְכוּתִי	פִּשְׁרַי	מַלְכְוָתִי
2m	פִּשְׁרָךְ	מַלְכוּתָךְ	*פִּשְׁרָיךְ	מַלְכְוָתָךְ
2f	פִּשְׁרֵכִי	מַלְכוּתֵכִי	פִּשְׁרַיְכִי	מַלְכְוָתֵכִי
3m	פִּשְׁרֵהּ	מַלְכוּתֵהּ	פִּשְׁרוֹהִי	מַלְכְוָתֵהּ
3f	פִּשְׁרַהּ	מַלְכוּתַהּ	*פִּשְׁרַיהּ	מַלְכְוָתַהּ
plural 1c	פִּשְׁרַנָא	מַלְכוּתַנָא	*פִּשְׁרַינָא	מַלְכְוָתַנָא
2m	פִּשְׁרְכֹם (-כוֹן)	מַלְכוּתְכֹם (-כוֹן)	פִּשְׁרֵיכֹם (-כוֹן)	מַלְכְוָתְכֹם (-כוֹן)
2f	פִּשְׁרְכֵן	מַלְכוּתְכֵן	פִּשְׁרֵיכֵן	מַלְכְוָתְכֵן
3m	פִּשְׁרְהֹם (-הוֹן)	מַלְכוּתְהֹם (-הוֹן)	פִּשְׁרֵיהֹם (-הוֹן)	מַלְכְוָתְהֹם (-הוֹן)
3f	פִּשְׁרְהֵן	מַלְכוּתְהֵן	פִּשְׁרֵיהֵן	מַלְכְוָתֵן

As in Hebrew, these suffixes are attached to a shortened form of the noun, such as פִּשְׁר- (which is the same base as that used for the determined suffix— פִּשְׁרָא), rather than the absolute פְּשַׁר. Sometimes, however, they are added to irregular forms of the words. This happens most often with words that refer to family members, such as אַב (אֲבָהָתָנָא, אֲבוּהִי), אַח (אֲחָיךְ), and בַּר (בְּרֵהּ).

When these suffixes are attached to nouns, they express possession:

e.g., בֵּיתִי   my house

אֱלָהֵהּ   his god

חַבְרְתַהּ   her companion

This can help explain an Aramaic phrase which is preserved in the New Testament:

μαραναθα = מָרַנָא תָה   "Our master, come!" (1 Corinthians 16:22)**

Pronominal suffixes can also appear on prepositions and on verbs. The prepositions לְ-, מִן, עִם, בְּגוֹ, לְוָת, and לָקֳבֵל take the pronominal endings that go on singular nouns; others, such as עַל, אַחֲרֵי, בֵּין, קֳדָם, and תְּחוֹת, take those for plural nouns.

---

* These are really mixed forms. The י (which is not pronounced) belongs to the כְּתִיב, where it would have been part of a diphthong (e.g., פִּשְׁרָיךְ); cf. the 3rd person masculine singular suffix Hebrew uses for plural nouns, such as אֱלָהָיו.

** Cf. Revelation 22:20.

singular	1	לִי	עֲלַי
	2 masculine	לָךְ	עֲלָיךְ
	2 feminine	* לִכִי	* עֲלַיְכִי
	3 masculine	לֵהּ	עֲלוֹהִי
	3 feminine	לַהּ	עֲלַיהּ
plural	1	לַנָא	עֲלַינָא
	2 masculine	(לְכוֹן) לְכֹם	* עֲלֵיכֹם
	2 feminine	* לְכֵן	* עֲלֵיכֵן
	3 masculine	(לְהוֹן) לְהֹם	(עֲלֵיהוֹן) עֲלֵיהֹם
	3 feminine	* לְהֵן	* עֲלֵיהֵן

The suffixes for plural nouns are also used with the particle of existence (אִיתַי) and are then translated as the subject of a copula (see chapter 11):

לֵאלָהָיךְ לָא אִיתַנָא פָלְחִין   We do not worship your god. (Daniel 3:18)

הַאִיתָיךְ כָּהֵל לְהוֹדָעֻתַנִי   Are you able to inform me? (Daniel 2:26)

Pronominal suffixes commonly appear as direct objects of a verb. (This same structure occurs in Hebrew, although its pronominal suffixes can also be attached to אֵת in forms like אוֹתוֹ.) Because the exact form of the suffix (and the verbal base onto which it is attached) varies, it is not practical to try to memorize all possibilities. Here are some examples to demonstrate what such forms look like on one verb:

		Perfect	*Imperfect*
singular	1	הוֹדַעְתַּנִי	** יְהוֹדְעִנַּנִי
	2 masculine	הוֹדְעָךְ	_____
	3 masculine	_____	אֲהוֹדְעִנֵּהּ
plural	1	הוֹדַעְתֶּנָא	_____

---

* These are hypothetical forms, which do not actually occur in the Bible.

** Note that the נ is doubled before the pronominal suffix.

When a noun is emphasized by being placed at the beginning of a sentence or clause, its place in the sentence proper is taken by a subsequent (resumptive) pronoun. This usage is called "casus pendens" (lit. "the hanging case") because the noun is technically neither the subject nor the object of the sentence.

e.g., בַּיְתָא דְנָה סַתְרֵהּ   This house—he destroyed it. (Ezra 5:12)

VOCABULARY

To Be Learned		Reference	
another	אָחֳרָן	kill (H)	אבד
tell (D, H)	חוה/חוא	*H infinitive*	הוֹבָדָה
D imperfect 1 p	נְחַוֵּא	say	אמר
D imf 3 ms + 3 fs	יְחַוִּנַּהּ	*G imf 3 ms*	יֵאמַר
H imf 1 p	נְהַחֲוֵה	*G imperative*	אֱמַר
H imf 2 mp	תְּהַחֲוֹן	limb	הַדָּם
H imv mp + 1 s	הַחֲוֹֻנִי	buy	זבן
H inf	לְהַחֲוָיָא	inform (H)	ידע
wise	חַכִּים	*H imf 2 mp*	תְּהוֹדְעוּנַּנִי
dream	חֵלֶם	be able	יכל
therefore, except	לָהֵן	difficult	יַקִּיר
word, thing	מִלָּה	glory	יְקָר
time	עִדָּן	receive	קבל
answer	ענה	*D imf 2 mp*	תְּקַבְּלוּן
G pf 3 mp	עֲנוֹ	be angry	קצף
interpretation	פְּשַׁר	issue	שׂים
change (D)	שׁנה	*Gt (passive) imperfect*	
Dt (passive) imperfect		*3 mp*	יִתְשָׂמוּן
3 ms	יִשְׁתַּנֵּה		

FROM THE BIBLE (Daniel 2:4–13)

The opening section of Daniel (1:1–2:4) is written in Hebrew. Read it in the original or in translation before beginning the Aramaic selection for this chapter.

מַלְכָּא אֱמַר חֶלְמָא לְעַבְדָיךְ וּפִשְׁרָא נְחַוֵּא. עָנֵה מַלְכָּא וְאָמַר לְכַשְׂדָּיֵא: הֵן לָא

תְהוֹדְעוּנַּנִי חֶלְמָא וּפִשְׁרֵהּ הַדָּמִין תִּתְעַבְדוּן וּבָתֵּיכוֹן נְוָלִי יִתְּשָׂמוּן וְהֵן חֶלְמָא וּפִשְׁרֵהּ

תְּהַחֲוֹן יְקָר שַׂגִּיא תְּקַבְּלוּן מִן קֳדָמָי. לָהֵן חֶלְמָא וּפִשְׁרֵהּ הַחֲוֹנִי. עֲנוֹ וְאָמְרִין:

מַלְכָּא חֶלְמָא יֵאמַר לְעַבְדוֹהִי וּפִשְׁרָה נְהַחֲוֵה. עָנֵה מַלְכָּא וְאָמַר: יַדַּע אֲנָה דִּי עִדָּנָא

אַנְתּוּן זָבְנִין עַד דִּי עִדָּנָא יִשְׁתַּנֵּא. עֲנוֹ כַשְׂדָּיֵא קֳדָם מַלְכָּא וְאָמְרִין: לָא אִיתַי אֲנָשׁ

דִּי מִלַּת מַלְכָּא יוּכַל לְהַחֲוָיָה. כָּל מֶלֶךְ רַב מִלָּה כִדְנָה לָא שְׁאֵל לְכָל כַּשְׂדָּי וּמִלְתָא

דִּי מַלְכָּה שָׁאֵל יַקִּירָה. וְאָחֳרָן לָא אִיתַי דִּי יְחַוִּנַּהּ קֳדָם מַלְכָּא לָהֵן אֱלָהִין.

מַלְכָּא קְצַף שַׂגִּיא וַאֲמַר לְהוֹבָדָה לְכָל חַכִּימֵי בָבֶל.

Proper Names

כַּשְׂדָּי — This term, which originally designated the inhabitants of a geographic region, came to mean "magician"; it is used with both meanings in the book of Daniel (cf. 5:11 and 30 on pp. 126 and 137). Although it is spelled with a שׁ here and throughout the book of Daniel, it occurs with ס (כַּסְדָּי) in Ezra 5:12 (see p. 38). Over time, שׁ tended to be replaced by ס, even in words where the former was historically correct. A similar process took place in post-biblical Hebrew; however, it is only beginnng to occur in the Bible (cf. Artaxerxes' name, which is spelled with a ס in Ezra 7:21; see p. 64).

Although the forms אָמַר and יָדַע look like Hebrew perfects, they are participles in Aramaic (compare the syntactically parallel עָנֵה); the perfect would be אֲמַר and יְדַע. אֱמַר is imperative.

EXERCISES

Translate:

אֲבוּךְ	כָּהֲנוֹהִי
אַחֲרֵיהוֹן	עַבְדָּיךְ
אִיתֵיכוֹן	עֲלַי
אִיתוֹהִי	עֲלָיךְ
אֱלָהִי	עִמֵּהּ
אֱלָהֵהּ	לָקֳבְלָךְ
בָּתְרָךְ	קֳדָמוֹהִי
בֵּינֵיהוֹן	רֵאשְׁהוֹן
בַּיְתֵהּ	שָׁמֵהּ
בְּרֵהּ	שְׁמָהָתְהֹם
בְּגַוַּהּ	תְּחֹתוֹהִי
הֵיכְלִי	תְּלָתְהוֹן
יָתְהוֹן	

Translate into Aramaic:

(1) The king will be a servant in another time.

(2) The wise men answered the head of the province.

(3) The interpretation will change if the scribe goes out from the city.

(4) There is a word in my dream that I did not know.

(5) We will tell everything except the name of our god.

(6) His house is on a dunghill.

Chapter 14

DEMONSTRATIVE, RELATIVE, AND INTERROGATIVE PRONOUNS

Besides the personal pronouns, there are demonstratives ("this, that," etc.), relatives (which, that), and interrogatives (who, what). In Hebrew, the singular forms of the demonstrative pronouns are built around the letter ז (זֶה, זֹאת); Aramaic uses ד:

		Singular	*Plural*
Near (this, these)	masculine	דְּנָה	אִלֵּין (also אֵלֶּה and אֵל)
	feminine	דָּא	
Far (that, those)	masculine	דֵּךְ	אִלֵּךְ
	feminine	דָּךְ	
	masculine and feminine	דִּכֵּן	

Third person pronouns can also be used as demonstratives:

הוּא צַלְמָא רֵאשֵׁהּ דִּי דְהַב

That statue—its head was of gold. (Daniel 2:32)

וּבְיוֹמֵיהוֹן דִּי מַלְכַיָּא אִנּוּן

And in the days of those kings   (Daniel 2:44)

As in Hebrew, the demonstratives can function either as nouns, which stand on their own, or act like adjectives, in which case they usually follow the noun they modify (which must be determined):

בַּיְתָא דְנָה	this house (Ezra 5:3, 12, 6:15)
כֹּל דְּנָה יְדַעְתָּ	you know all of this (Daniel 5:22)
כִּדְנָה תֵּאמְרוּן לְהוֹם	thus ("like this") shall you say to them (Jeremiah 10:11)

73

We have already encountered the Aramaic relative pronoun דִּי ("which, that"). It is especially common after verbs of perception and communication, such as אמר, ידע, and שמע, and frequently introduces direct quotations. It can also express purpose or cause.

הֵיכְלָא דִי בִירוּשְׁלֶם   the temple which is in Jerusalem (Ezra 5:14)

יָדַע אֲנָה דִּי עִדָּנָא אַנְתּוּן זָבְנִין   I know that you are buying time. (Daniel 2:8)

עָנֵה מַלְכָּא וְאָמַר לְחַכִּימֵי בָבֶל דִּי כָל אֱנָשׁ דִּי יִקְרֵה כְּתָבָה דְּנָה
וּפִשְׁרֵהּ יְחַוִּנַּנִי אַרְגְּוָנָא יִלְבַּשׁ

> The king answers and says to the wise men of Babylon: "Any man who will read this writing and tell me its interpretation will wear purple." (Daniel 5:7)

אַנְתְּ כָּהֵל דִּי רוּחַ אֱלָהִין קַדִּישִׁין בָּךְ

> You are able because the spirit of the holy gods is in you.
> (Daniel 4:15)

שְׁמָהָתְהֹן שְׁאֵלְנָא . . . דִּי נִכְתֻּב שֻׁם גֻּבְרַיָּא דִּי בְרָאשֵׁיהֹם

> We asked their names so that we can write the names of the men who are at their head. (Ezra 5:10)

In addition to standing on its own, דִּי is often attached to various prepositions to form a relative conjunction:

כְּדִי	when
מִן דִּי	after, because
כָּל קֳבֵל דִּי	inasmuch as, because
עַד דִּי	until

The interrogative pronouns are מַן ("who") and מָה ("what"). They can also be joined with the relative דִּי to form indefinite relative pronouns:

מַן דִּי	whoever
מָה דִּי	whatever

VOCABULARY

To Be Learned		*Reference*	
father	אַב	bless	בְּרַךְ
plural	אֲבָהָת	*D pass participle*	מְבָרַךְ
destroy (H)	אבד	power	גְּבוּרָה
H imf 3 mp	יְהוֹבְדוּן	companion	חֲבַר
H imf 2 ms	תְּהוֹבֵד	tell (D, H)	חוה/חוא
H infinitive	לְהוֹבָדָה	*D imf 1 s*	אַחֲוֵא
seek	בעה	*H infinitive*	לְהַחֲוָיָה
G infinitive	לְמִבְעֵה	inform (H)	ידע
reveal	גלה	*H perfect 3 ms*	הוֹדַע
passive perfect 3 ms	גְּלִי	thus	כֵּן
time	זְמַן	appoint (D)	מנה
wisdom	חָכְמָה	*D perfect 3 ms*	מַנִּי
enter	עלל	deep	עַמִּיק
G perfect 3 ms	עַל	establish, raise up (H)	קום
H imv 3 ms	הַעֵל	*H participle ms*	מְהָקֵים
thereupon	כָּל קֳבֵל דְּנָה	compassion	רַחֲמִין
secret	רָז	change (H—transitive)	שנה
praise (D)	שבח	*H participle ms*	מְהַשְׁנֵא
D participle ms	מְשַׁבַּח		

FROM THE BIBLE (Daniel 2:14–24)

בֵּאדַיִן דָּנִיֵּאל בְּעָה מִן מַלְכָּא דִּי זְמָן יִנְתֶּן לֵהּ וּפִשְׁרָא לְהַחֲוָיָה לְמַלְכָּא. אֱדַיִן דָּנִיֵּאל לְבַיְתֵהּ אֲזַל וְלַחֲנַנְיָה מִישָׁאֵל וַעֲזַרְיָה חַבְרוֹהִי מִלְּתָא הוֹדַע וְרַחֲמִין לְמִבְעֵא מִן קֳדָם אֱלָהּ שְׁמַיָּא עַל רָזָה דְּנָה דִּי לָא יְהֹבְדוּן דָּנִיֵּאל וְחַבְרוֹהִי עִם חַכִּימֵי בָבֶל.

אֱדַיִן לְדָנִיֵּאל רָזָה גֲלִי. אֱדַיִן דָּנִיֵּאל בָּרִךְ לֶאֱלָהּ שְׁמַיָּא. עָנֵה דָנִיֵּאל וְאָמַר.

לֶהֱוֵא שְׁמֵהּ דִּי אֱלָהָא מְבָרַךְ מִן עָלְמָא וְעַד עָלְמָא דִּי חָכְמְתָא וּגְבוּרְתָא דִּי לֵהּ הִיא

וְהוּא מְהַשְׁנֵא עִדָּנַיָּא וְזִמְנַיָּא. מְהָקֵים מַלְכִין יָהֵב חָכְמְתָא לְחַכִּימִין. הוּא גָּלֵא

עַמִּיקָתָא. לָךְ אֱלָהּ אֲבָהָתִי מְשַׁבַּח אֲנָה דִּי חָכְמְתָא וּגְבוּרְתָא יְהַבְתְּ לִי וּכְעַן הוֹדַעְתַּנִי

דִּי בְעֵינָא מִנָּךְ דִּי מִלַּת מַלְכָּא הוֹדַעְתֶּנָא. כָּל קֳבֵל דְּנָה דָּנִיֵּאל עַל עַל אַרְיוֹךְ דִּי מַנִּי

מַלְכָּא לְהוֹבָדָה לְחַכִּימֵי בָבֶל. אֲזַל וְכֵן אֲמַר לֵהּ. לְחַכִּימֵי בָבֶל אַל תְּהוֹבֵד. הַעֵלְנִי

קֳדָם מַלְכָּא וּפִשְׁרָא לְמַלְכָּא אֲחַוֵּא.

Proper Nouns

אַרְיוֹךְ — the captain of Nebuchadnezzar's guard.

דָּנִיֵּאל — a Jew who was taken to Babylon, where he served in the royal court, interpreting dreams and surviving great danger.

חֲנַנְיָה, מִישָׁאֵל, עֲזַרְיָה — young Judean exiles trained in the Babylonian court.

EXERCISES

Translate into English:

(1) יָדְעָנָא רָזַיָּא אִלֵּין.

(2) מַן בְּנָה הֵיכְלָא דֵךְ?

(3) סָפְרָא כְּתַב דִּי חָכְמָה אָבְדָה מִבָּבֶל בִּזְמַן נְבוּכַדְנֶצַּר.

(4) דָּנִיֵּאל עַל לְשָׁמַיָּא.

(5) כָּל קֳבֵל דְּנָה גַּלִי דִּי מְהָקֵים מַלְכָּא רֵאשׁ פֶּחָה עַל קִרְיְתָא דָא.

(6) אִיתַי אֱנָשׁ דִּי בָעֵה רַחֲמִין.

Translate into Aramaic:

(1) This father praises the law of God.

(2) I am authorized to seek that book in the treasure house.

(3) These provinces are under a strong king.

(4) They left that letter there.

(5) We are giving many vessels in the midst of the earth.

Chapter 15

G IMPERFECT

The verbal system of most Northwest Semitic languages has two major tenses (or aspects)—one formed by adding suffixes to the root (the perfect), while the other (the imperfect) adds prefixes, with suffixes used to indicate plurals and gender. (By contrast, Akkadian, which is an East Semitic language, has two distinct prefix tenses—one for the past, and the other for future action.)

Having already examined Aramaic's perfect conjugation, we can now consider the imperfect. Although the vowels are somewhat different, the basic structure is the same as in Hebrew:

G Imperfect

	Singular	*Plural*
1st person	אֶכְתֻּב	נִכְתֻּב
2d masculine	תִּכְתֻּב	תִּכְתְּבוּן
feminine	תִּכְתְּבִין	תִּכְתְּבָן
3d masculine	יִכְתֻּב	יִכְתְּבוּן
feminine	תִּכְתֻּב	יִכְתְּבָן

As in Hebrew, the theme vowel (the one under the second root letter) is not fixed, but can vary from root to root. Although *u* is the most common theme vowel (as in the case of כתב above), it is not universal:

e.g.,	יִפֵּל	(root נפל)	he will fall
	יִנְתֵּן *	(root נתן)	he will give
	יִשְׁלַט	(root שלט)	he will rule
	יִלְבַּשׁ	(root לבשׁ)	he will wear

---

* Notice that the initial נ does not assimilate in this form as it does in the Hebrew equivalent (יִתֵּן) and, indeed, in the form יִפֵּל given above.

A very important exception to this pattern involves the verb הוה (to be), in which several third person forms begin with ל-:

לֶהֱוֵא	he will be
לֶהֱוֹן	they (m) will be
לֶהֱוְיָן	they (f) will be

Thus:

אֱלָהּ רַב הוֹדַע לְמַלְכָּא מָה דִּי לֶהֱוֵא אַחֲרֵי דְנָה

The great God informed the king what will be after this. (Daniel 4:45)

The jussive appears to be the same as the imperfect, although final ן may fall off of some plural forms.

VOCABULARY

To Be Learned

stone	אֶבֶן
break off	גזר
is broken off	הִתְגְּזֶר
be crushed	דקק
H perfect 3 ms	הַדֵּק
see	חזה
clay	חֲסַף
mountain	טוּר
copper	נְחָשׁ
iron	פַּרְזֶל
statue	צְלֵם
foot	רְגַל

Reference

but	בְּרַם
exile	גָּלוּ
arm	דְּרָע
breast	חֲדֶה
inform (H)	ידע
H perfect 3 ms	הוֹדַע
H imperfect 3 mp	יְהוֹדְעוּן
be able	יכל
thigh	יַרְכָה
be able	כהל
hit	מחא
belly	מְעֵה
enter	עלל
H perfect 3 ms	הַנְעֵל
find	שכח
H perfect 1 s	הַשְׁכַּחַת
leg	שָׁק

FROM THE BIBLE (Daniel 2:25–36)

אֱדַיִן אַרְיוֹךְ הַנְעֵל לְדָנִיֵּאל קֳדָם מַלְכָּא וְכֵן אֲמַר לֵהּ: הַשְׁכַּחַת גְּבַר מִן בְּנֵי גָלוּתָא

דִּי יְהוּד דִּי פִשְׁרָא לְמַלְכָּא יְהוֹדַע. עָנֵה מַלְכָּא וְאָמַר לְדָנִיֵּאל דִּי שְׁמֵהּ בֵּלְטְשַׁאצַּר:

הַאִיתָיךְ כָּהֵל לְהוֹדָעֻתַנִי חֶלְמָא דִּי חֲזֵית וּפִשְׁרֵהּ? עָנֵה דָנִיֵּאל קֳדָם מַלְכָּא וְאָמַר:

רָזָה דִּי מַלְכָּא שָׁאֵל לָא חַכִּימִין יָכְלִין לְהַחֲוָיָה לְמַלְכָּא בְּרַם אִיתַי אֱלָהּ בִּשְׁמַיָּא

גָּלֵא רָזִין וְהוֹדַע לְמַלְכָּא נְבוּכַדְנֶצַּר מָה דִּי לֶהֱוֵא. וַאֲנָה לָא בְחָכְמָה דִּי אִיתַי בִּי

רָזָא דְנָה גֱּלִי לִי לָהֵן דִּי פִשְׁרָא לְמַלְכָּא יְהוֹדְעוּן. אַנְתְּ מַלְכָּא חָזֵה הֲוַיְתָ צֶלֶם

חַד שַׂגִּיא. צַלְמָא דִּכֵּן רַב. הוּא צַלְמָא — רֵאשֵׁהּ דִּי דְהַב טָב חֲדוֹהִי וּדְרָעוֹהִי

דִּי כְסַף מְעוֹהִי וְיַרְכָתֵהּ דִּי נְחָשׁ שָׁקוֹהִי דִּי פַרְזֶל רַגְלוֹהִי מִנְּהֵן דִּי פַרְזֶל וּמִנְּהֵן

דִּי חֲסַף. חָזֵה הֲוַיְתָ עַד דִּי הִתְגְּזֶרֶת אֶבֶן דִּי לָא בִידַיִן וּמְחָת לְצַלְמָא עַל רַגְלוֹהִי

דִּי פַרְזְלָא וְחַסְפָּא וְהַדֵּקֶת הִמּוֹן. בֵּאדַיִן דָּקוּ כַחֲדָה פַּרְזְלָא חַסְפָּא נְחָשָׁא כַּסְפָּא

וְדַהֲבָא. וְאַבְנָא דִּי מְחָת לְצַלְמָא הֲוָת לְטוּר רַב. דְּנָה חֶלְמָא וּפִשְׁרֵהּ נֵאמַר

קֳדָם מַלְכָּא.

EXERCISES

Conjugate the following verbs in the G imperfect:

		סגד		שׁבק
singular	1			
	2 m			
	2 f			
	3 m			
	3 f			
plural	1			
	2 m			
	2 f			
	3 m			
	3 f			

		שׁלט		נפל
singular	1			
	2 m			
	2 f			
	3 m			
	3 f			
plural	1			
	2 m			
	2 f			
	3 m			
	3 f			

Identify the form of the following imperfect verbs:

	Root	Person	Gender	Number
תֵּאכֵל				
נֵאמַר				
אֶבְעֵא				
תֶּהֱוֵא				
לֶהֱוֹן				
נִכְתֻּב				
תַּעַבְדוּן				
יִפְלְחוּן				
אֶקְרֵא				

Translate into Aramaic:

(1) I will write a letter on a stone from the mountain.

(2) She will send a message to the scribe.

(3) He broke the foot and the head off of the statue.

(4) That man sees vessels of clay which Daniel smashed.

(5) There is iron under the earth.

(6) We will ask to build a palace there.

(7) The Judeans left copper in Babylon.

Chapter 16

ADJECTIVES AND GENITIVE CONSTRUCTIONS (דִּי)

Aramaic adjectives behave very much like nouns—they have number and gender, and can be determined or undetermined. Moreover, their endings are exactly the same as those for nouns.

		Masculine	*Feminine*
singular	absolute	רַחִיק	רַחִיקָה
	determined	רַחִיקָא	רַחִיקְתָּא
plural	absolute	רַחִיקִין	רַחִיקָן
	determined	רַחִיקַיָּא*	רַחִיקָתָא

In general, adjectives must agree with the noun that they modify in number, gender, and determination; however, predicate adjectives are always undetermined.

Another way in which Aramaic expresses description is with nouns. This is done by using genitival constructions, such as construct phrases in which two nouns are joined together:

שֵׁם אֱלָהָא   the name of God

As in Hebrew, these word pairs are treated as if they were one word. Therefore, the first word loses its accent.

Another way of expressing genitival relationships is with the conjunction דִּי ("which, of"):

שֵׁם דִּי אֱלָהָא   the name of God

---

* The ending for plural determined gentilics is יֵ-.

Later on, Aramaic inserted a pronominal suffix (see chapter 13), which anticipates the genitive word, into this construction:

שְׁמֵהּ דִּי אֱלָהָא   His name, the one of God

i.e., the name of God

This construction eventually became almost normative in both Hebrew and Aramaic. However, it was still relatively uncommon in the biblical period, although it does sometimes occur (e.g., הִנֵּה מִטָּתוֹ שֶׁלִּשְׁלֹמֹה— "Behold, the bed of Solomon," Song of Songs 3:7).

Genitival constructions are not limited to possession. They can also indicate the composition of an object or what it is attached to:

שְׁבִיבִין דִּי נוּר   flames of fire (Daniel 7:9)

צְלֵם דִּי דְהַב   statue of gold (Daniel 3:1)

אֶצְבְּעָן דִּי יַד אֱנָשׁ   fingers of a human hand,

i.e., human fingers (Daniel 5:5)

VOCABULARY

To Be Learned			*Reference*	
another	אָחֳרִי	after	אַחֲרֵי
field	בַּר	face (*p*)	אֲנַף
dwell	דּוּר	finger	אֶצְבַּע
G participle mp	דָּאֲרִין	after (lit. "in place of")	בָּתַר
animal	חֵיוָה	reveal	גלה
be able	יכל	*G infinitive*	לְמִגְלֵא
fall	נפל	smash (H)	דקק
bow down	סגד	*H participle ms*	מְהַדֵּק
fourth	רְבִיעִי	destroy (D)	חבל
rule	שלט	*Dt (passive) imf 3 fs*	תִּתְחַבַּל
third	תְּלִיתָי	inform (H)	ידע
		H pf 3 ms	הוֹדַע
		day	יוֹם
		bird	עוֹף
		divided	פְּלִיגָה
		rise	קוּם
		H imf 3 ms	יְקִים
		foot	רְגַל
		leave, abandon	שבק
		Gt (passive) imf 3 fs	תִּשְׁתְּבִק
		breakable	תְּבִיר

FROM THE BIBLE (Daniel 2:37–49)

אַנְתְּ מַלְכָּא מֶלֶךְ מַלְכַיָּא דִּי אֱלָהּ שְׁמַיָּא מַלְכוּתָא יְהַב לָךְ וּבְכָל דִּי דָאֲרִין בְּנֵי אֲנָשָׁא

חֵיוַת בָּרָא וְעוֹף שְׁמַיָּא יְהַב בִּידָךְ וְהַשְׁלְטָךְ בְּכָלְּהֹן. אַנְתְּ הוּא רֵאשָׁה דִּי דַהֲבָא.

וּבָתְרָךְ תְּקוּם מַלְכוּ אָחֳרִי אֲרַעָא מִנָּךְ וּמַלְכוּ תְּלִיתָיָא אָחֳרִי דִּי נְחָשָׁא דִּי תִשְׁלַט בְּכָל

אַרְעָא. וּמַלְכוּ רְבִיעָיָה תֶּהֱוֵא תַקִּיפָה כְּפַרְזְלָא מְהַדֵּק כֹּלָּא. וְדִי חֲזַיְתָה רַגְלַיָּא

וְאֶצְבְּעָתָא מִנְּהֵן חֲסַף וּמִנְּהֵן פַּרְזֶל מַלְכוּ פְלִיגָה תֶּהֱוֵה וְאֶצְבְּעָת רַגְלַיָּא מִנְּהֵן פַּרְזֶל

וּמִנְּהֵן חֲסַף מִן מַלְכוּתָא תֶּהֱוֵא תַקִּיפָה וּמִנַּהּ תֶּהֱוֵה תְבִירָה. וּבְיוֹמֵיהוֹן דִּי מַלְכַיָּא אִנּוּן

יְקִים אֱלָהּ שְׁמַיָּא מַלְכוּ דִּי לְעָלְמִין לָא תִתְחַבַּל וּמַלְכוּתָה לְעַם אָחֳרָן לָא תִשְׁתְּבִק

וְהִיא תְּקוּם לְעָלְמַיָּא. כָּל קֳבֵל דִּי חֲזַיְתָ דִּי מִטּוּרָא אִתְגְּזֶרֶת אֶבֶן דִּי לָא בִידַיִן

וְהַדֶּקֶת פַּרְזְלָא נְחָשָׁא חַסְפָּא כַּסְפָּא וְדַהֲבָא. אֱלָהּ רַב הוֹדַע לְמַלְכָּא מָה דִּי לֶהֱוֵא

אַחֲרֵי דְנָה. בֵּאדַיִן מַלְכָּא נְבוּכַדְנֶצַּר נְפַל עַל אַנְפּוֹהִי וּלְדָנִיֵּאל סְגִד. עָנֵה מַלְכָּא

לְדָנִיֵּאל וְאָמַר. אֱלָהֲכוֹן הוּא אֱלָהּ אֱלָהִין וְגָלֵה רָזִין דִּי יְכֵלְתָּ לְמִגְלֵא רָזָה דְנָה.

אֱדַיִן מַלְכָּא הַשְׁלְטֵהּ עַל כָּל מְדִינַת בָּבֶל וְעַל כָּל חַכִּימֵי בָבֶל.

EXERCISES

Translate into English:

(1) אֲנַחְנָא דָאֲרִין בְּבַיִת דִּי דְהַב.

(2) יִשְׁלַט מַלְכָּא עַל מְדִינַת עֲבַר־נַהֲרָא.

(3) חַגַּי הַדֵּק חֵיוָה תַקִּיפָה.

(4) אֱנָשׁ רְבִיעִי אֲזַל.

(5) הִמּוֹ יִסְגְּדוּן לְרֵאשֵׁהּ דִּי צַלְמָא.

(6) אִיתַי אֶצְבְּעָן שַׂגִּיאָן עַל יַד דָּרְיָוֶשׁ.

Translate into Aramaic:

(1) The interpretation of the fourth decree is written in the temple.

(2) They fall from their feet and they pray to God.

(3) We went out to the distant field.

(4) The wise scribe came with a third message.

(5) We were able to build another house.

Chapter 17

NUMBERS

We have already encountered several Aramaic numerals which are etymologically related to their Hebrew equivalents. Thus "1" is חַד, which is only lacking the initial א of its Hebrew cognate אֶחָד. "3" and "6" are תְּלָת and שֵׁת, reflecting the Aramaic realization of Semitic *th* as ת, where Hebrew uses שׁ (hence שָׁלוֹשׁ and שֵׁשׁ).

As in Hebrew, Aramaic numerals, which can appear either before or after the nouns to which they refer, have both masculine and feminine forms.

	Masculine	*Feminine*
1	חַד	חֲדָה
2	תְּרֵין (תְּרֵי)	תַּרְתֵּין (תַּרְתֵּי)
3	תְּלָתָה	תְּלָת
4	אַרְבְּעָה	אַרְבַּע
5	חַמְשָׁא	חֲמֵשׁ
6	שִׁתָּה	שֵׁת (or שֶׁת)
7	שִׁבְעָה	שְׁבַע
8	תְּמָנְיָה	תְּמָנֶה
9	תִּשְׁעָה	תְּשַׁע
10	עֲשָׂרָה	עֲשַׂר

As in Hebrew, except for "1," the simpler form is used with feminine nouns, whereas the form ending with הָ- is used with masculine nouns:

e.g., גֻּבְרִין אַרְבְּעָא   4 men (Daniel 3:25)

אַמִּין שֵׁת   6 cubits (Daniel 3:1)

The number "2" has a construct form (תְּרֵי), which is used in the phrase for "12" (תְּרֵי־עֲשַׂר).

The decades between ten and one hundred are based on plural forms of the digits; thus twenty is עֶשְׂרִין, thirty is תְּלָתִין, and so on. Larger numbers include מְאָה (100), אֲלַף (1,000) and רִבּוֹ (10,000). (Recall that 200 is מָאתַיִן, as noted on p. 27.)

As the determined state became the "normal" form for nouns in later Aramaic, the language had to develop another way to indicate whether a word was determined or not. To do this, the numeral "one" (חַד) was used as a marker of *in*determinacy. Intimations of this practice can be found in the Bible:

צְלֵם חַד   an image (Daniel 2:31)

מְגִלָּה חֲדָה   a scroll (Ezra 6:2)

חַד is also used to indicate multiples:

חַד שִׁבְעָה   seven times more than. . . . (Daniel 3:19)

Ordinal numbers (except for "2") end with ִי-:

first   קַדְמָי

second   תִּנְיָן *

third   תְּלִיתָי

fourth   רְבִיעִי

---

*This form is much closer to the Hebrew שֵׁנִי than is the cardinal form תְּרֵין.

VOCABULARY

To Be Learned		*Reference*	
furnace	אַתּוּן	live (G)	חיה
music	זְמָר	strength	חַיִל
type	זַן	dedication	חֲנֻכָּה
burn	יקד	when	כְּדִי
fire	נוּר	gather	כנש
worship	פלח	*G infinitive*	לְמִכְנַשׁ
sound	קָל	*Dt participle mp*	מִתְכַּנְּשִׁין
horn	קֶרֶן	herald	כָּרוֹז
throw	רמה	prefect	סְגַן
Gt imf 3 ms	יִתְרְמֵא	rise	קוּם
hear	שמע	*G participle mp*	קָאֲמִין
		H perfect 3 ms	הֲקֵים
		call	קרא
		approach	קרב
		pay attention	שִׂים טְעֵם

FROM THE BIBLE (Daniel 3:1–12)

נְבוּכַדְנֶצַּר מַלְכָּא עֲבַד צְלֵם דִּי דְהַב וּשְׁלַח לְמִכְנַשׁ לְסִגְנַיָּא וּפַחֲוָתָא לַחֲנֻכַּת צַלְמָא דִּי

הֲקֵים נְבוּכַדְנֶצַּר מַלְכָּא. בֵּאדַיִן מִתְכַּנְּשִׁין סִגְנַיָּא וּפַחֲוָתָא לַחֲנֻכַּת צַלְמָא דִּי הֲקֵים

נְבוּכַדְנֶצַּר מַלְכָּא וְקָאֲמִין לָקֳבֵל צַלְמָא דִּי הֲקֵים נְבוּכַדְנֶצַּר וְכָרוֹזָא קָרֵא בְחָיִל:

לְכוֹן אָמְרִין עַמְמַיָּא: בְּעִדָּנָא דִּי תִשְׁמְעוּן קָל קַרְנָא וְכֹל זְנֵי זְמָרָא תִּפְּלוּן וְתִסְגְּדוּן

לְצֶלֶם דַּהֲבָא דִּי הֲקֵים נְבוּכַדְנֶצַּר מַלְכָּא וּמַן דִּי לָא יִפֵּל וְיִסְגֻּד יִתְרְמֵא לְגוֹא אַתּוּן

נוּרָא יָקִדְתָּא. כָּל קֳבֵל דְּנָה בֵּהּ זִמְנָא כְּדִי שָׁמְעִין כָּל עַמְמַיָּא קָל קַרְנָא וְכֹל זְנֵי

זְמָרָא נָפְלִין כָּל עַמְמַיָּא סָגְדִין לְצֶלֶם דַּהֲבָא דִּי הֲקֵים נְבוּכַדְנֶצַּר מַלְכָּא. כָּל קֳבֵל

דְּנָה בֵּהּ זִמְנָא קְרִבוּ גֻּבְרִין כַּשְׂדָּאִין. עֲנוֹ וְאָמְרִין לִנְבוּכַדְנֶצַּר מַלְכָּא: מַלְכָּא לְעָלְמִין

חֱיִי. אַנְתְּ מַלְכָּא שָׂמְתָּ טְעֵם דִּי כָל אֱנָשׁ דִּי יִשְׁמַע קָל קַרְנָא וְכֹל זְנֵי זְמָרָא יִפֵּל וְיִסְגֻּד

לְצֶלֶם דַּהֲבָא וּמַן דִּי לָא יִפֵּל וְיִסְגֻּד יִתְרְמֵא לְגוֹא אַתּוּן נוּרָא יָקִדְתָּא. אִיתַי גֻּבְרִין

יְהוּדָאִין שַׁדְרַךְ מֵישַׁךְ וַעֲבֵד־נְגוֹ. גֻּבְרַיָּא אִלֵּךְ לָא שָׂמוּ עֲלָיִךְ מַלְכָּא טְעֵם. לֵאלָהָיִךְ

לָא פָלְחִין וּלְצֶלֶם דַּהֲבָא דִּי הֲקֵימְתָּ לָא סָגְדִין.

Proper Nouns

שַׁדְרַךְ, מֵישַׁךְ, עֲבֵד־נְגוֹ — Names given to Hananiah, Mishael, and Azariah by
Babylonian officials

EXERCISES

How many different pairs of numbers can you list that add up to 10?

_____ + _____   _____ + _____

_____ + _____   _____ + _____

_____ + _____

Fill in the blank with the correct Aramaic numbers:

4 + 5 = _____ 10^3 = _____

7 - _____ = 6   2 + _____ = 5

8 ÷ 4 = _____   20 × 10 = _____

20 ÷ _____ = 2   4 + 2 = _____

8 - 3 = _____ 3^2 = _____

1 + 2 = _____   56 ÷ 8 = _____

2 × 3 = _____   10 - 2 = _____

8 ÷ 2 = _____   60 + 40 = _____

_____ + 1 = 6   17 ÷ 17 = _____

11 - 9 = _____   24 - _____ = 16

7 + 0 = _____   19,286 + _____ = 29,286

_____ - 4 = 2   10 × 2 = _____

17 - _____ = 13   6 + 6 _____

Translate into Aramaic:

(1) The first man is the head of the province.

(2) We pray to the God of heaven.

(3) Five secrets were in the dream.

(4) The sound went out from Babylon like a fire.

(5) They will worship a statue of iron.

(6) There are 10,000 books burning in the palace.

(7) One horn is thrown into the furnace.

(8) They heard four kinds of music.

Chapter 18

G-Imperative and Infinitive

As in Hebrew, Aramaic imperatives are based on the corresponding imperfect forms, from which the (pronominal) prefix has been removed and some necessary adjustments made for shifting vowels. The resulting forms are:

	Singular	*Plural*
masculine	כְּתֻב	כְּתֻבוּ
feminine	כְּתֻבִי	כְּתֻבָה

Technically, the forms derive from the jussive, which is very much like the imperfect except without the final ן on plural forms. It is, therefore, understandable, that negative commands are expressed by the full jussive along with אַל:

חֶלְמָא וּפִשְׁרֵא אַל יְבַהֲלָךְ

> Don't let the dream and interpretation frighten you. (Daniel 4:16)

That leaves only one G form which has not yet been described—the infinitive. It is characterized by a prefixed -מִ:

מִכְתַּב

The infinitive frequently appears with the preposition -לְ and sometimes with the negative לָא to express a prohibition (see the inscription on p. 172).

Interestingly, the infinitive of the verb בנה ("build") occurs with both a prefixed -לְ (לִבְּנֵא in Ezra 5:3, 13) and, sometimes, an additional מ (לְמִבְנֵא in Ezra 5:2, 6:8). This form is expanded still further in one passage by the addition of a feminine (or perhaps determinative) ending: לְמִבְנְיָה (Ezra 5:9).

95

VOCABULARY

To Be Learned		*Reference*	
heat	אזה	see	חזה
G infinitive	לְמֵזֵא	*G pass ptc* ("proper")	חֲזֵה
pass ptc	אֲזֵה	urgent	מַחְצְפָה
come	אתה	because	מִן דִּי
H (bring) passive		go up	סלק
perfect 3 mp	הֵיתָיוּ	*H pf 3 mp* (sacrifice)	הַסִּקוּ
H infinitive	לְהַיְתָיָה	true	צְדָּא
need	חשח	rise	קוּם
hand	יַד	*H perfect 1 s*	הֲקֵימֶת
very, excellent	יַתִּיר	anger	רְגַז
bind (D)	כפת	throw	רמה
D infinitive	לְכַפָּתָה	*Gt imperfect 2 mp*	תִּתְרְמוֹן
D pass ptc mp	מְכַפְּתִין	seven	שִׁבְעָה
ready	עֲתִיד	seven times	חַד שִׁבְעָה
kill (D)	קטל	reply (H)	תוב
he saves	יְשֵׁיזִב	*H infinitive + 2 ms*	לַהֲתָבוּתָךְ
imf 3ms + 2 mp	יְשֵׁיזְבִנְכוֹן		
infinitive + 1 p	לְשֵׁיזָבוּתַנָא		
hour	שָׁעָה		

FROM THE BIBLE (Daniel 3:13–23)

בֵּאדַיִן נְבוּכַדְנֶצַּר בִּרְגַז אֲמַר לְהַיְתָיָה לְשַׁדְרַךְ מֵישַׁךְ וַעֲבֵד־נְגוֹ. בֵּאדַיִן גֻּבְרַיָּא אִלֵּךְ

הֵיתָיוּ קֳדָם מַלְכָּא. עָנֵה נְבוּכַדְנֶצַּר וְאָמַר לְהוֹן: הַצְדָּא שַׁדְרַךְ מֵישַׁךְ וַעֲבֵד־נְגוֹ

לֵאלָהַי לָא אִיתֵיכוֹן פָּלְחִין וּלְצֶלֶם דַּהֲבָא דִּי הֲקֵימֶת לָא סָגְדִין? כְּעַן הֵן אִיתֵיכוֹן

עֲתִידִין דִּי בְעִדָּנָא דִּי תִשְׁמְעוּן קָל קַרְנָא וְכֹל זְנֵי זְמָרָא תִּפְּלוּן וְתִסְגְּדוּן לְצַלְמָא דִּי

עַבְדֵת וְהֵן לָא תִסְגְּדוּן בַּהּ שַׁעֲתָה תִּתְרְמוֹן לְגוֹא אַתּוּן נוּרָא יָקִדְתָּא. וּמַן הוּא אֱלָהּ דִּי

יְשֵׁיזְבִנְכוֹן מִן יְדָי. עֲנוֹ שַׁדְרַךְ מֵישַׁךְ וַעֲבֵד־נְגוֹ וְאָמְרִין לְמַלְכָּא: נְבוּכַדְנֶצַּר לָא
חַשְׁחִין אֲנַחְנָה עַל דְּנָה פִּתְגָם לַהֲתָבוּתָךְ. הֵן אִיתַי אֱלָהַנָא דִּי אֲנַחְנָא פָלְחִין יָכִל
לְשֵׁיזָבוּתַנָא מִן אַתּוּן נוּרָא יָקִדְתָּא וּמִן יְדָךְ מַלְכָּא יְשֵׁיזִב וְהֵן לָא יְדִיעַ לֶהֱוֵא לָךְ
מַלְכָּא דִּי לֵאלָהָיךְ לָא אִיתַינָא פָלְחִין וּלְצֶלֶם דַּהֲבָא דִּי הֲקֵימְתָּ לָא נִסְגֻּד. בֵּאדַיִן
נְבוּכַדְנֶצַּר עֲנֵה וְאָמַר לְמֵזֵא לְאַתּוּנָא חַד שִׁבְעָה עַל דִּי חֲזֵה לְמֵזְיֵהּ וּלְכַפָּתָה לְשַׁדְרַךְ
מֵישַׁךְ וַעֲבֵד־נְגוֹ לְמִרְמֵא לְאַתּוּן נוּרָא יָקִדְתָּא. כָּל קֳבֵל דְּנָה מִן דִּי מִלַּת מַלְכָּא
מַחְצְפָה וְאַתּוּנָא אֵזֵה יַתִּירָא גֻּבְרַיָּא אִלֵּךְ דִּי הַסִּקוּ לְשַׁדְרַךְ מֵישַׁךְ וַעֲבֵד־נְגוֹ קַטִּל הִמּוֹן
נוּרָא. וְגֻבְרַיָּא אִלֵּךְ תְּלָתֵּהוֹן שַׁדְרַךְ מֵישַׁךְ וַעֲבֵד־נְגוֹ נְפַלוּ לְגוֹא אַתּוּן נוּרָא יָקִדְתָּא
מְכַפְּתִין.

NOTE that 3d person plural verbs are often used indefinitely ("they . . ."); in such cases, they are often best translated into English with passive verbs. For example, גֻּבְרַיָּא אִלֵּךְ הֵיתָיוּ liter-ally means "they [indefinite] brought those men," but is better rendered, "those men were brought."

EXERCISES

Fill in the complete conjugation of the verb כתב:

	Perfect	*Imperfect*	*Participles*		*Imperative*
			Active	*Passive*	
1 cs					
2ms		ms			
2fs		fs			
3ms					
3fs		mp			
fp		fp			
1cp					
2mp					
2fp			*Infinitive:*		
3mp					
3fp					

What form are the following verbs?

	Root	Form	Person	Gender	Number	Meaning
מֶעְבַּד						
שְׁבַקוּ						
מֶחֱזֵא						
אָכְלִי						
מִגְלֵא						
אֱמַר						
מִבְנֵא						
מִכְנַשׁ						
מִבְעֵא						
מִקְרֵא						
מְפַשַּׁר						

Translate into Aramaic:

(1) Do not kill these strong men.

(2) God is ready to make a place in the heavens.

(3) The hand will write a very good letter.

(4) The king needs to burn this city with fire.

(5) Hear the sound of music in the distant field.

(6) They brought the bound scribe to a dunghill.

(7) The people will save many treasures.

Chapter 19

D CONJUGATION

The second major conjugation in Aramaic is called D because the middle letter of the root is *doubled*. (It is also known as *pa^{cc}el*.) As in the Hebrew *pi^cel*, a *dagesh* is used to indicate the doubled letter. Also as in Hebrew, the first root letter of Aramaic verbs in the D conjugation always has a vowel. (This is not true of G forms, such as כְּתַבוּ.) These two features are related: since the first of the two letters indicated by the *dagesh* always has a *sh'va*, it must be preceded by a vowel.

In other regards, the prefixes and suffixes are the same in the D as in the G conjugation:

			Perfect	*Imperfect*
Singular	1		קַבְּלֵת	אֲקַבֵּל
	2	masculine	קַבֵּלְתְּ	תְּקַבֵּל
	2	feminine	קַבֵּלְתִּי	תְּקַבְּלִין
	3	masculine	קַבֵּל	יְקַבֵּל
	3	feminine	קַבְּלַת	תְּקַבֵּל
Plural	1		קַבֵּלְנָא	נְקַבֵּל
	2	masculine	קַבֵּלְתּוּן	תְּקַבְּלוּן
	2	feminine	קַבֵּלְתֵּן	תְּקַבְּלָן
	3	masculine	קַבִּלוּ	יְקַבְּלוּן
	3	feminine	קַבִּלָה	יְקַבְּלָן

If the second consonant is a guttural and cannot, therefore, be doubled (i.e. take a *dagesh*), the preceding vowel is usually lengthened:

e.g.,   בָּרְכֵת   perfect, 1 singular

בָּרֵךְ   perfect, 3 masculine singular

100

As one would expect, imperative forms correspond to those for the second person imperfect, without the prefixed ‎תְּ-:

D Imperative

	Masculine	Feminine
Singular	קַבֵּל	קַבְּלִי
Plural	קַבְּלוּ	קַבֵּלְה

Finally, the participle and infinitive forms follow patterns which, as we shall see, are typical of all the derived (non-G) conjugations: participles begin with ‎מְ-, and infinitives end with the suffix ‎ה:‎-

D Participle

	Masculine	Feminine
Singular	מְקַבֵּל	מְקַבְּלָה
Plural	מְקַבְּלִין	מְקַבְּלָן

D Infinitive   קַבָּלָה

VOCABULARY

To Be Learned		*Reference*	
four	אַרְבַּע	sign	אָת
body	גְּשֶׁם	bless (D)	ברך
generation	דָּר	resemble	דמה
damage	חֲבָל	behold	הָא
surely	יַצִּיב	is it not (interrogative)	הֲלָא
how	כְּמָה	scorch	חרך
grow great (G)	שׂגא	*Dt (passive) pf 3 ms* הִתְחָרַךְ	

To Be Learned			*Reference*	
hair	שְׂעַר		angel	מַלְאַךְ
dominion	שָׁלְטָן		make, do	עבד
loosen	שׁרה		*Gt (pass) imperfect*	
pass participle mp	שְׁרַיִן		*3ms*	יִתְעֲבֵד
			go out	נפק
			imperative mp	פֻּקוּ
			cause to prosper (H)	צלח
			blasphemy	שָׁלָה
			three	תְּלָת

FROM THE BIBLE (Daniel 3:24–33)

אֱדַיִן נְבוּכַדְנֶצַּר מַלְכָּא קָם עָנֵה וְאָמַר: הֲלָא גֻבְרִין תְּלָתָא רְמֵינָא לְגוֹא נוּרָא מְכַפְּתִין?

עָנַיִן וְאָמְרִין לְמַלְכָּא: יַצִּיבָא מַלְכָּא. עָנֵה וְאָמַר: הָא אֲנָה חָזֵה גֻבְרִין אַרְבְּעָה שְׁרַיִן

מַהְלְכִין בְּגוֹא נוּרָא וַחֲבָל לָא אִיתַי בְּהוֹן וְרֵבִיעָיָא דָּמֵה לְבַר אֱלָהִין. בֵּאדַיִן קְרֵב

נְבוּכַדְנֶצַּר לִתְרַע אַתּוּן נוּרָא יָקִדְתָּא עָנֵה וְאָמַר: שַׁדְרַךְ מֵישַׁךְ וַעֲבֵד־נְגוֹ עַבְדוֹהִי דִּי אֱלָהָא

פֻּקוּ וֶאֱתוֹ. בֵּאדַיִן נָפְקִין שַׁדְרַךְ מֵישַׁךְ וַעֲבֵד־נְגוֹ מִן גּוֹא נוּרָא. לָא שְׁלֵט נוּרָא

בְּגֶשְׁמְהוֹן וּשְׂעַר רֵאשְׁהוֹן לָא הִתְחָרַךְ. עָנֵה נְבוּכַדְנֶצַּר וְאָמַר: בְּרִיךְ אֱלָהֲהוֹן דִּי

שַׁדְרַךְ מֵישַׁךְ וַעֲבֵד־נְגוֹ דִּי שְׁלַח מַלְאֲכֵהּ וְשֵׁיזִב לְעַבְדוֹהִי דִּי יְהַבוּ גֶשְׁמְהוֹן דִּי לָא

יִפְלְחוּן וְלָא יִסְגְּדוּן לְכָל אֱלָהּ לָהֵן לֵאלָהֲהוֹן. וּמִנִּי שִׂים טְעֵם דִּי כָל עַם דִּי יֵאמַר

שָׁלָה עַל אֱלָהֲהוֹן דִּי שַׁדְרַךְ מֵישַׁךְ וַעֲבֵד־נְגוֹ בַיְתֵהּ נְוָלִי יִתְעֲבֵד כָּל קֳבֵל דִּי לָא אִיתַי

אֱלָהּ אָחֳרָן כִּדְנָה. בֵּאדַיִן מַלְכָּא הַצְלַח לְשַׁדְרַךְ מֵישַׁךְ וַעֲבֵד־נְגוֹ בִּמְדִינַת בָּבֶל.

נְבוּכַדְנֶצַּר מַלְכָּא לְכָל עַמְמַיָּא דִּי דָאֲרִין בְּכָל אַרְעָא: שְׁלָמְכוֹן יִשְׂגֵּא. אָתַיָּא דִּי

עֲבַד עִמִּי אֱלָהָא כְּמָה תַקִּיפִין. מַלְכוּתֵהּ מַלְכוּת עָלַם וְשָׁלְטָנֵהּ עִם דָּר וְדָר.

EXERCISES

Identify the form of the following verbs which appear in the Bible in the D conjugation:

	Root	Tense	Person	Gender	Number
מְמַלֵּל					
בַּטִּלוּ					
יְטַעֲמוּן					
שַׁבַּחֵת					
מְהַדַּר					
חַבְּלוּ					
לְנַסָּכָה					
הַדְּרֵת					
חַבְּלָה					
יְבַקַּר					
מְמַלְלָא					
מְהַלֵּךְ					
מַנִּיתָ					
מְפַשַּׁר					
תְּקַבְּלוּן					
קַטֵּל					

	Root	Tense	Person	Gender	Number
יְשַׁמְּשׁוּן					
שַׁבַּחְתָּ					
מְצַבְּעִין					
לְקַטָּלָה					
יְמַלֵּל					
מְשָׁרֵא					
יְבַהֲלוּ					
בַּדַּרוּ					
מְשַׁבַּח					

Fill in the full conjugation of the verb חבל ("damage") in the D:

	Perfect	Imperfect	Participle	Imperative
1 cs				
2ms			ms	
2fs			fs	
3ms				
3fs			mp	
fp			fp	
1cp				
2mp				
2fp			Infinitive:	
3mp				
3fp				

Translate into Aramaic:

(1) They bound his body from head to foot.

(2) Surely, we will destroy four provinces.

(3) The king gave dominion to his son for eternity.

(4) How wise you are to leave the rebellious city in peace.

(5) She is praising the judge, who grew great in this generation.

(6) I searched in the treasure house, and there was damage there.

(7) He will tell us the interpretation of your dream.

(8) The wise men said to loosen the hair from my head.

Chapter 20

H CONJUGATION

Semitic languages have four basic verbal conjugations, which are generally identified by the letters G, D, H, and N on the basis of their form. (The Hebrew terms *pi‘el, hif‘il,* and *nif‘al* correspond to the vocalization of the 3d person masculine singular perfect of each conjugation; according to this system, the *qal,* which literally means "simple," would be called *pa‘al.*) We have already considered the Aramaic G (chapters 8, 9, 15, and 18) and D (chapter 19) conjugations. Since biblical Aramaic has no N (*nif‘al*) conjugation, that leaves only the H.

Its general pattern is the same as that of the other conjugations, except for the obvious presence of the prefixed -הַ. Since that usually has an "*a*" vowel, the conjugation is sometimes called the *haf‘el* in contrast to the *hif‘il.* However, unlike Hebrew, the initial ה is usually retained in Aramaic participles and imperfects. (It typically elides in Hebrew so that מְהַשְׁלִיךְ becomes מַשְׁלִיךְ and תְּהַשְׁלִיךְ becomes תַּשְׁלִיךְ).

			Perfect	*Imperfect*
Singular	1		הַשְׁלֵטֶת	אֲהַשְׁלֵט
	2	masculine	הַשְׁלֵטְתְּ	תְּהַשְׁלֵט
	2	feminine	הַשְׁלֵטְתִּי	תְּהַשְׁלְטִין
	3	masculine	הַשְׁלֵט	יְהַשְׁלֵט
	3	feminine	הַשְׁלֵטַת	תְּהַשְׁלֵט
Plural	1		הַשְׁלֵטְנָא	נְהַשְׁלֵט
	2	masculine	הַשְׁלֵטְתּוּן	תְּהַשְׁלְטוּן
	2	feminine	הַשְׁלֵטְתֵּן	תְּהַשְׁלְטָן
	3	masculine	הַשְׁלִטוּ	יְהַשְׁלְטוּן
	3	feminine	הַשְׁלֵטָה	יְהַשְׁלְטָן

Having said this, we should add that the -הַ does sometimes elide in biblical Aramaic, precisely as in Hebrew. (This may be due to Hebrew influence.)

106

As was true with the G and D conjugations, in Aramaic as in Hebrew, the imperative forms are based on the imperfect, without the pronominal prefixes:

H Imperative

	Masculine	*Feminine*
Singular	הַשְׁלֵט	הַשְׁלֵטִי
Plural	הַשְׁלֵטוּ	הַשְׁלֵטָה

The prefixed -הַ, which is characteristic of this conjugation, is also retained in the participles:

H Participle

	Masculine	*Feminine*
Singular	מְהַשְׁלֵט	מְהַשְׁלְטָה
Plural	מְהַשְׁלְטִין	מְהַשְׁלְטָן

Finally, the H infinitive is, like the D, characterized by the ending הָ-:

הַשְׁלָטָה

VOCABULARY

To Be Learned		*Reference*	
tree	אִילָן	last	אָחֳרֵין
behold	אֲלוּ	trouble	אֲנַס
disturb (D)	בהל	vision	חֱזוּ
fear (D—scare)	דחל	seek shade (H)	טלל
magician	חַרְטֹם	food	מָזוֹן
foliage	עֳפִי	reach	מטא

To Be Learned			Reference	
holy	קַדִּישׁ	enter	עלל	
grow	רבה	*G participle ms*	עָל	
wind	רוּחַ	*G participle mp*	עָלִין	
under	תְּחוֹת	*H infinitive*	*לְהַנְעָלָה	
		branch	עֲנַף	
		bird	צִפַּר	
		height	רוּם	
		beautiful	שַׁפִּיר	

FROM THE BIBLE (Daniel 4:1–9)

אֲנָה נְבוּכַדְנֶצַּר שְׁלֵה הֲוֵית בְּבֵיתִי. חֵלֶם חֲזֵית וִידַחֲלִנַּנִי. וְחֶזְוֵי רֵאשִׁי יְבַהֲלֻנַּנִי וּמִנִּי שִׂים

טְעֵם לְהַנְעָלָה קָדָמַי לְכֹל חַכִּימֵי בָבֶל דִּי פְשַׁר חֶלְמָא יְהוֹדְעֻנַּנִי. בֵּאדַיִן עָלִּין

חַרְטֻמַּיָּא וְכַשְׂדָּיֵא וְחֶלְמָא אָמַר אֲנָה קָדָמֵיהוֹן וּפִשְׁרֵהּ לָא מְהוֹדְעִין לִי. וְעַד אָחֳרֵין

עַל קָדָמַי דָּנִיֵּאל דִּי שְׁמֵהּ בֵּלְטְשַׁאצַּר כְּשֻׁם אֱלָהִי וְדִי רוּחַ אֱלָהִין קַדִּישִׁין בֵּהּ וְחֶלְמָא

קָדָמוֹהִי אַמְרֵת: בֵּלְטְשַׁאצַּר רַב חַרְטֻמַּיָּא דִּי אֲנָה יִדְעֵת דִּי רוּחַ אֱלָהִין קַדִּישִׁין בָּךְ

וְכָל רָז לָא אָנֵס לָךְ. חֶזְוֵי חֶלְמִי דִי חֲזֵית וּפִשְׁרֵהּ אֱמַר. וְחֶזְוֵי רֵאשִׁי חָזֵה הֲוֵית

וַאֲלוּ אִילָן בְּגוֹא אַרְעָא וְרוּמֵהּ שַׂגִּיא. רְבָה אִילָנָא וּרוּמֵהּ יִמְטֵא לִשְׁמַיָּא. עָפְיֵהּ

שַׁפִּיר וְאִנְבֵּהּ שַׂגִּיא וּמָזוֹן לְכֹלָּא בֵהּ. תְּחֹתוֹהִי תַּטְלֵל חֵיוַת בָּרָא וּבְעַנְפוֹהִי יְדֻרָן צִפֲּרֵי שְׁמַיָּא.

Proper Names

בֵּלְטְשַׁאצַּר — The Babylonian name given to Daniel (see Daniel 1:7), which means "May he protect his life" in Akkadian.

---

*This form is explained on p. 119.

EXERCISES

Identify the form of the following H verbs:

	Root	Tense	Person	Gender	Number
מַהְלְכִין					
לְהַחֲוָיָה					
נְהַחֲוֵה					
הַשְׁפָּלָה					
הֶחֱסַנוּ					
לְהַשְׁנָיָה					
הוֹדַעְנָא					
מְהוֹדְעִין					
מְהַנְזְקַת					
תְּהַנְזִק					
הַצְלַח					
מְהַחְצְפָה					
יְהַשְׁפֵּל					
הַרְגִזוּ					
הַרְגִּשׁוּ					
הַשְׁכַּחַת					
לְהַשְׁכָּחָה					
מְהַשְׁנֵא					

Fill in the full conjugation of the verb קְרֵב in the H:

	Perfect	*Imperfect*	*Participle*	*Imperative*
1 cs				
2ms			ms	
2fs			fs	
3ms				
3fs			mp	
fp			fp	
1cp				
2mp				
2fp			*Infinitive:*	
3mp				
3fp				

Translate into Aramaic:

(1) The sound of the horn reaches the heavens.

(2) Behold, the wind is smashing the vessels under the palace.

(3) The hair grew like foliage.

(4) The bird brought gold out of the tree.

(5) The word of the king will frighten the holy men of Babylon.

(6) The magicians fear that God will make Daniel ruler over them.

(7) The scribes said to bring the message before God.

Chapter 21

WEAK VERBS

Weak verbs contain letters that cause phonological problems when they occur in certain situations. For example, some letters cannot take certain vowels, while others tend to assimilate with adjoining consonants. Because the "weaknesses" which cause problems for these roots typically have to do with the pronunciation of specific consonants, many irregularities are common to Hebrew and Aramaic.

Some letters encounter problems when they occur at the beginning of a root. For example, when the letter נ is preceded by a vowel but has none of its own (i.e. when it has a silent *sh'va*), it often assimilates to the following letter. Thus, the imperfect of the root נפל (fall) includes forms like יִפֵּל (compare the Hebrew יִפֹּל). Since the imperative is based on this form (without the pronominal prefix), it frequently has no נ at all (e.g., שָׂא from נשא and פֻּק from נפק). However, Aramaic is not as consistent in this as is Hebrew. Thus, the נ remains in several forms of the verb נתן, such as תִנְתֵּן and יִנְתֵּן (the *dagesh* in the ת is *lene*) and frequently in H forms (הַנְפֵּק, תְּהַנְזִיק, etc.). Alternatively, it is possible that these forms are actually secondary developments. In other words, rather than having been retained, the נ may have initially assimilated and then later returned through a process of nasalized dissimilation. This process can be seen in other Aramaic verbs; for example, the H infinitives הַנְסָקָה and הַנְעָלָה are derived from the roots סלק and עלל respectively (see chapter 22). If a similar process was at work with נתן, the imperfect would have developed in something like the following stages:

יִנְתֵּן → יִתֵּן (assimilation) → יִנְתֵּן (dissimilation/nasalization)

A similar development takes place with the root ידע. Its imperfect, 2 masculine singular form should have been תִידַע, but that apparently became תִדְּדַע, with the י assimilating to the ד), and then תִנְדַּע, as the first ד dissimilated, becoming a (nasal) נ. In the same way, the 3 masculine plural form יִידְעוּן became יִנְדְּעוּן. This process also lies behind the name of the Mandeans, which comes from the root ידע and is used for a gnostic group that claims special religious knowledge (cf. מַנְדַּע, "knowledge," in Daniel 4:31 and 33 on p. 120).

The verb יד׳ע demonstrates another characteristic of the Northwest Semitic languages, namely the shift of initial ו to י. (The root was originally ודע.) Sometimes the initial י is lost altogether, as in the infinitive and imperative (e.g., הַב; see p. 49 above). However, under other circumstances, the shift to י never takes place at all. Hebrew examples include *hif'il* and *nif'al* forms such as הוֹלִיד and נוֹלַד, both of which come from the root ילד. Analogously, Aramaic has H forms such as הוֹתֵב and לְהוֹדָעָה from the roots יתב and ידע.

Gutturals and the letter ר often cause nearby vowels to shift to an *ah* sound (i.e. a *pataḥ* or *qames*). We have already seen examples of this in the G active participle (אָמַר). The same phenomenon is responsible for D participles such as מְשַׁבַּח, G perfect forms like עַבְדֵת ("I made"), and G imperfects such as תַּעַבְדוּן.

"Hollow" verbs have a long vowel—either *î* or *û*—instead of a middle consonant. Because their roots do not have three consonants, these verbs inevitably encounter problems fitting into "regular" conjugations. (This clearly does not apply to verbs such as חוה, "tell," in which the middle ו or י is consonantal.) Hollow roots have no middle letter at all in the G perfect (e.g., שָׂמֵת, "I ordered"). However, the G participle often developed an א in the middle position, apparently in an effort to make the verb more clearly triliteral—e.g., קָאֵם (he rises).* (In some verbs the *kĕtîv* has an א but the *qĕrê* a י, e.g., דָּאֲרִין/דָּיְרִין in Ezra 7:25 and דָּאֲנִין/דָּיְנִין in Daniel 2:38.) The long middle vowel does appear in the imperfect, where the pronominal prefix takes a *sh'va* (e.g., יְקוּם; contrast Hebrew, where the pronominal prefix takes a *qames*, reflecting how that language treats short vowels in syllables preceding the accent).

Final ה and א are not as distinct in Aramaic as they are in Hebrew. One of them may appear in forms attributed to roots derived from the other, such as מִשְׁרֵא from the root שרה and הִתְמְלִי from the root מלא. This blurring also occurs in the suffixes used for feminine and determined forms, which should be הָ- and אָ- respectively, but are not consistently distinguished. This ambiguity is compounded by the tendency of א to become quiescent and even fall away. This is evident in the root אתא, the H conjugation of which, as we have seen, has forms such as the infinitive לְהֵיתָיָה and the masculine singular third person perfect הֵיתִי, where there is a י instead of the expected א. As a consequence, the following forms are all derived from initial-א verbs:

---

* The same form occurs in the Hebrew passage Hosea 10:14.

תְּהוֹבֵד (Daniel 2:24)—from the root אבד in the H conjugation, with the א acting like a י, which then "becomes" a ו.

מְהֵימַן (Daniel 2:45, 6:5)—an H passive participle from the root אמן, where the א has become and remained a י (just like הַיְתִי).

מֵמַר (Ezra 5:11)—the א in this G infinitive has dropped (so too in the infinitives מֵזֵא and מֵחֵא); the same form occurs in Daniel 2:9 with the א intact (מֵאמַר).

Final ה verbs (which were originally final י) follow patterns familiar from Hebrew, except that the perfect, 3 plural suffix is ו- (e.g., בְּנוֹ, "they built"):

		Perfect	Imperfect		Participles		Imperative
					Active	Passive	
singular	1 c	בְּנֵית	אֶבְנֵא	ms	בָּנֵה	בְּנֵה	בְּנִי
	2m	בְּנַיְתָ	תִּבְנֵא	fs	בָּנְיָה	בַּנְיָה	
	2f	בְּנַיְתִי	תִּבְנַיִן	mp	בָּנַיִן	בְּנַיִן	בְּנוֹ
	3m	בְּנָה	יִבְנֵא	fp	בָּנְיָן	בַּנְיָן	
	3f	בְּנָת	תִּבְנֵה				
plural	1c	בְּנֵינָא	נִבְנֵא	*Infinitive*	מִבְנֵא		
	2m	בְּנֵיתוּן	תִּבְנוֹן				
	2f	בְּנֵיתֵן	תִּבְנְיָן				
	3m	בְּנוֹ	יִבְנוֹן				
	3f	בְּנָה	יִבְנְיָן				

Geminate verbs (those in which the second and third root consonants are the same) are handled in a variety of ways:

(1) Sometimes these roots behave as if they were perfectly regular (e.g., קַצְצוּ, יְמַלִּל, הַטְלֵל, שַׁכְלִלוּ, מְרָעַע).

(2) Often, the repeated consonant appears only once, sometimes without any indication that it is doubled. In those cases, the vowel pattern may shift (e.g., גֻּדּוּ, תְּרֹעַ, נְדַת, מְחָן).

(3) In certain cases, the doubling (gemination) one would have expected in the final letter of the root shifts to the first letter (this is most common in H forms of the root דקק, such תַּדֵּק, מְהַדֵּק, and הַדֵּקוּ).

VOCABULARY

To Be Learned		*Reference*	
cut down	גדד	but	בְּרַם
dew	טַל	in order that	דִּבְרָה (עַד)
be able	כהל	living	חַי
heart	לְבַב	give	יהב
reach	מטא	*Gt imf 3 ms*	יִתְיְהִב
descend	נחת	food	מָזוֹן
Most High	עֶלְי	flee	נוד
want	צבה	enemy	עָר
be wet	צבע	call	קרא
Dt	יִצְטַבַּע	greatness	רְבוּ
		be appalled	שׁמם
		ʾitpolel pf	אֶשְׁתּוֹמַם
		root	שְׁרֵשׁ

FROM THE BIBLE (Daniel 4:10–19)

חָזֵה הֲוֵית בְּחֶזְוֵי רֵאשִׁי עַל־מִשְׁכְּבִי וַאֲלוּ עִיר וְקַדִּישׁ מִן־שְׁמַיָּא נָחִת. קָרֵא בְחַיִל וְכֵן אָמַר: גֹּדּוּ אִילָנָא תֻּנְד

חֵיוְתָא מִן־תַּחְתּוֹהִי בְּרַם עִקַּר שָׁרְשׁוֹהִי בְּאַרְעָא שְׁבֻקוּ וּבְטַל שְׁמַיָּא יִצְטַבַּע. לִבְבֵהּ מִן

אֲנָשָׁא יְשַׁנּוֹן וּלְבַב חֵיוָה יִתְיְהִב לֵהּ עַד דִּי יִנְדְּעוּן חַיַּיָּא דִּי־שַׁלִּיט עִלָּיָא

בְּמַלְכוּת אֲנָשָׁא וּלְמַן־דִּי יִצְבֵּא יִתְּנִנַּהּ. דְּנָה חֶלְמָא חֲזֵית אֲנָה מַלְכָּא נְבוּכַדְנֶצַּר וְאַנְתְּ

בֵּלְטְשַׁאצַּר פִּשְׁרֵא אֱמַר כָּל קֳבֵל דִּי כָל חַכִּימֵי מַלְכוּתִי לָא יָכְלִין פִּשְׁרָא לְהוֹדָעֻתַנִי

וְאַנְתְּ כָּהֵל דִּי רוּחַ אֱלָהִין קַדִּישִׁין בָּךְ. אֱדַיִן דָּנִיֵּאל דִּי שְׁמֵהּ בֵּלְטְשַׁאצַּר אֶשְׁתּוֹמַם

כְּשָׁעָה חֲדָה. עָנֵה מַלְכָּא וְאָמַר. בֵּלְטְשַׁאצַּר חֶלְמָא וּפִשְׁרֵא אַל יְבַהֲלָךְ.

עָנֵה בֵלְטְשַׁאצַּר וְאָמַר. חֶלְמָא וּפִשְׁרֵהּ לְעָרָיךְ. אִילָנָא דִּי חֲזַיְתָ דִּי רְבָה וּמְטָא

לִשְׁמַיָּא וּמְזוֹן לְכֹלָּא בֵהּ, תְּחֹתוֹהִי תְּדוּר חֵיוַת בָּרָא—אַנְתְּ הוּא מַלְכָּא דִּי רְבַית

וּרְבוּתָךְ רְבָת וּמְטָת לִשְׁמַיָּא.

EXERCISES

Identify the form of the following verbs:

	Root	Conjugation	Tense	Person	Gender	Number
טְאֵב						
דַּע						
מִנְתַּן						
יִקְרוֹן						
יְהוֹבְדוּן						
יָדַע						
יַחְלְפוּן						
תִּפְּלוּן						
הַדֵּקֶת						

	Root	Conjugation	Tense	Person	Gender	Number
הוֹתֵב						
שָׂם						
מְהָקֵים						
אֶבְעֵא						
פֵּקוּ						
אֵתוֹ						
הֵיבֵל						
נֵאמַר						
הוֹבָדָה						
יִנְדְּעוּן						
יִפֵּל						

Translate into Aramaic:

(1) Then the magicians knew that the king heard the dream.

(2) I am able to bind the body on top of the mountain.

(3) Wisdom is like a burning fire.

(4) The interpretation damaged all who heard it.

(5) One man builds a house, and another man smashes it.

(6) My hair is wet with dew.

(7) The interpretation of the dream changed the king's heart.

(8) A holy one came down when he heard the word of the Most High.

(9) They cut down the tree that reached into the heavens.

(10) We went to praise them.

Chapter 22

UNUSUAL VERBS

There are several common verbs with idiosyncratic forms. Some of these have already been described.

הוה (to be)—As noted in chapter 15, imperfect 3d person forms often use a prefixed ל- (thus לֶהֱוֵא, לֶהֱוֹן, לֶהֶוְיָן). Although in biblical Aramaic this involves only the verb הוה, the prefix is more extensively attested in later dialects, including rabbinic Aramaic, Syriac, and Mandaic.

הלך (go)—Participles are conjugated in the D and H (מְהַלְּכִין and מְהַלֵּךְ). Imperfect and infinitive forms are kept in the G conjugation, where they act as if they were derived from a hollow root (הוך) with no middle consonant nor any evidence of assimilation—thus, יְהָךְ (he will go) and לִמְהָךְ (to go).

יכל (be able) has several different forms. The imperfect follows the pattern יִכֻּל, תִּכֻּל, although some Aramaic passages have the same form (יוּכַל) as is known from Hebrew. Participles can be based on either יכל (יָכֵל, יָכְלָה, יָכְלִין, יָכְלָן) or כהל (כָּהֵל, כָּהֲלָה, כָּהֲלִין, כָּהֲלָן).

סלק (go up)—Whenever the initial ס has a silent *sh'va*, the ל assimilates to it. This happens in several H forms, such as הַסִּקוּ (lift up!) and הֻסַּק (be lifted up). In the H infinitive, the double ס then *dissimilates*, resulting in the form הַנְסָקָה through a process of nasalization:

הַנְסָקָה ← הַסָּקָה ← הַסְלָקָה

עלל (enter)—The G participle of this geminate root has two forms, with the *kĕtîv* showing both ל's (עָלֲלָת and עָלֲלִין), but the *qĕrê* only one (עָלַת and עָלִין). Nasalization sometimes occurs in the H forms of this verb, yielding the perfect, 3d person masculine singular form הַנְעֵל and the infinitive הַנְעָלָה, which exists alongside of הֶעָלָה.

119

VOCABULARY

To Be Learned			*Reference*	
bless, kneel (D)	בְּרַךְ	living	חַי
strength, army	חַיִל	pass by	חֲלַף
drive out	טְרַד	add	יְסַף
day	יוֹם	*H pass pf 3 fs*	הוּסְפַת
dwelling	מְדוֹר	month	יְרַח
lift	נְטַל	because	מִן דִּי
pass away (G)	עֲדָה	understanding	מַנְדַּע
mouth	פֻּם	eye	עַיִן
end	קְצָת	enduring	קַיָּם
return	תּוֹב	greatness	רְבוּ
		seven	שִׁבְעָה
		root	שְׁרֹשׁ
		restore (H)	תְּקַן
		H passive	הָתְקְנַת
		twelve	תְּרֵי עֲשַׂר

FROM THE BIBLE (Daniel 4:20–34)

וְדִי חֲזָה מַלְכָּא קַדִּישׁ נָחִת מִן שְׁמַיָּא וְאָמַר גֹּדּוּ אִילָנָא וְחַבְּלוּהִי בְּרַם עִקַּר שָׁרְשׁוֹהִי בְּאַרְעָא שְׁבֻקוּ וּבֶאֱסוּר דִּי־פַרְזֶל וּנְחָשׁ בְּדִתְאָא דִּי בָרָא וּבְטַל שְׁמַיָּא יִצְטַבַּע. דְּנָה פִשְׁרָא דִּי מְטָה עַל מַלְכָּא: לָךְ טָרְדִין מִן אֲנָשָׁא וְעִם חֵיוַת בָּרָא לֶהֱוֵה מְדֹרָךְ וּמִטַּל שְׁמַיָּא לָךְ מְצַבְּעִין וְשִׁבְעָה עִדָּנִין יַחְלְפוּן עֲלָיךְ עַד דִּי תִנְדַּע דִּי שַׁלִּיט עִלָּיָא בְּמַלְכוּת אֲנָשָׁא וּלְמַן דִּי יִצְבֵּא יִתְּנִנַּהּ. וְדִי אֲמַרוּ לְמִשְׁבַּק עִקַּר שָׁרְשׁוֹהִי דִּי אִילָנָא —מַלְכוּתָךְ לָךְ קַיָּמָה מִן דִּי תִנְדַּע דִּי שַׁלִּטִן שְׁמַיָּא. כֹּלָּא מְטָא עַל נְבוּכַדְנֶצַּר מַלְכָּא.

לִקְצָת יַרְחִין תְּרֵי־עֲשַׂר עַל הֵיכַל מַלְכוּתָא דִּי בָבֶל מְהַלֵּךְ הֲוָה. עָנֵה מַלְכָּא וְאָמַר: הֲלָא דָא הִיא בָּבֶל רַבְּתָא דִּי אֲנָה בֱנַיְתַהּ לְבֵית מַלְכוּ? מִלְּתָא בְּפֻם מַלְכָּא וְקָל מִן שְׁמַיָּא נְפַל. לָךְ אָמְרִין נְבוּכַדְנֶצַּר מַלְכָּא: מַלְכוּתָה עֲדָת מִנָּךְ וּמִן אֲנָשָׁא לָךְ טָרְדִין וְעִם חֵיוַת בָּרָא מְדֹרָךְ וְשִׁבְעָה עִדָּנִין יַחְלְפוּן עֲלָיךְ עַד דִּי תִנְדַּע דִּי שַׁלִּיט עִלָּיָא בְּמַלְכוּת אֲנָשָׁא וּלְמַן דִּי יִצְבֵּא יִתְּנִנַּהּ. בַּהּ שַׁעֲתָא מִן אֲנָשָׁא טְרִיד וּמִטַּל שְׁמַיָּא גִּשְׁמֵהּ יִצְטַבַּע. וְלִקְצָת יוֹמַיָּה אֲנָה נְבוּכַדְנֶצַּר עַיְנַי לִשְׁמַיָּא נִטְלֵת וּמַנְדְּעִי עֲלַי יְתוּב וּלְעִלָּיָא בָּרְכֵת וּלְחַי עָלְמָא שַׁבְּחֵת דִּי שָׁלְטָנֵהּ שָׁלְטָן עָלַם וּמַלְכוּתֵהּ עִם דָּר וְדָר וּכְמִצְבְּיֵהּ עָבֵד בְּחֵיל שְׁמַיָּא וְדָאֲרֵי אַרְעָא וְלָא אִיתַי דִּי יְמַחֵא בִידֵהּ וְיֵאמַר לֵהּ: מָה עֲבַדְתְּ? בֵּהּ זִמְנָא מַנְדְּעִי יְתוּב עֲלַי וְעַל מַלְכוּתִי הַתְקְנַת. וּרְבוּ יַתִּירָה הוּסְפַת לִי.

EXERCISES

Identify the form of the following verbs:

	Root	Conjugation	Tense	Person	Gender	Number
הַנְעֵל						
הֶעַל						
לֶהֱוֵה						
הֲווֹ						
הַסִּקוּ						
הַנְסָקָה						
מַהְלְכִין						
מְהַלֵּךְ						
יְהָךְ						
יְכֵלְתָּ						
יְכֵל						
תֻּכַל						
יוּכַל						
כָּהֲלִין						

Translate into Aramaic:

(1) The priests drove the governor from the city.

(2) The animal's dwelling is in a tree.

(3) At the end of the day his strength passed away.

(4) The magician lifted his hands and blessed the silver statue.

(5) I returned to bring the letter up to the top of the mountain.

Chapter 23

SYNTAX

Aramaic syntax differs from that of biblical Hebrew in some important ways. For example, we have already pointed out that Aramaic's definite object marker (יָת), which is cognate to the Hebrew אֶת, occurs only once in the Bible (Daniel 3:12; see p. 62). More often, definite direct objects are marked with the preposition -ל:

אֱדַיִן אַרְיוֹךְ . . . הַנְעֵל לְדָנִיֵּאל קֳדָם מַלְכָּא

Then Arioch . . . brought Daniel before the king. (Daniel 2:25)

Many times, however, definite direct objects stand alone, without any indicator at all:

. . . כָּל אֱנָשׁ דִּי יְהַשְׁנֵא פִּתְגָמָא דְנָא . . .

Anyone who will change this message. . . . (Ezra 6:11)

On the other hand, the relationship between nouns and adjectives is very much like that in Hebrew. Adjectives follow the nouns they modify and must agree not only with respect to number and gender, but determination as well (just as in Hebrew both must have or lack the definite article). However, as in Hebrew, this applies only if the adjective is attributive, that is, if it describes the noun; when it is predicative, they need agree only with respect to number and gender:

מַלְכָּא רַבָּא the great king

מַלְכָּא רַב the king is great

Similar rules apply to demonstratives. When they function as adjectives, they normally follow the noun they modify, which *must* be definite (i.e. determined). However, demonstrative pronouns need not be directly adjacent to the noun to which they refer, and the noun may or may not be determined:

גַּבְרַיָּא אִלֵּין	these men
אִלֵּין גֻּבְרִין	these are men
אִלֵּין גֻּבְרַיָּא	these are the men

Aramaic sentence structure is, overall, far looser than Hebrew's. To be sure, there are numerous cases of the familiar verb-subject-object word order:

מְהוֹדְעִין אֲנַחְנָה לְמַלְכָּא   We inform the king. (Ezra 4:16)

However, it is more common for the object to come first:

פִּתְגָמָא שְׁלַח מַלְכָּא עַל רְחוּם . . . וְשִׁמְשַׁי

The king sent a message to Rehum and Shimshai. (Ezra 4:17)

Frequently, it is reiterated by a resumptive pronoun:

גֻּבְרַיָּא אִלֵּךְ . . . קַטִּל הִמּוֹן שְׁבִיבָא דִּי נוּרָא

Those men—the flame of fire killed them. (Daniel 3:22)

Sometimes, the subject comes at the very beginning of a sentence:

רְחוּם . . . וְשִׁמְשַׁי . . . כְּתַבוּ אִגְּרָה חֲדָה עַל יְרוּשְׁלֶם לְאַרְתַּחְשַׁשְׁתְּא מַלְכָּא

Rehum and Shimshai wrote a letter concerning Jerusalem to Artaxerxes, the king. (Ezra 4:8)

Finally, both the particle אִיתַי (functioning as a copula) and the verb הוה are often used with Aramaic participles. Although in such situations the participles are technically predicate nouns or adjectives, the resulting verb phrases come very close to comprising compound tenses:

e.g.,   לֵאלָהָיךְ לָא אִיתַנָא פָלְחִין   We *do not worship* your god. (Daniel 3:18)

אַנְתְּ מַלְכָּא חָזֵה הֲוַיְתָ   Oh king, you *were seeing*. (Daniel 2:31)

VOCABULARY

To Be Learned		*Reference*	
finger	אֶצְבַּע	wood	אָע
splendor	זִיו	purple	אַרְגְּוָן
wine	חֲמַר	disturb (D)	בהל
wear	לבש	*Dt (pass) ptc ms*	מִתְבָּהַל
meal	לְחֶם	taste	טְעֵם
interpret (D)	פשר	understanding	מַנְדַּע
read, call	קרא/קרה	wall	כְּתַל
Gt (pass) imf 3 ms	יִתְקְרֵי	banquet	מִשְׁתְּא
thought	רַעְיוֹן	illumination	נַהִירוּ
find	שכח	palm (of hand)	פַּס
Gt (pass) pf 3 fs	הִשְׁתְּכַחַת	change (G)	שנה
drink	שתה	*Dt (pass) imf 3 mp*	יִשְׁתַּנּוֹ
		ruler (over 1/3 kingdom)	תַּלְתִּי

FROM THE BIBLE (Daniel 5:1–12)

בֵּלְשַׁאצַּר מַלְכָּא עֲבַד לְחֶם רַב וְחַמְרָא שָׁתֵה. בֵּלְשַׁאצַּר אֲמַר בִּטְעֵם חַמְרָא לְהַיְתָיָה

לְמָאנֵי דַּהֲבָא וְכַסְפָּא דִּי הַנְפֵּק נְבוּכַדְנֶצַּר אֲבוּהִי מִן הֵיכְלָא דִּי בִירוּשְׁלֵם וְיִשְׁתּוֹן

בְּהוֹן. בֵּאדַיִן הַיְתִיו מָאנֵי דַהֲבָא דִּי הַנְפִּקוּ מִן הֵיכְלָא דִּי בֵית אֱלָהָא דִּי בִירוּשְׁלֵם

וְשַׁבַּחוּ לֵאלָהֵי דַהֲבָא וְכַסְפָּא נְחָשָׁא פַרְזְלָא אָעָא וְאַבְנָא. בַּהּ שַׁעֲתָה נְפַקָה אֶצְבְּעָן

דִּי יַד אֱנָשׁ וְכָתְבָן עַל כְּתַל הֵיכְלָא דִּי מַלְכָּא וּמַלְכָּא חָזֵה פַּס יְדָה דִּי כָתְבָה.

אֱדַיִן מַלְכָּא זִיוֹהִי שְׁנוֹהִי וְרַעְיֹנֹהִי יְבַהֲלוּנֵּהּ. קָרֵא מַלְכָּא בְּחַיִל לְהֶעָלָה כַּשְׂדָּיֵא.

עָנֵה מַלְכָּא וְאָמַר לְחַכִּימֵי בָבֶל דִּי כָל אֱנָשׁ דִּי יִקְרֵה כְּתָבָה דְנָה וּפִשְׁרֵהּ יְחַוִּנַּנִי

אַרְגְּוָנָא יִלְבַּשׁ וְתַלְתִּי בְמַלְכוּתָא יִשְׁלַט. אֱדַיִן עָלְלִין כֹּל חַכִּימֵי מַלְכָּא וְלָא כָהֲלִין

כְּתָבָא לְמִקְרֵא וּפִשְׁרֵהּ לְהוֹדָעָה לְמַלְכָּא. אֱדַיִן מַלְכָּא בֵּלְשַׁאצַּר שַׂגִּיא מִתְבָּהַל

וְזִיוֹהִי שָׁנַיִן עֲלוֹהִי. מַלְכְּתָא לָקֳבֵל מִלֵּי מַלְכָּא לְבֵית מִשְׁתְּיָא עַלַּת.

עֲנָת מַלְכְּתָא וַאֲמֶרֶת: מַלְכָּא לְעָלְמִין חֱיִי אַל יְבַהֲלוּךְ רַעְיוֹנָךְ וְזִיוָיךְ אַל יִשְׁתַּנּוֹ.

אִיתַי גְּבַר בְּמַלְכוּתָךְ דִּי רוּחַ אֱלָהִין קַדִּישִׁין בֵּהּ וּבְיוֹמֵי אֲבוּךְ נַהִירוּ וְחָכְמָה כְּחָכְמַת

אֱלָהִין הִשְׁתְּכַחַת בֵּהּ וּמַלְכָּא נְבֻכַדְנֶצַּר אֲבוּךְ רַב חַרְטֻמִּין וְכַשְׂדָּאִין הֲקִימֵהּ אֲבוּךְ

מַלְכָּא. כָּל קֳבֵל דִּי רוּחַ יַתִּירָה וּמַנְדַּע מְפַשַּׁר חֶלְמִין הִשְׁתְּכַחַת בֵּהּ בְּדָנִיֵּאל דִּי מַלְכָּא

שָׂם שְׁמֵהּ בֵּלְטְשַׁאצַּר. כְּעַן דָּנִיֵּאל יִתְקְרֵי וּפִשְׁרָה יְהַחֲוֵה.

EXERCISES

Rewrite the following sentences twice, expressing the direct object differently each time:

(1) מַלְכָּא כְּפַת חַרְטֻמַּיָּא.

(a)

(b)

(2) יַת חֶלְמָא פְּשַׁר דָּנִיֵּאל.

(a)

(b)

(3) קְטַלוּ גֻּבְרַיָּא לְכָהֲנַיָּא.

(a)

(b)

Now rearrange each of the original sentences above twice, beginning with a different word each time.

(1a)

(1b)

(2a)

(2b)

(3a)

(3b)

Translate each sentence into English:

(1)

(2)

(3)

Translate into Aramaic:

(1) They drank wine with the meal.

(2) The big finger wrote a message.

(3) The golden vessels were found in the temple.

(4) The priest called the people to pray.

(5) The queen wore gold on her head.

(6) The strong thoughts frightened me.

(7) The wall of the house is wood.

(8) The splendor of his wisdom went out to the whole land.

Chapter 24

PASSIVE CONJUGATIONS

The G passive participle (e.g., כְּתִיב), which was described in chapter 9, is only a small part of a far more elaborate system, one which is significantly more developed in Aramaic than in biblical Hebrew. There one finds a *qal* (G) passive participle (e.g., בָּרוּךְ) as well as two passive conjugations—the *puʿal* and the *hofʿal*. These latter two really belong to the *piʿel* (D) and the *hifʿil* (H), as is evident from the fact that they share the characteristic features of those conjugations—the doubled middle root letter of the *piʿel* and the prefixed ה of the *hifʿil*. Where they differ from the active forms is in their vowel pattern, for which both use *u-a*. These conjugations are, therefore, called *internal* passives of the *piʿel* and *hifʿil*.

Although biblical Hebrew's *qal* has only a passive participle, some anomalous forms have led scholars to suspect that at one time it too must have had a full internal passive. Whatever the facts about that, there are internal passives for all the major conjugations in biblical Aramaic.

The G passive is characterized by the theme vowel *î*. It is found in both the participle and perfect forms. (There are no imperfect forms for any of the internal passive conjugations in the Bible.)

G PASSIVE	*Perfect*				*Participle*	
	Singular	*Plural*				
1	כְּתִיבֵת	כְּתִיבְנָא	singular	masculine		כְּתִיב
2 masculine	כְּתִיבְתָ	כְּתִיבְתּוּן		feminine		כְּתִיבָה
feminine	כְּתִיבְתִּי	כְּתִיבְתֵּן				
3 masculine	כְּתִיב	כְּתִיבוּ	plural	masculine		כְּתִיבִין
feminine	כְּתִיבַת	כְּתִיבָה		feminine		כְּתִיבָן

The D passive resembles the Hebrew *puᶜal*, except that the participle has a *pataḥ (a)* theme vowel instead of *u*. Since Aramaic rules of pronunciation call for this vowel to be reduced to a *sh'va* in all forms of the passive participle except the masculine singular, that is the only participial form in which the active and the passive differ.

D PASSIVE	*Perfect*				*Participle*
	Singular	*Plural*			
1	קֻבְּלֵת	קֻבַּלְנָא	singular	masculine	מְקַבַּל
2 masculine	קֻבַּלְתָּ	קֻבַּלְתּוּן		feminine	מְקַבְּלָה
feminine	קֻבַּלְתִּי	קֻבַּלְתֵּן			
3 masculine	קֻבַּל	קֻבַּלוּ	plural	masculine	מְקַבְּלִין
feminine	קֻבְּלַת	קֻבַּלָה		feminine	מְקַבְּלָן

The H internal passive follows the same pattern in the perfect as the Hebrew *hofᶜal*, while the passive participle is identical with its active counterpart, except that the theme vowel shifts from *ṣere* to *pataḥ* (when it shows), precisely as occurs in the D passive.

H PASSIVE	*Perfect*				*Participle*
	Singular	*Plural*			
1	הֻשְׁלְטֵת	הֻשְׁלַטְנָא	singular	masculine	מְהֻשְׁלַט
2 masculine	הֻשְׁלַטְתָּ	הֻשְׁלַטְתּוּן		feminine	מְהֻשְׁלְטָה
feminine	הֻשְׁלַטְתִּי	הֻשְׁלַטְתֵּן			
3 masculine	הֻשְׁלַט	הֻשְׁלַטוּ	plural	masculine	מְהֻשְׁלְטִין
feminine	הֻשְׁלְטַת	הֻשְׁלַטָה		feminine	מְהֻשְׁלְטָן

As in Hebrew, the initial vowel in the perfect may be either a short *ŏ* (הָ) or *ŭ* (הֻ).

VOCABULARY

To Be Learned		*Reference*	
glory	יְקָר	purple	אַרְגְּוָן
throne	כָּרְסֵא	lacking	חַסִּיר
master	מָרֵא	proclaim (H)	כרז
greatness	רְבוּ	count (G)	מנה
rise	רום	remove (H)	עדה
G pass ptc ms	רִים	divide	פרס
H (causative) ptc ms	מָרִים	chiefs	רַבְרְבָנִין
Hitpolel (reflexive)		weigh	תקל
pf 2 ms	הִתְרוֹמַמְתָּ		
write	רשם		
be like	שוה		
be finished	שלם		
be low (*H causative*)	שפל		
rule (over 1/3 of kingdom)	תַּלְתָּא		

FROM THE BIBLE (Daniel 5:13–29)

בֵּאדַיִן דָּנִיֵּאל הֻעַל קֳדָם מַלְכָּא. עָנֵה מַלְכָּא וְאָמַר לְדָנִיֵּאל: אַנְתְּ הוּא דָנִיֵּאל דִּי מִן

בְּנֵי יְהוּד דִּי הַיְתִי מַלְכָּא אַבִי מִן יְהוּד. וְשִׁמְעֵת עֲלָיךְ דִּי רוּחַ אֱלָהִין בָּךְ וְחָכְמָה

יַתִּירָה הִשְׁתְּכַחַת בָּךְ. וּכְעַן הֻעַלּוּ קָדָמַי חַכִּימַיָּא דִּי כְתָבָה דְנָה יִקְרוֹן וּפִשְׁרֵהּ

לְהוֹדָעֻתַנִי וְלָא כָהֲלִין פְּשַׁר מִלְּתָא לְהַחֲוָיָה. וַאֲנָה שִׁמְעֵת עֲלָיךְ דִּי תִּכּוּל פִּשְׁרִין

לְמִפְשַׁר. כְּעַן הֵן תִּכּוּל כְּתָבָא לְמִקְרֵא וּפִשְׁרֵהּ לְהוֹדָעֻתַנִי אַרְגְּוָנָא תִלְבַּשׁ וְתַלְתָּא

בְּמַלְכוּתָא תִּשְׁלַט. בֵּאדַיִן עָנֵה דָנִיֵּאל וְאָמַר קֳדָם מַלְכָּא: כְּתָבָא אֶקְרֵא לְמַלְכָּא

וּפִשְׁרָא אֲהוֹדְעִנֵּהּ. אַנְתְּ מַלְכָּא אֱלָהָא עִלָּיָא מַלְכוּתָא וּרְבוּתָא וִיקָרָא יְהַב לִנְבֻכַדְנֶצַּר

אֲבוּךְ. וּמִן רְבוּתָא דִּי יְהַב לֵהּ כֹּל עַמְמַיָּא הֲווֹ דָחֲלִין מִן קֳדָמוֹהִי. דִּי הֲוָה צָבֵא

הֲוָא קָטֵל וְדִי הֲוָה צָבֵא הֲוָה מָרִים וְדִי הֲוָה צָבֵא הֲוָה מַשְׁפִּיל. וּכְדִי רִם לִבְבֵהּ

וְרוּחֵהּ הָנְחַת מִן כָּרְסֵא מַלְכוּתֵהּ וִיקָרָה הֶעְדִּיו מִנֵּהּ. וּמִן בְּנֵי אֲנָשָׁא טְרִיד וְלִבְבֵהּ עִם

חֵיוְתָא שַׁוִּי וּמִטַּל שְׁמַיָּא גִּשְׁמֵהּ יִצְטַבַּע עַד דִּי יְדַע דִּי שַׁלִּיט אֱלָהָא עִלָּיָא בְּמַלְכוּת

אֲנָשָׁא וּלְמַן דִּי יִצְבֵּה יְהָקֵים עֲלַיהּ. וְאַנְתְּ בְּרֵהּ בֵּלְשַׁאצַּר לָא הַשְׁפֵּלְתְּ לִבְבָךְ כָּל

קֳבֵל דִּי כָל דְּנָה יְדַעְתָּ. וְעַל מָרֵא שְׁמַיָּא הִתְרוֹמַמְתָּ וּלְמָאנַיָּא דִי בַיְתֵהּ הַיְתִיו קָדָמָיךְ

וְאַנְתְּ וְרַבְרְבָנָיךְ חַמְרָא שָׁתַיִן בְּהוֹן וְלֵאלָהֵי כַסְפָּא וְדַהֲבָא נְחָשָׁא פַרְזְלָא אָעָא וְאַבְנָא

דִּי לָא חָזַיִן וְלָא שָׁמְעִין וְלָא יָדְעִין שַׁבַּחְתָּ. בֵּאדַיִן מִן קֳדָמוֹהִי שְׁלִיחַ יְדָא וּכְתָבָא

דְנָה רְשִׁים. וּדְנָה כְתָבָא דִּי רְשִׁים: מְנֵא מְנֵא תְּקֵל וּפַרְסִין. דְּנָה פְּשַׁר מִלְּתָא:

מְנֵא—מְנָה אֱלָהָא מַלְכוּתָךְ וְהַשְׁלְמַהּ. תְּקֵל—תְּקִילְתָּה וְהִשְׁתְּכַחַתְּ חַסִּיר. פְּרֵס—

פְּרִיסַת מַלְכוּתָךְ וִיהִיבַת לְמָדַי וּפָרָס. בֵּאדַיִן אֲמַר בֵּלְשַׁאצַּר וְהַלְבִּישׁוּ לְדָנִיֵּאל

אַרְגְּוָנָא וְהַכְרִזוּ עֲלוֹהִי דִּי לֶהֱוֵא שַׁלִּיט תַּלְתָּא בְּמַלְכוּתָא.

Proper Names

מָדַי — Region in western Iran from which a powerful kingdom emerged in the seventh century, but was conquered by Cyrus of Persia in the sixth century.

EXERCISES

Identify the form of the following passive verbs:

	Root	Conjugation (G, D, H)	Tense	Person	Gender	Number
שְׁלִיחַ						
יְהִיב						
קְטִילַת						
מְפָרַשׁ						
עֲשִׂית						

	Root	Conjugation (G, D, H)	Tense	Person	Gender	Number
מְעָרַב						
שִׂים						
הֻסְפַת						
יְהִיבַת						
חֲשִׁיבִין						
זְקִיף						
זְהִירִין						
שְׁמַת						
דְּחִיל						
גְּמִיר						
יְהִיבוּ						
פְּרִיסַת						
מְכַפְתִין						
שְׁלִם						

Translate into Aramaic:

(1) The letter was written in Jerusalem.

(2) He is raising the palace on the mountain.

(3) The throne was lowered from the heavens.

(4) The master's dream was interpreted there.

(5) The great gods are praised on earth.

(6) They asked him to bring the silver to the big palace.

(7) Daniel became ruler, and his glory was like a king.

(8) God gave greatness to the province and to its governor.

(9) The earth was finished in six days.

Chapter 25

REFLEXIVE CONJUGATIONS

Just as each major conjugation has an internal passive, so can each theoretically be made reflexive by adding the prefix -הִתְ. Hebrew normally does this only for the D (*piˤel*) conjugation (for other possibilities, see pp. 32–33). Aramaic, however, uses this prefix as a passive for both G and D.* We have already seen examples of verbs in both of these conjugations (e.g., הִתְבְּנֵה, הִתְיְהֵב, הִתְבַּקַּר, הִתְעֲבֵד).

There are some clues that can help determine which conjugation is involved:

(a) Spelling—whether the middle root letter is doubled (D) or not (G)

(b) Etymology—whether the verbal root normally appears in the G or D

In any case, these conjugations follow the same general principles as other Aramaic conjugations and their Hebrew equivalents:

(1) Perfect forms use the standard suffixes.

(2) The prefixed -ה elides in the imperfect and the participle because of its location between a prefix (pronominal in the case of the imperfect; -מ for the participle) and the following ת.**

(3) Infinitives end with the suffix הָ-.

(4) Initial sibilants (שׁ, שׂ, צ, ס, ז) switch places (metathesize) with the ת of the prefix, which becomes ט (a sharpened dental) when the root begins with צ (a sharpened sibilant) and ד (a voiced dental) when the first root letter is ז (a voiced sibilant).

---

* The Bible may contain a trace of this for the H conjugation if the words מַלְכִים תְּהַנְזִק in Ezra 4:13 are redivided to read מַלְכִי מִתְהַנְזִק ("my king is damaged"), as some have suggested.

** Compare the Hebrew definite article, which elides when it is preceded by a preposition (e.g., בַּבַּיִת←בְּהַבַּיִת) and the prefixed ה of the H conjugation both in Hebrew and sometimes in Aramaic (see p. 106). In talmudic Aramaic, the ת also elides.

135

The actual forms are exactly what one would expect:

			Gt	Dt
PERFECT				
	Singular	1	הִתְקְטֵלֵת	הִתְחַבְּלֵת
		2 masculine	הִתְקְטֵלְתְּ	הִתְחַבַּלְתְּ
		2 feminine	הִתְקְטֵלְתִּי	הִתְחַבַּלְתִּי
		3 masculine	הִתְקְטֵל	הִתְחַבַּל
		3 feminine	הִתְקַטְלַת	הִתְחַבְּלַת
	Plural	1	הִתְקְטֵלְנָא	הִתְחַבַּלְנָא
		2 masculine	הִתְקְטֵלְתּוּן	הִתְחַבַּלְתּוּן
		2 feminine	הִתְקְטֵלְתֵּן	הִתְחַבַּלְתֵּן
		3 masculine	הִתְקְטִלוּ	הִתְחַבַּלוּ
		3 feminine	הִתְקְטִלָה	הִתְחַבַּלָה
IMPERFECT				
	Singular	1	אֶתְקְטֵל	אֶתְחַבַּל
		2 masculine	תִּתְקְטֵל	תִּתְחַבַּל
		2 feminine	תִּתְקַטְלִין	תִּתְחַבְּלִין
		3 masculine	יִתְקְטֵל	יִתְחַבַּל
		3 feminine	תִּתְקְטֵל	תִּתְחַבַּל
	Plural	1	נִתְקְטֵל	נִתְחַבַּל
		2 masculine	תִּתְקַטְלוּן	תִּתְחַבְּלוּן
		2 feminine	תִּתְקַטְלָן	תִּתְחַבְּלָן
		3 masculine	יִתְקַטְלוּן	יִתְחַבְּלוּן
		3 feminine	יִתְקַטְלָן	יִתְחַבְּלָן
PARTICIPLES				
	Singular	masculine	מִתְקְטֵל	מִתְחַבַּל
		feminine	מִתְקַטְלָה	מִתְחַבְּלָה
	Plural	masculine	מִתְקַטְלִין	מִתְחַבְּלִין
		feminine	מִתְקַטְלָן	מִתְחַבְּלָן
INFINITIVE			הִתְקְטָלָה	הִתְחַבָּלָה

VOCABULARY

To Be Learned		*Reference*	
satrap	אֲחַשְׁדַּרְפַּן	petition	בָּעוּ
be faithful (H)	אמן	take counsel (Dt)	יעט
H pass ptc	מְהֵימַן	hundred	מְאָה
lion	אַרְיֵה	suffer damage	נזק
pit	גּוֹב	distinguish self (Dt)	נצח
night	לֵילֵי	chief	סָרֵךְ
pretext	עִלָּה	above	עֵלָּא
receive (D)	קבל	twenty	עֶשְׂרִין
statute	קְיָם	intend	עשׁת
assemble (H)	רגשׁ	establish (D)	קום
please	שׁפר	*D infinitive*	לְקַיָּמָה
		negligence	שָׁלוּ

FROM THE BIBLE (Daniel 5:30–6:10)

בֵּהּ בְּלֵילְיָא קְטִיל בֵּלְאשַׁצַּר מַלְכָּא כַשְׂדָּיָא וְדָרְיָוֶשׁ מָדָיָא קַבֵּל מַלְכוּתָא כְּבַר שְׁנִין
שִׁתִּין וְתַרְתֵּין. שְׁפַר קֳדָם דָּרְיָוֶשׁ וַהֲקִים עַל מַלְכוּתָא לַאֲחַשְׁדַּרְפְּנַיָּא מְאָה וְעֶשְׂרִין
דִּי לֶהֱוֹן בְּכָל מַלְכוּתָא. וְעֵלָּא מִנְּהוֹן סָרְכִין תְּלָתָא דִּי דָנִיֵּאל חַד מִנְּהוֹן דִּי לֶהֱוֹן
אֲחַשְׁדַּרְפְּנַיָּא אִלֵּין יָהֲבִין לְהוֹן טַעְמָא וּמַלְכָּא לָא לֶהֱוֵא נָזִק. אֱדַיִן דָּנִיֵּאל דְּנָה הֲוָא
מִתְנַצַּח עַל סָרְכַיָּא וַאֲחַשְׁדַּרְפְּנַיָּא כָּל קֳבֵל דִּי רוּחַ יַתִּירָא בֵּהּ וּמַלְכָּא עֲשִׁית לַהֲקָמוּתֵהּ
עַל כָּל מַלְכוּתָא. אֱדַיִן סָרְכַיָּא וַאֲחַשְׁדַּרְפְּנַיָּא הֲווֹ בָעַיִן עִלָּה לְהַשְׁכָּחָה לְדָנִיֵּאל וְכָל
עִלָּה לָא יָכְלִין לְהַשְׁכָּחָה כָּל קֳבֵל דִּי מְהֵימַן הוּא וְכָל שָׁלוּ לָא הִשְׁתְּכַחַת עֲלוֹהִי.
אֱדַיִן גֻּבְרַיָּא אִלֵּךְ אָמְרִין דִּי לָא נְהַשְׁכַּח לְדָנִיֵּאל כָּל עִלָּה לָהֵן הַשְׁכַּחְנָה עֲלוֹהִי
בְּדָת אֱלָהֵהּ. אֱדַיִן סָרְכַיָּא וַאֲחַשְׁדַּרְפְּנַיָּא אִלֵּן הַרְגִּשׁוּ עַל מַלְכָּא וְכֵן אָמְרִין לֵהּ:
דָּרְיָוֶשׁ מַלְכָּא לְעָלְמִין חֱיִי. אִתְיָעַטוּ כֹּל סָרְכֵי מַלְכוּתָא וַאֲחַשְׁדַּרְפְּנַיָּא וּפַחֲוָתָא
לְקַיָּמָה קְיָם מַלְכָּא דִּי כָל דִּי יִבְעֵה בָעוּ מִן כָּל אֱלָהּ וֶאֱנָשׁ עַד יוֹמִין תְּלָתִין לָהֵן מִנָּךְ
מַלְכָּא יִתְרְמֵא לְגֹב אַרְיָוָתָא. כְּעַן מַלְכָּא תְּרְשֻׁם כְּתָבָא דִּי לָא לְהַשְׁנָיָה כְּדָת מָדַי
וּפָרַס דִּי לָא תֶעְדֵּא. כָּל קֳבֵל דְּנָה מַלְכָּא דָּרְיָוֶשׁ רְשַׁם כְּתָבָא.

EXERCISES

Identify the base conjugation and form of the following Aramaic verbs:

	Root	Base Conjugation (G or D)	Tense	Person	Gender	Number
מִתְיְהֵב						
הִתְמְלִי						
יִצְטַבַּע						
הִתְחָרַךְ						
מִתְנַשְּׂאָה						
הִזְדְּמִנְתּוּן						
מִשְׁתַּכַּל						
יִתְקְרֵי						
תִּשְׁתְּבִק						
תִּתְעַבְדוּן						
הִשְׁתְּכַחַת						
יִתְעֲבֵד						
יִשְׁתַּמְעוּן						
הִתְנַדַּבוּ						
יִתְבַּקַּר						

	Root	Base Conjugation (G or D)	Tense	Person	Gender	Number
מִתְכַּנְּשִׁין						
יִשְׁתַּנֵּא						
הִתְגְּזֶרֶת						
יִתְבְּנֵא						
תִּתְחַבַּל						
הִתְרְחִצוּ						

Translate into Aramaic:

(1) The wise father wrote a statute at night.

(2) A strong lion fell into the big pit.

(3) The satraps assembled before the throne.

(4) The message was received in the rebellious city.

(5) Surely, the faithful priest will be pleasing to the people.

(6) The governor sought a pretext to kill the men.

Chapter 26

OTHER CONJUGATIONS

Alongside the major conjugations (G, D, and H) and their passive variations (*p*e*ˤil*, *puˤal*, *hofˤal*, *hitpeˤel*, and *hitpaˤal*) are a host of others. Many of these are familiar from Hebrew. For example, since hollow roots cannot occur in the D inasmuch as they do not have a middle root letter to double, they often use the *polel* conjugation, in which the final letter is doubled, as if to compensate for the lack of a middle letter:

e.g., מְרוֹמֵם (masc. sing. participle from the root רוּם), "raise up"

The related *ʾetpolel* conjugation is used for the geminate root שׁמם:

אֶשְׁתּוֹמַם, "be disturbed"

This word illustrates another phenomenon, which became characteristic of later Aramaic through a process that is only beginning to be evident in the Bible. We can see it by looking closely at the biblical passage where אֶשְׁתּוֹמַם occurs:

אֱדַיִן דָּנִיֵּאל דִּי שְׁמֵהּ בֵּלְטְשַׁאצַּר אֶשְׁתּוֹמַם כְּשָׁעָה חֲדָה   (Daniel 4:16)

Since דָּנִיֵּאל is the subject of אֶשְׁתּוֹמַם, the verb must be 3 masculine singular perfect ("then Daniel . . . was disturbed"); however, one would have expected the first letter of a perfect verb to be ה (for *hit-polel*) instead of א. A similar anomaly occurs in several other words:

אִתְגְּזֶרֶת	(Daniel 2:45)	Root גזר; perfect 3 feminine singular
אֶתְכְּרִיַּת	(Daniel 7:15)	Root כרה; perfect 3 feminine singular
אֶשְׁתַּנִּי	(Daniel 3:19)	Root שׁנה; perfect 3 masculine singular
אֲקִימֵהּ	(Daniel 3:1)	Root קוּם; perfect 3 masculine singular with
		3 masculine singular pronominal suffix
אַתַּרוּ	(Daniel 4:11)	Root נתר; imperative masculine plural
אֲחֵת	(Ezra 5:15)	Root נחת; imperative masculine singular

141

All of these forms would have been expected to begin with ה. When they were written, the letter ה must have weakened to the point that it was not heard. This weakening may also account for the vacillation between ה and א in final weak roots as well as in the feminine and determined endings (see pp. 26 and 113). Over time, then, the H conjugation became an א conjugation (i.e., *ʾafʿel* rather than *hafʿel*); analogously, Gt became *ʾitpeʿel* rather than *hitpeʿel*, and Dt became *ʾitpaʿʿal* rather than *hitpaʿʿal.* To be sure, this process is only beginning in the Bible, where a handful of initial-א forms exist alongside others with initial -ה. (Thus the perfect 3 masculine singular is given as אֲקֵימָה in Daniel 3:1, but הֲקֵימֶה in 5:11, and the perfect 3 feminine singular is אִתְגְּזֶרֶת in Daniel 2:45 but הִתְגְּזֶרֶת in 2:34.) However, it may be more widespread than we can tell, since other examples of these conjugations could be obscured by the elision of the א with the participle's prefixed -מ or with the imperfect pronominal prefixes, so that we cannot identify all the words which belong to initial -א conjugations with certainty.*

The form אֶשְׁתִּיו (Daniel 5:3–4) also has a prefixed א; however, it does not occur in place of a ה, since the word means "he drank," which is normally expressed with the G conjugation of שׁתה. That א must, therefore, be regarded as prosthetic (see p. 15), rather than signalling a different conjugation.

Several other peculiar forms suggest that biblical Aramaic may have had yet another conjugation. These verbs begin with שׁ, which appears to be a prefix attached to more familiar 3-letter roots:

שֵׁיזִב	save (Daniel 3:28; cf. vv. 15, 17; 16:15, 17, 21, 28), root: עזב	
שֵׁיצִיא	complete (Ezra 6:15), root: יצא	
שַׁכְלֵל	complete (Ezra 4:12; 5:3, 9, 11; 6:14), root: כלל	
מְסוֹבְלִין	laid (Ezra 6:3), root: יבל, passive	

Both Akkadian and Ugaritic have causative conjugations that begin with שׁ rather than ה. It is, therefore, reasonable to connect these words with a distinct conjugation. However, there are several reasons to regard them as Akkadian loanwords rather than evidence that there was a functioning *shafʿel* in Aramaic:

(1) the paucity of such forms, which are limited to a mere handful of roots;

(2) the fact that the causative conjugation normally begins with a prefixed -ה in the Northwest Semitic group of languages, to which Aramaic belongs;

(3) the ample evidence of a *hafʿel* (and *ʾafʿel*) in Aramaic;

---

* אֶשְׁתּוֹלְלוּ (Ps 76:6) may demonstrate the same process in Hebrew.

(4) the presence of ס in one of these words (מְסֹובְלִין), where the others have a שׁ; this is especially striking given that the same root occurs several times in the *hafᶜel* (viz., הֵיבֵל in Ezra 5:14; 6:5, and לְהֵיבָלָה in Ezra 7:15);

(5) the י in שֵׁיזִב, which is etymologically derived from the Semitic root עזב. Akkadian is unique among Semitic languages in not representing ע (although its presence can often be inferred from the shift of nearby vowels to *e*, another mark of Akkadian influence), so this form must have been taken over from Akkadian rather than generated within Aramaic.

For all these reasons, biblical Aramaic appears to have borrowed these verbs directly from Akkadian. They are, therefore, best regarded as loanwords from Akkadian *shafᶜel* forms rather than evidence of an Aramaic *shafᶜel*.

As a result of these separate processes, we can identify three distinct prefixes that can be added to roots in biblical Aramaic in order to make them causal and thus list three separate, if related, causal conjugations:

ה   *hafᶜel*

א   *ʾafᶜel*

שׁ   *shafᶜel*

VOCABULARY

To Be Learned		*Reference*	
prohibition	אֱסָר	also	אַף
exile	גָּלוּ	bottom	אַרְעִית
living	חַי	sign	אָת
when	כְּדִי	be evil	בְּאֵשׁ
speak (D)	מלל	is it not (*interrogative*)	הֲלָא
close	סגר	innocence	זָכוּ
go up	סלק	damage	חֲבוּלָה
make prosper (H)	צלח	angel	מַלְאַךְ
formerly	קַדְמָה	flee	נדד
approach	קרב	women	נְשִׁין
		piece	קְרַץ
		accuse	אכל קרץ
		pay attention	שִׂים טְעֵם
		sleep	שְׁנָה

FROM THE BIBLE (Daniel 6:11–29)

וְדָנִיֵּאל כְּדִי יְדַע דִּי רְשִׁים כְּתָבָא עַל לְבַיְתֵהּ וְכַוִּין פְּתִיחָן לֵהּ בְּעִלִּיתֵהּ נֶגֶד יְרוּשְׁלֶם וְזִמְנִין תְּלָתָה בְיוֹמָא הוּא בָּרֵךְ וּמְצַלֵּא

קֳדָם אֱלָהֵהּ כָּל קֳבֵל דִּי הֲוָא עָבֵד מִן קַדְמַת דְּנָה. אֱדַיִן גֻּבְרַיָּא אִלֵּךְ הַרְגִּשׁוּ וְהַשְׁכַּחוּ

לְדָנִיֵּאל בָּעֵא קֳדָם אֱלָהֵהּ. בֵּאדַיִן קְרִיבוּ וְאָמְרִין קֳדָם מַלְכָּא עַל אֱסָר מַלְכָּא:

הֲלָא אֱסָר רְשַׁמְתָּ דִּי כָל אֱנָשׁ דִּי יִבְעֵה מִן כָּל אֱלָהּ וֶאֱנָשׁ עַד יוֹמִין תְּלָתִין לָהֵן מִנָּךְ

מַלְכָּא יִתְרְמֵא לְגוֹב אַרְיָוָתָא? עָנֵה מַלְכָּא וְאָמַר: יַצִּיבָא מִלְּתָא כְּדָת מָדַי וּפָרַס דִּי

לָא תֶעְדֵּא. בֵּאדַיִן עֲנוֹ וְאָמְרִין קֳדָם מַלְכָּא דִּי: דָּנִיֵּאל דִּי מִן בְּנֵי גָלוּתָא דִּי יְהוּד

לָא שָׂם עֲלַיךְ מַלְכָּא טְעֵם וְעַל אֱסָרָא דִּי רְשַׁמְתָּ וְזִמְנִין תְּלָתָה בְיוֹמָא בָּעֵא. אֱדַיִן

מַלְכָּא כְּדִי מִלְּתָא שְׁמַע שַׂגִּיא בְּאֵשׁ עֲלוֹהִי. בֵּאדַיִן גֻּבְרַיָּא אִלֵּךְ הַרְגִּשׁוּ עַל מַלְכָּא

וְאָמְרִין לְמַלְכָּא דַּע מַלְכָּא דִּי דָת לְמָדַי וּפָרַס דִּי כָל אֱסָר וּקְיָם דִּי מַלְכָּא יְהָקֵים

לָא לְהַשְׁנָיָה. בֵּאדַיִן מַלְכָּא אֲמַר וְהַיְתִיו לְדָנִיֵּאל וּרְמוֹ לְגֻבָּא דִּי אַרְיָוָתָא.

עָנֵה מַלְכָּא וְאָמַר לְדָנִיֵּאל: אֱלָהָךְ דִּי אַנְתְּ פָּלַח לֵהּ הוּא יְשֵׁיזְבִנָּךְ. וְהֵיתָיִת אֶבֶן

חֲדָה וְשֻׂמַת עַל פֻּם גֻּבָּא. אֱדַיִן אֲזַל מַלְכָּא לְהֵיכְלֵהּ וּבָת טְוָת וְדַחֲוָן לָא הַנְעֵל קָדָמוֹהִי וְשִׁנְתֵּהּ נַדַּת עֲלוֹהִי.

בֵּאדַיִן מַלְכָּא יְקוּם וּבְהִתְבְּהָלָה לְגֻבָּא דִּי אַרְיָוָתָא אֲזַל וּכְמִקְרְבֵהּ לְגֻבָּא לְדָנִיֵּאל עָנֵה

מַלְכָּא וְאָמַר לְדָנִיֵּאל: דָּנִיֵּאל עֲבֵד אֱלָהָא חַיָּא אֱלָהָךְ דִּי אַנְתְּ פָּלַח לֵהּ הֲיָכִל

לְשֵׁיזָבוּתָךְ מִן אַרְיָוָתָא. אֱדַיִן דָּנִיֵּאל עִם מַלְכָּא מַלִּל: מַלְכָּא לְעָלְמִין חֱיִי.

אֱלָהִי שְׁלַח מַלְאֲכֵהּ וּסֲגַר פֻּם אַרְיָוָתָא וְלָא חַבְּלוּנִי כָּל קֳבֵל דִּי קָדָמוֹהִי זָכוּ הִשְׁתְּכַחַת

לִי וְאַף קָדָמַיךְ מַלְכָּא חֲבוּלָה לָא עַבְדֵת. בֵּאדַיִן מַלְכָּא שַׂגִּיא טְאֵב עֲלוֹהִי וּלְדָנִיֵּאל

אֲמַר לְהַנְסָקָה מִן גֻּבָּא. וְהֻסַּק דָּנִיֵּאל מִן גֻּבָּא וְכָל חֲבָל לָא הִשְׁתְּכַח בֵּהּ דִּי הֵימִן

בֵּאלָהֵהּ. וַאֲמַר מַלְכָּא וְהַיְתִיו גֻּבְרַיָּא אִלֵּךְ דִּי אֲכַלוּ קַרְצוֹהִי דִּי דָנִיֵּאל וּלְגֹב אַרְיָוָתָא

רְמוֹ אִנּוּן בְּנֵיהוֹן וּנְשֵׁיהוֹן וְלָא מְטוֹ לְאַרְעִית גֻּבָּא עַד דִּי שְׁלִטוּ בְהוֹן אַרְיָוָתָא.

בֵּאדַיִן דָּרְיָוֶשׁ מַלְכָּא כְּתַב לְכָל עַמְמַיָּא אֻמַיָּא וְלִשָּׁנַיָּא דִּי דָארִין בְּכָל אַרְעָא שְׁלָמְכוֹן יִשְׂגֵּא.

מִן קֳדָמַי שִׂים טְעֵם דִּי בְּכָל שָׁלְטָן מַלְכוּתִי לֶהֱוֹן זָאעִין וְדָחֲלִין מִן קֳדָם אֱלָהֵהּ דִּי דָנִיֵּאל

דִּי הוּא אֱלָהָא חַיָּא וְקַיָּם לְעָלְמִין וּמַלְכוּתֵהּ דִּי לָא תִתְחַבַּל מְשֵׁיזִב וּמַצִּל וְעָבֵד אָתִין

בִּשְׁמַיָּא וּבְאַרְעָא דִּי שֵׁיזִיב לְדָנִיֵּאל מִן יַד אַרְיָוָתָא. וְדָנִיֵּאל דְּנָה הַצְלַח בְּמַלְכוּת

דָּרְיָוֶשׁ וּבְמַלְכוּת כּוֹרֶשׁ פָּרְסָיָא.

EXERCISES

Identify the root and conjugation of the following verbs:

נְפַקָה	הַב
הֵיבֵל	מְעַבַּד
קָאֵם	תְּקַבְּלוּן
מְשֵׁיזֵב	הַסַּק
יִפֵּל	דְּאָנִין
יְדִיעַ	מְכַפְּתִין
אַחֲוְיָה	תּוּכַל
יִשְׁתַּנֵּא	מַנִּיתָ
הִתְחָרַךְ	פְּקוּ
הַנְעֵל	חֲזֵיתוּן
אֶשְׁתַּנִּי	אֲקִימֵהּ
שֵׁיצִיא	מְבָרַךְ
הֲוַת	יִשְׁתַּכְלְלוּן
פְּתִיחוּ	בְּעֵינָא
אָנְדַּע	הוֹתֵב
תְּהַשְׁכַּח	מֵמַר
תְּהוֹבֵד	יְשֵׁיזֵב

לְהֵוֹן		הַיְתִי	
יִתְקְרֵי		מְהַקְרְבִין	
יְהָקֵים		תְּרַע	
שָׂמֶת		יְהוֹדַע	
תֶּעְדֵּא		עֲנוֹ	
תִּתְבְּנֵא		הַדֵּקֶת	
נְחַוֵּא		יְהָךְ	
יְשַׁנּוֹן		הִתְרוֹמַמְתָּ	

Explain the *grammatical* difference between the following pairs of forms:

יְקִים (Daniel 2:44) and יְקוּם (Daniel 7:24)

לְהֶעָלָה (Daniel 4:3) and לְהַנְעָלָה (Daniel 5:7)

הִתְבְּהָלָה (Daniel 5:9) and מִתְבָּהַל (Daniel 2:25)

אֲמַר (Daniel 4:11) and אֲמַר (Ezra 5:15)

תִּתְיְהִב (Ezra 6:4) and תִּתְחַבַּל (Daniel 2:44)

מִתְנַשְּׂאָה (Ezra 4:19) and מִתְעֲבֵד (Ezra 5:8)

מִתְקַטְּלִין (Daniel 2:13) and לְהִתְקְטָלָה (Daniel 2:13)

הִתְגְּזֶרֶת (Daniel 2:34) and אִתְגְּזֶרֶת (Daniel 2:45)

Translate into Aramaic:

(1) The father saved his son from the wild animals (lit. "of the field").

(2) The scribe completed the work on the fourth kingdom.

(3) The king assembled the people to praise God at night.

(4) I sought to leave the city when the king issued that prohibition.

(5) I went up on the mountain when a lion approached.

(6) We are closing the statue's mouth.

(7) The Jews succeeded when they were driven out into exile.

(8) The living God spoke in former times.

Chapter 27

DANIEL 7

The biblical texts in the preceding chapters have all been changed from the original, if only to reduce the amount of new vocabulary they require to a reasonable level. In this chapter, we will read Daniel 7, the last Aramaic passage in the Bible, exactly as it appears. All the necessary vocabulary can be found in the glossary at the end of this book.

The chapter describes Daniel's vision of four animals, which symbolize a succession of four empires. The history of this theme is discussed in "The Theory of the Four Monarchies: Opposition History Under the Roman Empire" by J. W. Swain in *Classical Philology* 35 (1940) 1–21, "The Four Empires in the Fourth Sibyl and in the Book of Daniel" by David Flusser in *Israel Oriental Studies* 2 (1972) 148–75, and the commentaries by James Montgomery (International Critical Commentary; New York: Charles Scribner's Sons, 1927), Louis Hartman and Alexander Di Lella (Anchor Bible; Garden City, NY: Doubleday & Co., 1978), and John Collins (Hermeneia; Minneapolis: Fortress Press, 1993).

(1) בִּשְׁנַת חֲדָה לְבֵלְאשַׁצַּר מֶלֶךְ בָּבֶל דָּנִיֵּאל חֵלֶם חֲזָה וְחֶזְוֵי רֵאשֵׁהּ עַל מִשְׁכְּבֵהּ

בֵּאדַיִן חֶלְמָא כְתַב רֵאשׁ מִלִּין אֲמַר׃

Translate into English:

רֵאשׁ מִלִּין is understood by some scholars as meaning a "complete account"; others think it refers to the "essential contents." There is a similar Hebrew phrase in Psalm 119:160.

NOTICE the -לְ prefixed to לְבֵלְאשַׁצַּר, which expresses possession, just like a construct phrase. The name itself is Babylonian (Bel-shar-uṣur) and means

"Bel guards the king." In Daniel 5 it occurs with the א following the שׂ (verses 1, 2, 9, 22, and 29); that kind of inconsistency is to be expected in the transliteration of a foreign name (compare our spellings Eileen and Ilene).

List all the verbs in this sentence and identify the form of each:

Verbal forms	Root	Conjugation	Tense	Person	Gender	Number

Translate each of the following words into Hebrew:

חֲדָה

רֵאשֵׁהּ

חֶלְמָא

מִלִּין

(2) עָנֵה דָנִיֵּאל וְאָמַר חָזֵה הֲוֵית בְּחֶזְוִי עִם לֵילְיָא וַאֲרוּ אַרְבַּע רוּחֵי שְׁמַיָּא מְגִיחָן לְיַמָּא רַבָּא. (3) וְאַרְבַּע חֵיוָן רַבְרְבָן סָלְקָן מִן יַמָּא שָׁנְיָן דָּא מִן דָּא.

Translate into English:

NOTICE: The meaning of עִם is apparently temporal ("at the time of") as in Daniel 3:33 and 4:31 (עִם דָּר וְדָר, see chapters 19 and 22).

"Wind" (רוּחַ) and "sea" (יַם) are common elements in ancient Near Eastern stories about primeval time, including the creation story in Genesis 1.

What form are the following verbs:

	Root	Conjugation	Tense	Person	Gender	Number
עֲנֵה						
חָזֵה						
הֲוֵית						
סְלִקָן						
שָׁנְיָן						
מְגִיחָן						

The subject of מְגִיחָן is _____; although that noun does not have a formal feminine ending (ה‍ָ- or ת-), the verb's feminine ending makes its gender clear.

אֲמַר is equivalent to the Hebrew form _____.

The phrase חָזֵה הֲוֵית means _____.

(4) קַדְמָיְתָא כְאַרְיֵה וְגַפִּין דִּי נְשַׁר לַהּ חָזֵה הֲוֵית עַד דִּי מְּרִיטוּ גַפַּיהּ וּנְטִילַת מִן אַרְעָא וְעַל רַגְלַיִן כֶּאֱנָשׁ הֳקִימַת וּלְבַב אֱנָשׁ יְהִיב לַהּ. (5) וַאֲרוּ חֵיוָה אָחֳרִי תִנְיָנָה דָּמְיָה לְדֹב וְלִשְׂטַר חַד הֳקִמַת וּתְלָת עִלְעִין בְּפֻמַּהּ בֵּין שִׁנַּיהּ וְכֵן אָמְרִין לַהּ קוּמִי אֲכֻלִי בְּשַׂר שַׂגִּיא. (6) בָּאתַר דְּנָה חָזֵה הֲוֵית וַאֲרוּ אָחֳרִי כִּנְמַר וְלַהּ גַּפִּין אַרְבַּע דִּי עוֹף עַל גַּבַּיהּ וְאַרְבְּעָה רֵאשִׁין לְחֵיוְתָא וְשָׁלְטָן יְהִיב לַהּ.

Translate into English:

Translate the following words into Hebrew:

עִלְעִין

(The singular occurs in the Garden of Eden story.)

אָמְרִין

לְחֵיוְתָא

נְשַׁר

What form are the following verbs:

	Root	Conjugation	Tense	Person	Gender	Number
מְּרִיטוּ						
נְטִילַת						
הָקֵמַת						
דָּמְיָה						
יְהִיב						

What is the subject of הָקֵמַת in verse 5? _____

This passage includes a series of ordinal numbers:

      "first"   קַדְמָיְתָא

      "second"   תִּנְיָנָה

  (for "third"   תְּלִיתָיָא, see Daniel 2:39 on p. 87.)

      "fourth"   רְבִיעָיָה (see verse 7 below)

In post-biblical Aramaic, the ד in קַדְמָא ("first") assimilated to the מ, leaving the form קַמָּא; thus the three subdivisions of the talmudic tractate נְזִיקִין are called:

      בָּבָא בַתְרָא   בָּבָא מְצִיעָא   בָּבָא קַמָּא

בַתְרָא is an adjectival form, which developed from בָּאתַר ("after," see verse 6 and p. 62), itself a composite of the preposition בְּ- ("in") and the noun אֲתַר ("place").

(7) בָּאתַר דְּנָה חָזֵה הֲוֵית בְּחֶזְוֵי לֵילְיָא וַאֲרוּ חֵיוָה רְבִיעָיָה דְּחִילָה וְאֵימְתָנִי וְתַקִּיפָא

יַתִּירָא וְשִׁנַּיִן דִּי פַרְזֶל לַהּ רַבְרְבָן אָכְלָה וּמַדֱּקָה וּשְׁאָרָא בְּרַגְלַיהּ רָפְסָה וְהִיא מְשַׁנְּיָה

מִן כָּל חֵיוָתָא דִּי קָדָמַיהּ וְקַרְנַיִן עֲשַׂר לַהּ. (8) מִשְׂתַּכַּל הֲוֵית בְּקַרְנַיָּא וַאֲלוּ קֶרֶן אָחֳרִי

זְעֵירָה סִלְקָת בֵּינֵיהֵן וּתְלָת מִן קַרְנַיָּא קַדְמָיָתָא אֶתְעֲקַרָה מִן קֳדָמַיהּ וַאֲלוּ עַיְנִין

כְּעַיְנֵי אֲנָשָׁא בְּקַרְנָא דָא וּפֻם מְמַלִּל רַבְרְבָן.

Translate into English:

NOTICE the suffix on יַתִּירָא (verse 7), which functions adverbially; it may be a remnant of an old accusative ending.

The adjectives אֵימְתָנִי (verse 7) and אָחֳרִי (verse 8) are both feminine singular.

What are the number and gender of:

		Number	Gender
רַבְרְבָן	(verses 7 and 8)		
חֵיוָתָא	(verse 7)		

What does the phrase מִשְׂתַּכַּל הֲוֵית (verse 8) mean?

What part of the sentence are the following words in verse 8?

פֻּם

מְמַלִּל

רַבְרְבָן

NOTICE the word order in the various clauses found in these sentences.

What form are the following verbs:

	Root	Conjugation	Tense	Person	Gender	Number
דְּחִילָה						
רָפְסָה						
מְשַׁנְּיָה						
מִשְׂתַּכַּל						
סִלְקָת						
אֶתְעֲקַרָה						

The subject of אֶתְעֲקַרָה (verse 8) is _____. Since this Gt verb is in the perfect, which normally begins with הִתְ, the prefixed א must have weakened from an original ה.

מַדְּקָה and אָכְלָה (verse 7) are both the same form, albeit in different conjugations. To what conjugations do they belong?

אָכְלָה

מַדְּקָה

What form are they? _____

NOTE that the root of מַדְּקָה is דקק. The (doubling) *dagesh* would normally be expected in the ק rather than the ד; Hebrew has analogous forms (e.g., יִסֹּב, which comes from the root סבב).

קַרְנַיִן עֲשַׂר לַהּ expresses possession ("it had 10 horns"); this chapter of Daniel contains several other examples of this construction:

גַּפִּין דִּי נְשַׁר לַהּ (verse 4) means _____.

לַהּ גַּפִּין אַרְבַּע דִּי עוֹף (verse 6) means _____.

שִׁנַּיִן דִּי פַרְזֶל לַהּ רַבְרְבָן (verse 7) means _____.

(9) חָזֵה הֲוֵית עַד דִּי כָרְסָוָן רְמִיו וְעַתִּיק יוֹמִין יְתִב לְבוּשֵׁהּ כִּתְלַג חִוָּר וּשְׂעַר רֵאשֵׁהּ כַּעֲמַר נְקֵא כָּרְסְיֵהּ שְׁבִיבִין דִּי נוּר גַּלְגִּלּוֹהִי נוּר דָּלִק. (10) נְהַר דִּי נוּר נָגֵד וְנָפֵק מִן קֳדָמוֹהִי אֶלֶף אַלְפִים יְשַׁמְּשׁוּנֵּהּ וְרִבּוֹ רִבְבָן קֳדָמוֹהִי יְקוּמוּן דִּינָא יְתִב וְסִפְרִין פְּתִיחוּ.

Translate into English:

List all the passive verbs in this passage:

List all the active participles in this passage:

NOTICE that יְתִב is in the perfect; the *ḥiriq* is the theme vowel. The phrase דִּינָא יְתִב means "the court sat."

What other verbs can you find in this passage?

Verb	Root	Conjugation	Tense	Person	Gender	Number

Identify the suffixes on the following words:

כָּרְסָוָן   (verse 9)

לְבוּשֵׁהּ   (verse 9)

גַּלְגִּלּוֹהִי   (verse 9)

שְׁבִיבִין   (verse 10)

דִּינָא   (verse 10)

This passage, which is widely regarded as a poem (note the parallelistic sentence structure), is one of several throne visions in the Bible (compare 1 Kings 22:19, Isaiah 6, and Ezekiel 1, 3:23–34 and 10:1, as well as 1 Enoch 14:18–23). "The ancient of days" (עַתִּיק יוֹמִין) is God.

(11) חָזֵה הֲוֵית בֵּאדַיִן מִן קָל מִלַּיָּא רַבְרְבָתָא דִּי קַרְנָא מְמַלֱּלָה חָזֵה הֲוֵית עַד דִּי קְטִילַת חֵיוְתָא וְהוּבַד גִּשְׁמַהּ וִיהִיבַת לִיקֵדַת אֶשָּׁא. (12) וּשְׁאָר חֵיוָתָא הֶעְדִּיו שָׁלְטָנְהוֹן וְאַרְכָה בְחַיִּין יְהִיבַת לְהוֹן עַד זְמַן וְעִדָּן.

Translate into English:

קָל is equivalent to the Hebrew word _____.

קְטִילַת and הוּבַד are both passive forms; what are their roots and to what conjugations do they belong?

	Root	Conjugation
קְטִילַת		
הוּבַד		

What form are the following verbs:

	Root	Conjugation	Tense	Person	Gender	Number
מְמַלֱּלָה						
הֶעְדִּיו						

Identify the suffixes on the following words:

מַלְיָא

אֶשָּׁא

גִּשְׁמֵהּ

רַבְרְבָתָא

What is the difference between חֵיוָתָא (verse 11) and חֵיוָתָא (verse 12)?

זְמַן and עִדָּן are synonyms; the phrase זְמַן וְעִדָּן should, therefore, probably be understood as a hendiadys, meaning "a time and a(nother) time," i.e., "two times."

(13) חָזֵה הֲוֵית בְּחֶזְוֵי לֵילְיָא וַאֲרוּ עִם עֲנָנֵי שְׁמַיָּא כְּבַר אֱנָשׁ אָתֵה הֲוָה וְעַד עַתִּיק יוֹמַיָּא מְטָה וּקְדָמוֹהִי הַקְרְבוּהִי. (14) וְלֵהּ יְהִיב שָׁלְטָן וִיקָר וּמַלְכוּ וְכֹל עַמְמַיָּא אֻמַיָּא וְלִשָׁנַיָּא לֵהּ יִפְלְחוּן שָׁלְטָנֵהּ שָׁלְטָן עָלַם דִּי לָא יֶעְדֵּה וּמַלְכוּתֵהּ דִּי לָא תִתְחַבַּל.

Translate into English:

What is the function of the suffix on לֵילְיָא (verse 13)? The י corresponds to the final ה on the Hebrew form לַיְלָה, which cannot be a feminine ending since that invariably carries the accent; note the Hebrew form לֵיל, which occurs in Isaiah 16:3.

The phrase אָתֵה הֲוָה (verse 13) means _____ .

What is the relationship between מַלְכוּ and מַלְכוּתֵהּ (verse 14)?

What form are the following verbs:

	Root	Conjugation	Tense	Person	Gender	Number
אָתֵה						
מְטָה						
יֶעְדֵּה						
תִּתְחַבַּל						
יִפְלְחוּן						
הַקְרְבוּהִי						

What is the subject of:

הַקְרְבוּהִי   (verse 13)

יִפְלְחוּן   (verse 14)

The phrase כְּבַר אֱנָשׁ is famous, but problematic. בַּר is used in Aramaic, as בֶּן is in Hebrew, to indicate the possessor of a quality or the member of a class, in this case "human being" (אֱנָשׁ; cf. בֶּן אֱנוֹשׁ in Ps 144:3). The equivalent phrase (υἱὸς τοῦ ἀνθρώπου) occurs in the New Testament, where its meaning is widely debated. For further discussion, see "The Son of Man" by John Bowker in *Journal of Theological Studies* new series 28 (1977) pp. 19–48, and "The New Testament Title 'Son of Man' Philologically Considered" by Joseph A. Fitzmyer in *A Wandering Aramean: Collected Aramaic Essays* (Missoula, MT: Scholars Press, 1979) pp. 143–60.

(15) אֶתְכְּרִיַּת רוּחִי אֲנָה דָנִיֵּאל בְּגוֹא נִדְנֶה וְחֶזְוֵי רֵאשִׁי יְבַהֲלֻנַּנִי. (16) קִרְבֵת עַל חַד מִן קָאֲמַיָּא וְיַצִּיבָא אֶבְעֵא מִנֵּהּ עַל כָּל דְּנָה וַאֲמַר לִי וּפְשַׁר מִלַּיָּא יְהוֹדְעִנַּנִי.

(17) אִלֵּין חֵיוָתָא רַבְרְבָתָא דִּי אִנִּין אַרְבַּע אַרְבְּעָה מַלְכִין יְקוּמוּן מִן אַרְעָא.

(18) וִיקַבְּלוּן מַלְכוּתָא קַדִּישֵׁי עֶלְיוֹנִין וְיַחְסְנוּן מַלְכוּתָא עַד עָלְמָא וְעַד עָלַם עָלְמַיָּא.

Translate into English:

NOTICE how the phrase אֲנָה דָנִיֵּאל functions as an appositive to the pronominal suffix of רוּחִי in verse 15, resulting in the meaning: "my spirit—me, Daniel. . . ."

The reference to Daniel's spirit as having a sheath (נִדְנֶה) suggests a distinction between the body and the mind, which emerged only late in the biblical period.

What form are the following verbs:

	Root	Conjugation	Tense	Person	Gender	Number
קִרְבֵת						
אֶבְעֵא						
יְהוֹדְעִנַּנִי						
יְקַבְּלוּן						
קָאֲמַיָּא						

NOTICE how the weak middle letter of the hollow root קוּם has been "strengthened" to an א.

Although אֶתְכְּרִיַּת (verse 15) clearly belongs to the Gt conjugation, the fact that it is perfect demonstrates that the א is not a pronominal prefix (the form is 3d person feminine singular), but softened from ה, making this an *ʾitpeʿel* form (compare the *hafʿel* conjugation, which sometimes weakens into *ʾafʿel*).

אִנִּין (verse 17) literally means _____; in this sentence, it functions as a copula, as pronouns often do in Aramaic and later Hebrew.

קַדִּישֵׁי (verse 18) is a term with a long and important history. In ancient Canaanite texts it refers to gods; however, the Hebrew Bible uses it primarily for angels (e.g., Psalm 89:6 and Job 15:15). Jews later applied it to themselves. In the Middle Ages, the Latin equivalent (*sanctus*) was used for "saints." (The English word is derived from the same Latin root.) For further reading on this term, see "The Saints of the Most High and Their Kingdom" by C. H. W. Brekelmans in *Oudtestamentische Studiën* 14 (1965) 305–29, and "The Identity of 'the Saints of the Most High' in Daniel 7" by G. F. Hasel in *Biblica* 56 (1975) 173–92.

(19) אֱדַיִן צְבִית לְיַצָּבָא עַל חֵיוְתָא רְבִיעָיְתָא דִּי הֲוָת שָׁנְיָה מִן כָּלְּהֵן דְּחִילָה יַתִּירָה שִׁנַּיַּה דִּי פַרְזֶל וְטִפְרַיַּה דִּי נְחָשׁ אָכְלָה מַדֲּקָה וּשְׁאָרָא בְּרַגְלַיהּ רָפְסָה. (20) וְעַל קַרְנַיָּא עֲשַׂר דִּי בְרֵאשַׁהּ וְאָחֳרִי דִּי סִלְקַת וּנְפַלָה מִן־קֳדָמַיהּ תְּלָת וְקַרְנָא דִכֵּן וְעַיְנִין לַהּ וּפֻם מְמַלִּל רַבְרְבָן וְחֶזְוַהּ רַב מִן־חַבְרָתַהּ. (21) חָזֵה הֲוֵית וְקַרְנָא דִכֵּן עָבְדָה קְרָב עִם קַדִּישִׁין וְיָכְלָה לְהוֹן. (22) עַד דִּי אֲתָה עַתִּיק יוֹמַיָּא וְדִינָא יְהִב לְקַדִּישֵׁי עֶלְיוֹנִין וְזִמְנָא מְטָה וּמַלְכוּתָא הֶחֱסִנוּ קַדִּישִׁין.

Translate into English:

דְּכֵן (verse 20) is what part of speech: _____

     gender _____

     number _____

What form are the following verbs:

	Root	Conjugation	Tense	Person	Gender	Number
צָבִית						
שָׁנְיָה						
דְּחִילָה						
מַדְּקָה						
סִלְקָת						
נְפַלָה						
מְטָה						

The subject of נְפַלָה is _____.

NOTE that the description of the fourth beast in verse 19 includes the phrase טִפְרַיה דִּי נְחָשׁ ("claws of bronze"), which is not found in verse 7 where it may, therefore, have been accidentally omitted.

(23) כֵּן אֲמַר חֵיוְתָא רְבִיעָיְתָא מַלְכוּ רְבִיעָיָא תֶּהֱוֵא בְאַרְעָא דִּי תִשְׁנֵא מִן כָּל מַלְכְוָתָא וְתֵאכֻל כָּל אַרְעָא וּתְדוּשִׁנַּהּ וְתַדְּקִנַּהּ. (24) וְקַרְנַיָּא עֲשַׂר מִנַּהּ מַלְכוּתָה עַשְׂרָה מַלְכִין יְקֻמוּן וְאָחֳרָן יְקוּם אַחֲרֵיהוֹן וְהוּא יִשְׁנֵא מִן קַדְמָיֵא וּתְלָתָה מַלְכִין יְהַשְׁפִּל. (25) וּמִלִּין לְצַד עִלָּיָא יְמַלִּל וּלְקַדִּישֵׁי עֶלְיוֹנִין יְבַלֵּא וְיִסְבַּר לְהַשְׁנָיָה זִמְנִין וְדָת וְיִתְיַהֲבוּן בִּידֵהּ עַד עִדָּן וְעִדָּנִין וּפְלַג עִדָּן. (26) וְדִינָא יִתִּב וְשָׁלְטָנֵהּ יְהַעְדּוֹן לְהַשְׁמָדָה וּלְהוֹבָדָה עַד סוֹפָא. (27) וּמַלְכוּתָה וְשָׁלְטָנָא וּרְבוּתָא דִּי מַלְכְוָת תְּחוֹת כָּל שְׁמַיָּא יְהִיבַת לְעַם קַדִּישֵׁי עֶלְיוֹנִין מַלְכוּתֵהּ מַלְכוּת עָלַם וְכֹל שָׁלְטָנַיָּא לֵהּ יִפְלְחוּן וְיִשְׁתַּמְּעוּן.

Translate into English:

NOTICE the difference between אָחֳרָן ("another") and אַחֲרֵיהֹן ("after them") in verse 24, which are comparable to the Hebrew pair אַחֵר ("other") and אַחֲרֵי ("after").

לְצַד (lit. "to the side of") apparently means "against" in verse 25.

עִדָּן וְעִדָּנִין וּפְלַג עִדָּן (verse 25) refers to the three and one half units of time (1 + 2 + 1/2) which are also mentioned in Daniel 8:14 and 9:27.

What form are the following verbs:

	Root	Conjugation	Tense	Person	Gender	Number
תְּחֱוֵה						
יִתְיַהֲבוּן						
יְהִיבַת						
יְהַשְׁפֵּל						

NOTICE that the ה is retained in this last form, as in the grammatically similar יְהַעְדּוֹן (verse 26).

To what conjugation does each of the following verbs belong:

יְמַלִּל

יְבַלֵּא

יִסְבַּר

What is the root of:

לְהַשְׁנָיָה

לְהַשְׁמָדָה

לְהוֹבָדָה

All three of these words are _____.

What are the roots and the conjugations for the following verbs?

	Conjugation	*Root*
יִפְלְחוּן		
יִשְׁתַּמְּעוּן		
יְהַעֲדּוֹן		

(28)   עַד כָּה סוֹפָא דִי מִלְּתָה אֲנָה דָנִיֵּאל שַׂגִּיא רַעְיוֹנַי יְבַהֲלֻנַּנִי וְזִיוַי יִשְׁתַּנּוֹן עֲלַי וּמִלְּתָא בְּלִבִּי נִטְרֵת.

Translate into English:

NOTICE the similar phrase near the end of Ecclesiastes (12:13).

List all the verbs in this verse and give the form of each:

Verb	*Root*	*Conjugation*	*Tense*	*Person*	*Gender*	*Number*

Chapter 28

INSCRIPTIONS

The oldest surviving texts in Aramaic are inscriptions. We will consider three of these, one from the language's earliest known period, another that was found in a modern collection so that its original date and location are unknown, and a third that comes from a seventh-century synagogue.

The following words are common in inscriptions and should be learned:

brother	אח
evil (sometimes באש) . .	ביש
remember	דכר
see	חמה
direct object marker	ית
thus	כן
is not	לישה
open	פתח

Our earliest evidence of Aramaic's long history comes from a series of inscriptions which were found in northern Syria and had been written during the time of Israel's divided monarchy.* Several of these are from the rulers of a country known as Samʾal, a petty kingdom of the ninth and eighth centuries, a time during which the Arameans established several small countries in this region. (The Bible mentions Damascus, Zobah, Beth Rechob, and Maacah.) The example which follows is by one Barrakib, who apparently ruled Samʾal towards the end of the eighth century, about the same time that Amos, Hosea, Micah, and Isaiah were active in Israel. It was found at Zinjirli in northwest Syria at the end of the last century. A relief with his picture (see p. 168) is inscribed with the words אנה בר רכב בר פנמו at the top. This same phrase opens the much longer inscription which we will read here.

---

*These are conveniently collected in H. Donner and W. Röllig's *Kanaanäische und Aramäische Inschriften* (Wiesbaden: Otto Harrassowitz, 1966).

167

אנה בר רכב בר פנמו מלך שמאל עבד תגלתפליסר מרא רבעי ארקא.

בצדק אבי ובצדקי הושבני מראי רכבאל ומראי תגלתפליסר על כרסא אבי.

ובית אבי עמל מן כל. ורצת בגלגל מראי מלך אשור במצעת מלכן

רברבן בעלי כסף ובעלי זהב. ואחזת בית אבי והיטבתה מן בית חד

מלכן רברבן. והתנאבו אחי מלכיא לכל מה טבת ביתי. ובי טב

לישה לאבהי מלכי שמאל הא בית כלמו להם פהא בית שתוא להם

והא בית כיצא. ואנה בנית ביתא זנה.

Vocabulary

settle (H)	ישב	desire (Htn)	אבה
summer	קיץ	grasp	אחז
middle	מצעת	*dialect form of* בית	בי
exert oneself, toil	עמל	wheel	גלגל
and	פ-	behold	הא

Vocabulary (cont.)

righteousness	צדק	gold	זהב
quarter	רבע	this	זנה
run	רוץ	goodness	טבה
winter	שתו	be pleasing (H)	יטב

Use the biblical vowel system to vocalize the above text.

Translate it into English:

Proper Names

בר רכב — This name is pronounced Barrakib according to an inscribed Hittite seal, where it is spelled out syllabically (*Orientalia* 20 [1957] 345).

פנמו — Pronounced Panamuwa according to cuneiform inscriptions from several Assyrian rulers (e.g., Tiglath Pilesar III; see James Pritchard, *Ancient Near Eastern Texts Relating to the Old Testament*, pp. 282 and 283); *-muwa* was a common ending for names in Asia Minor (see כלמו below).

שמאל — The ancient name of the land in which Zinjirli is located; it may also have been called Yaudi.

תגלתפליסר — Tiglath Pilesar III, who is mentioned several times in the Bible (2 Kings 15:29; 16:7, 10; 1 Chronicles 5:6, 26; 2 Chronicles 28:20); he is called by the Babylonian throne name Pul in 2 Kings 15:19.

רכבאל — The patron god of Samʾal.

כלמו — An earlier ruler of Samʾal from the ninth century, who is apparently the author of another inscription found in Zinjirli (see H. Donner and W. Röllig, *Kanaanäische und Aramäische Inschriften*, no. 24, and James Pritchard, *Ancient Near Eastern Texts Relating to the Old Testament*, p. 654).

NOTICE that we have already encountered ארקא in Jeremiah 10:11, where it is juxtaposed with the more common form ארעא, demonstrating two different realizations of the Semitic consonant *ḍ*, which appears as צ in Hebrew (i.e. ארץ).* The title מרא רבעי ארקא is a translation from Assyrian (*shar kibrat arbaʾi*).

מצעת (middle) can be compared with mishnaic אֶמְצַע; the second section of the talmudic tractate נְזִיקִין is called בָּבָא מְצִיעָא (the first section is בָּבָא קַמָּא and the last section בָּבָא בַתְרָא, as explained on p. 153).

התנאבו appears to be a *hitnafʿal* form from a root related to אבה and יאב (wish); its meaning would be something like "envy" or "be jealous."

The most conspicuous features of this early inscription are the number of forms which agree with Hebrew, rather than biblical Aramaic:

הושבני contrast the form הותב (e.g., Ezra 4:10) from the root יתב.

לישה corresponding to the Akkadian *lā išu*, comes from the words לא יש ("it is not"); however it appears as לית in other Aramaic sources, including the massoretes' marginal notes to the biblical text, where its abbreviation ל is used to identify forms that are spelled uniquely in the Hebrew text (see p. 55).

זהב is common in the Aramaic sections of the Bible, but appears there as דְהַב (e.g., Ezra 5:14; 6:5, and often in Daniel 2, 3, and 5).

אחז usually spelled אחד in Aramaic.

זנה typically דְנָה (but compare Hebrew זֶה).

---

*The two forms are juxtaposed in the Elephantine letter (Cowley 6) presented in chapter 29.

רצת is from the root רוץ, which appears as רהט in Aramaic (compare Targum Onkelos with the original Hebrew in Genesis 24:27, 20, 28, and 29).

These are all cases in which original Semitic sounds that came to be realized differently in Hebrew and in Aramaic (e.g., *t* as שׁ or ת, *ṭ* as ט or צ, and *d* as ז or ד) here follow the "Hebrew" (really Canaanite) spelling. This inscription may, therefore, have been written before these two branches of Northwest Semitic had fully separated. Thus the original *t* appears as שׁ in הושב and ליש, *ṭ* as צ in רץ and כיץ, and *d* as ז in זהב, אחז, and זנה.

כיצא   spelled קיט in biblical Aramaic (Daniel 2:35), but קיץ in Hebrew. The use of כ instead of ק may reflect a certain fluidity in spelling (so also שׁתו appears as סְתָו in Song of Songs 2:11). However, since the same spelling is found in several other inscriptions, it is more likely that dissimilation caused the ק to shift to כ, inasmuch as the word already had one emphatic letter (צ) in it.

Several other features in this inscription are characteristically Aramaic:

SOUNDS: The *â* sound is evident in אנה (as opposed to Hebrew אֲנִי) and words like טב, where it shifted to *ô* in Hebrew.

WORDS: בר חד כרסא מרא רברבן

FORMS: The determined state (ארקא, ביתא, מלכיא);

    masculine plural suffixes ending with *nun* (e.g., מלכן);

    perfect, 1st person singular forms ending with *-ēt* rather than *-tî*

    (e.g., בנית and אחזת).

The next inscription was found on a stone plaque in a nineteenth-century collection of antiquities at the Russian convent on Jerusalem's Mount of Olives. It mentions Judah's King Uzziah, who reigned during the early part of the eighth century; however, its "Aramaic style" script was not adopted by Jews until the Babylonian Exile, when it replaced the "Phoenician" (Paleo-Hebrew) script that had been used during the monarchy period. The inscription itself was probably written sometime around the first century.

לכה התית טמי עוזיה מלך יהודה ולא למפתח.

Vocabulary

bones . . . . טם

here . . . . כה

Use the biblical vowel system to vocalize the above text.

Translate it into English:

התית   is an H passive form of the common root אתה ("come," cf. Daniel 6:18).

טמי is equivalent to the Hebrew word עֶצֶם ("bone"). The loss of the ע suggests that it was not pronounced in this period; there are several reports
in the Talmud indicating that the letters ע and א were often not distinguished in pronunciation during the early centuries of this era (*j.
Berakhot* 2:4, *b. Berakhot* 32a, *b. Megillah* 24b, *b. Erubin* 53b).

למפתח the מ in this word is shaped like the form (ם) which is used today at the
end of words (see the illustration on p. 172). Apparently, the two shapes
we use for the letter מ were originally interchangeable (see Isaiah 9:6);
over time, one of them (ם) was reserved for the end of words, probably
on the basis of analogy with other letters in which medial (כ, נ, פ, צ)
and final forms (ך, ן, ף, ץ) had come to be distinguished. Thus ם is the
only final form that does not have a tail.

The prohibition against opening the vessel containing Uzziah's bones is typical of
many inscriptions (for several Phoenician examples, see James Pritchard, *Ancient Near
Eastern Texts Relating to the Old Testament,* pp. 661–62). 2 Chronicles 26:23 reports that
King Uzziah, who suffered from leprosy, was buried in a special location outside Jerusalem's
city wall (cf. Josephus, *Antiquities* 9:10.4 §227 and Nehemiah 3:15). This inscription, then,
attests to his bones' having been moved some time after their initial burial.

A final inscription comes from the mosaic floor of a seventh-century synagogue located in ʿEin Gedi, along the western coast of the Dead Sea between Qumran and Masada. (An
earlier, Hebrew section of the inscription lists several ancient biblical luminaries and the signs
of the zodiac.)

דכירין לטב יוסה ועירון וחזיקיו בנוה דחלפי. כל מן דיהיב פלגו בן גבר לחבריה

הי אמר לשן ביש על חבריה לעממיה הי גניב צבותיה דחבריה הי מן דגלי רזה

דקרתה לעממיה דין דעינוה משוטטן בכל ארעה וחמי סתירתה הוא יתן אפוה

בגברה ההו ובזרעיה ויעקור יתיה מן תחות שומיה. וימרון כל עמה אמן ואמן

סלה. רבי יוסה בן חלפי חזקיו בן חלפי דכירין לטב דרגי סגי

אנון עבדו לשמה דרחמנה שלום.

Vocabulary

selah *(liturgical term)*	סלה	amen *(liturgical term)*	אמן
hidden thing	סתירה	nose, anger	אף
uproot	עקר	between (בין)	בן
discord	פלג	steal	גנב
property	(ת)צבו	of	ד-
Merciful One	רחמן	stair	דרג
wander	שטט	or	הי
		seed	זרע

Proper Names

חזיקיו — This form conforms to a normal northern pattern for spelling the divine element at the end of names rather than the more familiar (southern) יהו-.

חלפי

יוסה

עירון

Use the biblical vowel system to vocalize the above text.

Translate it into English:

NOTICE the phrase דין דעינוה (lit. "This one, which his eyes,"
i.e. "the one whose eyes . . .").

Several features of this inscription are familiar from other Aramaic texts we have studied. For example, תחות occurs in the book of Daniel (also Jeremiah 10:11), as does the direct object marker ית (Daniel 3:12) in contrast to biblical Hebrew's את. דכירין and ארעה also reflect common Aramaic forms (contrast the Hebrew words זכרן and ארץ), as does דין. Surprisingly, זרע is closer to the Hebrew form of the word for "arm" (זְרוֹעַ) than biblical Aramaic's (אֶ)דְרָע; note also שלום rather than שלם. Other notable spellings include:

> בן for בין (between)
> שומיא for שמיא (sky)
> ימרון from the root אמר (say)
> סגי for שגיא (much)

The last two examples, along with הי rather than the more common היא, suggest that the pronunciation of several consonants was becoming weaker. (See p. 70 regarding שׁ becoming ס; examples are mentioned on pp. 171 and 206.)

On the other hand, this inscription contains several unfamiliar phenomena:

– passive participles (גניב and יהיב) used in apparently active contexts.
– the particle דְ־ where biblical Aramaic uses דִי.
– final י in words the Bible spells with ה (e.g., גלי and חמי).
– the determined suffix marked with ה rather than the biblical א.

Chapter 29

LETTERS

Several Aramaic letters have survived from various periods of antiquity. Although our interest here is linguistic, they provide important evidence for understanding the nature of ancient letters in general.

Vocabulary To Be Learned

women	נשין	fire	אש
burnt offering	עלוה/עלתה	donkey	חמר
compassion	רחמן	month	ירח
break	תבר	to, with	לות
here	תנה	altar	מדבח
		self	נפש

The first letter was written in the fifth pre-Christian century at a Jewish settlement on the island of Yeb (Elephantine), which is north of the first cataract of the Nile, where the Aswan Dam is located today. The Persian Empire, which had conquered Egypt in 525 B.C.E., supported Jewish mercenaries in this military colony on the southern frontier of ancient Egypt. Their writings, on papyri, were discovered in the early part of the twentieth century. The following letter gives us a fair amount of information about the colony's history.

Lines 1–3

אל מראן בגוהי פחת יהוד. עבדיך ידניה וכנותה כהניא זי ביב בירתא:

שלם מראן אלה שמיא ישאל שגיא בכל עדן ולרחמן ישימנך קדם דריוהוש מלכא

ובני ביתא יתיר מן זי כען חד אלף. וחין אריכן ינתן לך וחדה ושריר הוי

בכל עדן.

Vocabulary

long .... אריך

fortress .... בירתה

who, which .... זי

happiness .... חדה

life .... חין

prosperous .... שריר

Use the biblical vowel system to vocalize the passage above.

Translate it into English:

Proper Nouns

בגוהי — governor of Judah, apparently after Nehemiah

ידניה — son of Gemariah, priest and leader of the Jewish community

דריהוש — Darius II, who ruled Persia from 423 to 403. The letter ends with the author's statement that he wrote this in the 17th year of Darius' reign, i.e. 407 B.C.E.

חד אלף — 1000 times; compare the phrase חַד שִׁבְעָה in Daniel 3:19 (see p. 90)

Lines 4–13

כען עבדך ידניה וכנותה כן אמרן: בירח תמוז שְׁנת 14 דריוהוש מלכא כזי ארשם

נפק ואזל על מלכא כמריא זי אלהא חנוב זי ביב בירתא המונית עם וידרנג

זי פרתרך תנה הוה. לם אגורא זי יהו אלהא זי ביב בירתא יהעדו מן תמה.

אחר וידרנג זך לחיא אגרת שלח על נפין ברה זי רבחיל הוה בסון בירתא לאמר:

אגורא זי ביב בירתא ינדשו. אחר נפין דבר מצריא עם חילא אחרנן אתו לבירת

יב עם תליהם עלו באגורא זך נדשוהי עד ארעא ועמודיא זי אבנא זי הוו תמה

תברו המו. אף הוה תרען זי אבן 5 בנין פסילה זי אבן זי הוו באגורא זך נדשו

ודשיהם קימן וציריהם זי דששיא אלך נחש ומטלל עקהן זי ארז כלא זי עם שירית

אשרנא ואחרן זי תמה הוה כלא באשה שרפו. ומזרקיא זי זהבא וכסף ומנדעממתא

זי הוה באגורא זך כלא לקחו ולנפשהום עבדו.

Vocabulary

roof	מטלל	temple	אגורא
anything	מנדעם	cedar	ארז
destroy	נדש	beams	אשרן
pillar	עמוד	lead (D)	דבר
wood	עק	door	דש
cut stone	פסיל	in agreement with	המונית עם
commander	פרתרך	that	זי, זך
pivot (of a door)	ציר	army	חיל
standing	קים	when (cf. כדי)	כזי
general	רבחיל	priest	כמר
burn	שׂרף	evil	לחיא
remainder	שׁירי	surely	לם
weapon	תלי	take	לקח
gate	תרע	basin	מזרק

Use biblical vowels to vocalize the passage above.

Translate it into English:

Proper Nouns

ארשם — Persian satrap over Egypt

חנוב — a male Egyptian god at Elephantine

וידרנג — commander of the Persian garrison at Elephantine and later *frataraka*

("foremost"), a position with judicial and military authority

יהו — the God of the Jews

נפין — son of Vidranga

מצריא — Egyptians

סון — Syene (ancient name of Elephantine); cf. Ezekiel 29:10 and 30:6

תמוז — a late summer month

רבחיל — the Bible includes several titles which are similarly constructed: -

רַב שָׁקֵה and ,רַב סָרִיס ,רַב מַג ,רַב טַבָּחִים ,רַב הַחֹבֵל

Lines 13–17

ומן יומי מלך מצרין אבהין בנו אגורא זך ביב בירתא. וכזי כנבוזי על למצרין
אגורא זך בנה השכחה. ואגורי אלהי מצרין כל מגרו ואיש מנדעם באגורא זך
לא חבל. וכזי כזנה עביד אנחנה עם נשין ובנין שקקן לבשן הוין וצימין ומצלין
ליהו מרא שמיא זי החוין בוידרנג זך. כלביא הנפקו כבלא מן רגלוהי וכל נכסין
זי קנה אבדו וכל גברין זי בעו באיש לאגורא זך כל קטילו וחזין בהום.

Vocabulary

be lost	אבד
chain	כבל
dog	כלב
throw down	מגר
property	נכס
fast	צום
buy	קנה
sackcloth	שקק

Use the biblical vowel system to vocalize the passage above.

Translate it into English:

Proper Nouns

כנבוזי — Cambyses, son of Cyrus; ruled Persia from 530 to 522 B.C.E. He apparently found the Jewish temple already standing when he conquered Egypt in 525 B.C.E. His destruction of Egyptian temples while letting the Jewish one stand may have contributed to tension between Jews and Egyptians.

Lines 17–22

אף קדמת זנה בעדן זי זא באישתא עביד לן אגרה שלחן על מראן ועל יהוחנן

כהנא רבא וכנותה כהניא זי בירושלם ועל אוסתן אחוהי זי ענני וחרי יהודיא.

אגרא חדה לא שלחו עלין. אף מן ירח תמוז שנת 14 דריהוש מלכא ועד זנה יומא

אנחנה שקקן לבשן וצימין. נשיא זילן כארמלה עבידין. משח לא משחין וחמר לא

שתין. אף מן זכי ועד יום שנת 17 דריהוש מלכא מנחה ולבונה ועלוה לא עבדו

באגורא זך.

Vocabulary

incense	לבונה	also	אף
grain offering	מנחה	widow	ארמלה
oil	משח	our	זילן
anoint	משח	that	זכי
until	עד	this	זנה
		noble	חרי

Proper Nouns

יהוחנן — the high priest, mentioned also in Nehemiah 12:22 and 13:28

אוסתן — a Jew, brother of Anani

ענני — scribe and chancellor to Arsame; 1 Chronicles 3:24 mentions a descendant of David who bore the same name

Use the biblical vowel system to vocalize the passage above.

Translate it into English:

This passage demonstrates that there were ties between the Jews of Elephantine and those in Jerusalem, an impression supported by the analogous links with those in Babylon described in the books of Ezra and Nehemiah.

Lines 22–30

כען עבדיך ידניה וכנותה ויהודיא כל בעלי יב כן אמרין. הן על מראן טב

אתעשת על אגורא זך למבנה בזי לא שבקן לן למבניה. חזי בעלי טבתך ורחמיך

זי תנה במצרין. אגרה מנך ישתלח עליהום על אגורא זי יהו אלהא למבניה

ביב בירתא לקבל זי בנה הוה זי קדמין. ומנחתא ולבונתא ועלותא יקרבון על

מדבחא זי יהו אלהא בשמך ונצלה עליך בכל עדן אנחנה ונשין ובנין ויהודיא

כל זי תנה. הן כן עבדו עד זי אגורא זך יתבנה וצדקה יהוה לך קדם יהו אלה

שמיא מן גבר זי יקרב לה עלוה ודבחן דמן כדמי כסף כנכרין אלף ועל זהב.

על זנה שלחן הודען. אף כלא מליא באגרה חדה שלחן בשמן על דליה ושלמיה

בני סנאבלט פחת שמרין. אף בזנה זי עביד לן כלא ארשם לא ידע.

ב־20 למרחשון שנת 17 דריהוש מלכא.

Vocabulary

a coin	כנכר	1000	אלף
grain offering (cf. מנחה)	מחתא	sacrifice	דבח
intend (Gt–take thought)	עשת	price	דמי
merit	צדקה	gold	זהב

Use the biblical vowel system to vocalize the passage above.

Translate it into English:

Proper Nouns

שלמיה and דליה — sons of Sanballat (people with the same names are mentioned in Ezra 2:60; 10:39, 41; and Nehemiah 3:30 and 13:13, supporting the picture of post-exilic Jewry presented both in this document and the Bible)

סנאבלט — (Akkadian Sin-uballiṭ)—governor of Samaria (cf. Nehemiah 2:19; 3:33; 6:1; etc.)

מרחשון — month in late fall

The most conspicuous linguistic feature in this letter is its use of ז where biblical Aramaic uses ד, especially for the demonstrative elements זנה, זך, and זכי as well as זי (cf. זיל). Note also זהב (biblical Aramaic has דהב). On the other hand, the spelling עק for "tree" contrasts with the Hebrew עץ; biblical Aramaic uses אע. (Compare the word ארקא that is found in Jeremiah 10:11 for the Hebrew ארץ, which Aramaic elsewhere presents as ארע.)

The redundant syntax of the phrase אחוהי זי ענני (lit. "his brother of Anani") is comparable to that found in biblical Aramaic, as described in chapter 16.

From almost six centuries later come a series of letters written by Simon bar Kosiba, who led a Jewish revolt against the Romans. He is better known by his title Bar Kochba (lit. "son of the star," based on Numbers 24:17). These documents, written in Hebrew, Aramaic, and Greek, were found in caves near those which produced the famous Dead Sea Scrolls. The following example raises interesting possibilities about his religious views:

שמעון ליהודה בר מנשה לקרית ערביה: שלחת לך תרי חמרין די תשלח עמהן
תרי גברין לות יהונתן בר בעין ולות מסבלה די יעמרן וישלחן למחניה לותך
ללבין ואתרגין. ואת שלח אחרנין מלותך וימטון לך הדסין וערבין. ותקן יתהן
ושלח יתהן למחניה הוא שלם.

Vocabulary

citron	אתרג
myrtle	הדס
palm	ללב
camp	מחנה
load	עמר
willow	ערבא
prepare	תקן

Use the biblical vowel system to vocalize the passage above.

Translate it into English:

Proper Nouns

יהודה בר מנשה

יהונתן בר בעין — with Masabala, apparently Bar Kochba's military commander of Ein Gedi, to whom most of Bar Kochba's letters are addressed

מסבלה — son of Shimon

קרית ערביה — lit. "town of the Arabs" or "willows," where Judah was posted between Ein Gedi and Bar Kochba's main camp (presumably at Betar)

The preposition לות is a compound made of up ל- and ות (from ית, which occurs in Daniel 3:12); in other words, it is a double direct object marker, which appears once (מלותך) with an additional preposition (-מֵ).

The reference to the palm (ללב), citron (אתרג), myrtle (הדס), and willow (ערבא) is reminiscent of the holiday of Sukkot (see traditional Jewish interpretations of Leviticus 23:40, as found in Targum Onkelos and *Mishnah Sukkah* 3–4, for example), at which time these four species are to be waved in celebration of a successful harvest.

Chapter 30

DEAD SEA SCROLLS

Several of the famous Dead Sea Scrolls, which were discovered during the 1940's and 1950's, are written in Aramaic. Many of these are the writings of a religious community that settled alongside the Wadi Qumran during the Hasmonean period (2d century B.C.E.), probably in order to avoid the wrath of the governing party in Jerusalem; other documents found there may have been the community's copies of more widely known writings.

The selections that follow are from a scroll called the Genesis Apocryphon (1QapGen) because it expands on passages in the book of Genesis. The sections here are based on Genesis 12, which describes Abraham and Sarah's visit to the land of Egypt. According to the Bible, Abraham was worried that the Pharaoh might have him killed so that he could have the beautiful Sarah for himself. In this passage, Abraham describes a dream he experienced as he entered Egypt, which foreshadows what he expected would happen there.

Vocabulary To Be Learned

face, nose	אֲנַף
wife	אַנְתָה
companion	חֲבַר
lovely	יָא
take	נְסַב
eye	עַיִן
love	רְחֵם

19:14–17

וחלמת אנה אברם חלם בלילה מעלי לארע מצרין. וחזית בחלמי והא ארז חד

ותמרא חדא יאיא שגיא. ובני אנוש אתו ובעון למקץ ולמעקר לארזא ולמשבוק

תמרתא בלחודיהה. ואכליאת תמרתא ואמרת אל תקוצו לארזא ארי תרינא

מן שרבא חדא. ושביק ארזא בטלל תמרתא ולא אתקץ.

186

Vocabulary

singly	לחוד	human	אנוש
uproot	עקר	cedar	ארז
cut down	קצץ	dream	חלם
family	שרב	shadow	טלל
palm	תמר	protest (*afʿel*)	כלא

Use the biblical vowel system to vocalize the above text.

Translate it into English:

מעלי — the G infinitive of עלל; other G infinitives in this passage are מעקר, משבוק,
   and מקץ.

-ל — marks the direct object (ארזא).

אכליאת — a perfect form from the root כלא, which must, therefore, belong to the
   ʾ*afʿel* conjugation.

אל — introduces a negative command.

The next column of the scroll describes Sarah in a way that justifies Abraham's con-
cern (Genesis 12:11), albeit one that seems more suitable to the Song of Songs than the book
of Genesis:

20:2–8

כמה נציח ושפיר לה צלם אנפיהא . . . . . וכמא רקיק לה שער ראישה כמא יאין להין

לה עיניהא ומא רגג הוא לה אנפהא וכול נץ אנפיהא . . . . . כמא יאא לה חדיה וכמא

שפיר לה כול לבנהא דרעיהא מא שפירן וידיהא כמא כלילן וחמיד כול מחזה

ידיהא. כמא יאין כפיה ומא אריכן וקטינן כול אצבעת ידיהא. רגליהא כמא

שפירן וכמא שלמא להן לה שקיא. וכל בתולן וכלאן די יעלן לגנון לא ישפרן

מנהא. ועל כול נשין שופר שפרה ועליא שפרהא לעלא מן כולהן ועם כול

שפרא דן חכמא שגיא עמהא ודלידיהא יאא.

Vocabulary

radiance, bloom	נץ		long	אריך
splendid	נציח		virgin	בתולה
form	צלם		bridal chamber	גנון
delicate	קטין		*possessive* (cf. זיל)	דיל־
pleasant	רגג		arm	דרע
soft	רקיק		breast	חדה
beauty	שופר		attractive	חמיד
perfect	שלם		bride	כלה
beautiful	שפיר		perfect	כליל
be beautiful	שפר		hand	כף
leg	שק		whiteness	לבן
			appearance	מחזה

Use the biblical vowel system to vocalize the above text.

Translate it into English:

דן is equivalent to the biblical demonstrative דְּנָה.

Although Abraham's statement about Sarah's beauty is surprising in light of the Bible's reference to her as having been 90 at the time Isaac was conceived (Genesis 17:17, cf. 18:12) and having lived in Canaan less than 25 years (cf. Genesis 12:4 and 17:1), her beauty was often noted in post-biblical literature. For example, the rabbis say that she lit up the entire land of Egypt (*Genesis Rabbah* 40:5).

20:8–11

וכדי שמע מלכא מלי חרקנוש ומלי תרין חברוהי די פם חד תלתהון ממללין שגי

רחמה ושלח לעובע דברהא וחזהא ואתמה על כול שפרהא ונסבהא לה לאנתא

ובעא למקטלני ואמרת שרי למלכא דאחי הוא כדי הוית מתגר על דילהא.

ושביקת אנה אברם בדילהא ולא קטילת. ובכית אנה אברם בכי תקיף אנה ולוט

בר אחי עמי בליליא כדי דבירת מני שרי באונס.

Vocabulary

force	אונס
cry	בכה
lead (away)	דבר
haste	עובע
wonder (A)	תמה

Use the biblical vowel system to vocalize the above text.

Translate it into English:

Proper Nouns

חרקנוש — an Egyptian noble, not mentioned in any other traditions about this incident.

לוֹט — Abraham's nephew

NOTICE that שֹגי is spelled both with and without א.

אנתה corresponds to the Hebrew word אִשָּׁה (woman), with *t* realized as ת in Aramaic (it is שׁ in Hebrew) and the root's נ retained.

This document includes both די (the relative pronoun found throughout biblical Aramaic and at Elephantine in the form זי) and the particle ־ד, as in the synagogue inscription from Ein Gedi.

מתגר ("benefit") is apparently an *ʾitpaʿal* of either אגר or תגר, both of which can mean "earn, gain."

Chapter 31

MIDRASH

Numerous passages in rabbinic literature are written in Aramaic, although not all texts use the same dialect and the language frequently shifts back and forth into Hebrew. The passage below is from *Genesis Rabbah,* a collection of rabbinic lore which was probably compiled in Palestine during the fifth century. It is arranged as a commentary on the book of Genesis. The following selection relates to the Bible's statement that Abraham's brother Haran died עַל פְּנֵי their father Terah (Genesis 11:28). That phrase is usually translated "in the presence of"; however, the rabbis understood it to mean that Haran had died "on account of" his father, who, they taught, had been an idol maker.

Vocabulary To Be Learned

place	אתר
bring (H)	יבל
when	כיון
die	מות
deliver	מסר
human	נש

תרח עובד צלמים הוה. חד זמן נפק לאתר הושיב אברהם מוכר תחתיו. הוה אתי

בר נש בעי דיזבון. אמר ליה: בר כמה שנין את? אמר ליה: בר חמשין. אמר

ליה: ווי להההוא גברא דאת בר חמשין ותסגוד לבר יומא. והוה מתבייש והולך לו.

Vocabulary
(Words marked with an asterisk are Hebrew.)

set (H)	ישב	embarrass (Dt)	בוש *
how many	כמה	that	ההוא
sell	מכר *	woe!	ווי
instead of	תחת *	buy	זבן
		fifty	חמשין

191

Use the biblical vowel system to vocalize the passage above.

Translate it into English:

NOTICE the intermingling of Hebrew and Aramaic. Forms like צלמים, and תחת are clearly Hebrew (perhaps הושיב, too, although it also occurs in the Barrakib inscription presented in chapter 29; the form הותיב is found throughout the book of Daniel); however, בר, נפק, זמן, חד, and לאתר are Aramaic, as is the particle ־ד.

בר is often used to indicate a quality, as in the phrase בר נש (human being). With a time span, it indicates age:

בר כמה שנין	how old
בר חמשין	fifty years old
בר יומא	one day old

סגד ("bow down") also occurs in Arabic, where it provides the root for the word *masjid,* which designates a place of worship, just as מַדְבַּח designates a place of sacrifice, i.e., an altar, and מִשְׁכַּב a place of lying, i.e., a bed. The Arabic word has come into English in the form "mosque."

חד זמן אתת איתתא טעינא חד פינך דסלת. אמרת ליה: הא לך קרב קדמיהון.

קם נסיב בוקלסה ותברהון ויהב ההוא בוקלסה בידוי דרבה דבהון. כיון דאתא

אבוה אמר ליה: מה עבד להון כדין? אמר ליה: מה נכפור לך? אתת חדא איתתא

טעינא חד פינך דסלת ואמרת לי: קרב קדמיהון. דין אמר: אנא אכיל קדמאי

ודין אמר: אנא אכיל קדמאי. קם הדין רבה נסיב בוקלסה ותברהון. אמר ליה:

מה את מפלה בי ידעין אינון. אמר ליה: ולא ישמעו אזניך מפיך.

Vocabulary
(Words marked with an asterisk are Hebrew.)

how	מה **	ear	אזן **
flour	סלת	eat	אכל
mouth	פה **	club	בוקלסא
plate	פינך	this	דין
trick	פלא	that	ההוא
first	קדמאי	carry	טען
sacrifice (D)	קרב	deny	כפר **

Vocalize the passage above using biblical vowels.

Translate it into English:

NOTICE the use of י as a vowel marker (*mater lectionis*), particularly in the participles (נפיק and טעין).

איתתא (woman) is the determined form, although its sense is indefinite (see p. 25). Its root is אנת, as shown by the form אנתה in the Genesis Apocryphon (chapter 30). In the Hebrew form of this word (אִשָּׁה) the נ has assimilated to the שׁ, as it does to the ת here. In the Genesis Apocryphon either the נ had not assimilated or the double ת dissimilated (like the H infinitive הנעלה, which comes from the root עלל; see p. 119).

נסתיה ומסרתיה לנמרוד. אמר ליה: נסגוד לנורא. אמר ליה: נסגוד למייא

דמטפין לנורא. אמר ליה: ונסגוד למיא. אמר ליה: נסגוד לעננ6 דטעני מיא.

אמר ליה: ונסגוד לעננא. אמר ליה: נסגוד לרוחא דמובלי עננא. אמר ליה:

ונסגוד לרוחא. אמר ליה: נסגוד לבר נשא דסביל רוחא. אמר ליה: מלין את

משתעי. לא נסגוד אלא לאור. הריני משליכך בו ויבא אלהיך שאתה משתחוה

לו ויצילך ממנו.

Vocabulary
(Words marked with an asterisk are Hebrew.)

lift (G) . . . . נסה		flame . . . . אור	
save (H) . . . . * נצל		except . . . . אלא	
endure . . . . סבל		god . . . . * אלוהים	
cloud . . . . ענן		behold . . . . * הרי	
throw (H) . . . . שלך		extinguish (ʾafʿel) . . . . טפה	
talk (Gt) . . . . שעה		water . . . . מייא	
		prostrate self . . . . * משתחוה	

Use the biblical vowel system to vocalize the passage.

Translate it into English:

The rabbis regarded Nimrod, who is mentioned in Genesis 10:8–10, as having been a powerful but wicked ruler who tried to impose his form of idolatry on all the ancient peoples under his control.

הוה תמן הרן קאים פליג. אמר: מה נפשך? אם נצח אברם אנא אמר מן דאברם

אנא אם נצח נמרוד אמר אנא מנמרוד אנא. כיון שירד אברם לכבשן האש ונוצל

אמרין ליה מן דמן את? אמר ליה: מן דאברם. נטלוהו והשליכוהו באש ונחמרו

מעיו ויצא ומת על פני אביו. הדא הוא דכתיב וימת הרן על פני תרח אביו.

Vocabulary
(Words marked with an asterisk are Hebrew.)

belly	מעין	parch	חמר
will	* נפש	go out	* יצא
win	* נצח	descend	* ירד
be saved (N)	* נוצל	furnace	* כבשן
divided	פליג	on the side of	מן דְ־

Use the biblical vowel system to vocalize the passage above.

Translate it into English:

הדא הוא דכתיב (this is what is written)—introduces a biblical quotation, in this case the passage from Genesis (11:28) that the preceding story is intended to explain.

NOTICE the interweaving of Hebrew and Aramaic in this selection. The verbs נוצל and נחמרו are *nifꜤal,* a conjugation which does not occur in biblical Aramaic. The following phrases are pure Hebrew:

הושיב אברהם מוכר תחתיו

ולא ישמעו אזניך מפיך

הריני משליכך בו ויבוא אלהיך שאתה משתחוה לו ויצילך ממנו

ויצא ומת על פני אביו

Chapter 32

Targum

With the spread of Aramaic among Jews after the Babylonian exile, the Hebrew Bible became increasingly inaccessible. It was, therefore, translated into Aramaic. Reciting such a translation was even required as part of liturgical Scripture reading (*Mishna Megillah* 4:4, cf. *Babylonian Talmud Berakhot* 8a). Several different translation traditions developed, some of which were eventually written down in what have come to be known as targumim (the root first occurs in Ezra 4:7, where it introduces the Aramaic section of that book). The most important of these are a translation of the Pentateuch attributed to Onkelos and one of the Prophets attributed to Jonathan. (These names may be related to Aquila and Theodotion, who were considered the authors of ancient Greek translations of the Bible; the latter means "God gives" in Greek, just as Jonathan does in Hebrew, while Aquila and Onkelos are phonetically close.) Although these versions tend to follow the original Hebrew rather closely, other Aramaic translations expand on the biblical text. Among these is a targum to the Pentateuch which appears to have reached its present form in Palestine sometime after the seventh century and has traditionally come to be ascribed to Jonathan (hence scholars' reference to it as Pseudo-Jonathan). Its rendering of the biblical text is considerably more expansive than that of Onkelos, as demonstrated by its translation of Genesis 22 (the binding of Isaac):

Vocabulary To Be Learned

inherit	ירת	after	בתר *
height	מרום	behold, how	האנא
slaughter	נכס	lift	זקף
on	עילוי	instead of	חולף
place	שוה	young servant	טליה

---

*From באתר; see p. 62 and Daniel 2:29 (p. 80) and 7:6–7 (pp. 152–54).

197

(1) והוה בתר פיתגמיא האילין מן דינצו יצחק וישמעאל. ישמעאל הוה אמר:
לי חמי למירות ית אבא דאנא בריה בוכרייא. ויצחק הוה אמר: לי חמי למירות
ית אבא דאנא בר שרה אינתתיה ואנת בר הגר אמתא דאימי. עני ישמעאל ואמר:
אנא זכאי יתיר מינך דאנא איתגזרית לתלסירי שנין ואין הוה צבותי למעכבא
לא הוינא מסר נפשי לאתגזרא. ואנת אתגזרת בר תמניא יומין אילו הוה בך מנדעא
דילמא לא הוית מסר נפשך לאתגזרא. מתיב יצחק ואמר: האנא יומנא בר תלתין
ושב שנין ואילו בעי קודשא בריך הוא לכולי איבריי לא הוותי מעכב. מן יד
אישתמעו פיתגמיא האילין קדם מרי עלמא ומן יד מימרא דייי נסי ית אברהם
ואמר ליה: אברהם.

Vocabulary

organ	איבר	immediately	מן יד
if	אילו	understanding	מנדע
if	אין	test (D)	נסי
mother	אם	quarrel	נצה
handmaid	אמתא	refuse	עכב
senior	בוכריא	wish	צבו
perhaps	דילמא	the Holy One	קודשא
worthy	זכאי	seven	(ע)שבב
today	יומנא	thirteen	תלסירי
word	מימרא	thirty	תלתין
after	מן די	eight	תמניא

Use the biblical vowel system to vocalize the passage above.

Translate it into English:

ייי is the way God's name is presented in this manuscript.

NOTE: (a) the use of י as a vowel letter (*mater lectionis*) in:

              nouns – אינת ,אימי ,מימרי, פיתגם

              Gt verbs – איתגזר ,אישתמע

              final ה verbs – עני

     (b) that the passive participle of חמי ("see") means "fitting," as does the passive form of the Hebrew verb ראה (ראוי)

     (c) the Hebrew definite article on the demonstrative element in the phrase פיתגמיא האילין

     (d) characteristically Aramaic features such as the direct object marker ית and the particle ד־.

ואמר ליה: האנא. (2) ואמר: דבר כדון ית ברך ית יחידך דאת רחים
ית יצחק ואיזל לך לארע פולחנא ואסיקהי תמן לעלתא על חד מן טווריא
דאימר לך. (3) ואקדים אברהם בצפרא וזריז ית חמריה ודבר ית תרין טלייוי
ית אליעזר וית ישמעאל עימיה וית יצחק בריה וקטע קיסין דזיתא ותאנתא ודיקלא
דחזיין לעלתא וקם ואזל לאתרא דאמר ליה ייי. (4) ביומא תליתאה וזקף
אברהם ית עינוי וחמא ענן איקרא קטיר על טוורא ואשתמודעיה מן רחיק
(5) ואמר אברהם לעולימוי: אוריכן לכון הכא עם חמרא ואנא ועולימא נתמטי
עד כא לבחוני אין יתקיים מה דאתבשרית כדין יהון בנך ונסגוד למרי עלמא ונתוב
לוותכון. (6) ונסיב אברהם ית קיסי דעלתא ושוי עילוי יצחק בריה ונסיב בידיה
ית אישתא וית סכינא ואזלו תרוויהום כחדא. (7) ואמר יצחק לאברהם אבוי
ואמר: אבא. ואמר: האנא. ואמר: הא אישתא וקיסין והאן אימרא לעלתא?
(8) ואמר אברהם: ייי יבחר ליה אימרא לעלתא ברי: ואזלו תרויהום בלב שלים
כחדא.

Vocabulary

here	כא	wait (ʾafˁel) ארך	אוריך
now	כדון	lamb	אימר
here	כה	if	אין
knife	סכין	glory	איקרא
youth	עולימו	(יקר with prosthetic א)	
cloud	ענן	recognize	אשתמודע
worship	פולחן	examine	בחן
morning	צפרא	choose	בחר
do early (H, ʾafˁel)	קדם.	announce (Gt)	בשׂר
Dt (התקיים) be fulfilled	קום	seize, take	דבר
cut	קטע	palm	דיקלא
rise in circle	קטר	behold	הא
twig	קיסא	here	הכא
perfect	שלים	olive	זית
fig	תאנה	saddle	זרז
		only	יחיד

Use the biblical vowel system to vocalize the passage above.

Translate it into English:

כדין יהון בנך is the targum's rendering of the biblical phrase כֹּה יִהְיֶה זַרְעֶךָ in Genesis 15:5, where God promises Abraham that his descendants will be as numerous as the stars.

The spelling עים and אישתא further demonstrate the generous use of vowel letters in this text.

אסיק is an *ʾafᶜel* form of the root סלק (cf. הַסִּקוּ in Daniel 3:23; see p. 119); note also אתבשׂר, which is *ʾitpeᶜel* (the form is 3d person masculine singular perfect), and אשתמודעין, which is a verb based on the noun מודע (in the "*ʾishtafᶜal*"). נתמטי is *nitpaᶜel,* a mixture of *hitpaᶜel* and *nifᶜal.*

חזי (fitting) is a passive participle of חזה (see), providing yet again an example of a verb which means "to see" being used for "fitting" in the passive (others are Aramaic חמי and Hebrew ראוי).

(9) ואתו לאתרא דאמר ליה ייי ובנא תמן אברהם ית מדבחא דבנא אדם ואיתפכר במוי דטובענא ותב נח ובנייה ואיתפכר בדרא דפלוגתא. וסדר עילוי ית קיסיא וכפת ית יצחק בריה ושוי יתיה על מדבחא לעיל מן קיסין. (10) ופשט אברהם ית ידיה ונסיבת סכינא למיכס ית בריה. עני ואמר יצחק לאבוי: כפת יתי יאות דלא נפרכס מן צערא דנפשי ונדחי לגובא דחבלא וישתכח פסולא בקרבנך. עינווי דאברהם מסתכלן בעינויי דיצחק ועיינויי דיצחק מסתכלן למלאכי מרומא. יצחק הוה חמי יתהום ואברהם לא חמי יתהום. עניין מלאכי מרומא: איתון חמון תרין יחידאין דאית בעלמא חד נכיס וחד מתנכיס. דנכיס לא מעכב ודמתנכיס פשיט צווריה. (11) וקרא ליה מלאכא דייי מן שמיא ואמר ליה: אברהם אברהם. ואמר: האנא . (12) ואמר: אל תושיט ידך לטלייא ולא תעביד ליה מידעם ביש. ארום כדון גלי קדמי ארום דחלא דייי אנת ולא עכיבתא ית ברך ית יחידך מיני. (13) וזקף אברהם ית עינוי וחזא והא דיכרא חד דאיתברי ביני שימשתא דשכלול עלמא אחיד בחרישותא דאילנא בקרנוי. ואזל אברהם ונסיב יתיה ואסיקהי לעלתא חולף בריה.

Vocabulary

arrange	סדר	catch	אחד
knife	סכין	*plural participle of* אתה	איתון
look (Dt)	סכל	behold	ארום
above	עיל	create	ברי
refuse	עכב	thrust	דחה
destroy	פכר	ram	דיכרא
division	פלוגתא	destruction	חבלה
blemish	פסולא	thicket	חרישותא
struggle	פרכס	flood	טובען
extend	פשט	well	יאות
neck	צוור	only	יחיד
pain	צער	stretch forth (H)	ישט
wood	קיסא	now	כדון
offering	קרבן	slaughter	כסס
place	שׁוה	water	מוי
sun	שמש	anything	מידעם
twilight	ביני שימשתא	(*see* מנדעם *on p. 178*)	
completion	שכלול	banish	נדח

Use the biblical vowel system to vocalize the passage above.

Translate it into English:

בנא must be understood as "rebuild" in this context.

פלוגתא (division) is a traditional term for the dispersion which took place after the confrontation with God involving the Tower of Babel.

נפרכס — this dialect of Aramaic uses -נ for the imperfect first person singular prefix.

עינוי דאברהם is a redundant construction, which literally means "his eye of Abraham," i.e., "Abraham's eye" (see p. 85).

איתברי — this Gt form is based on the root ברי (create), which corresponds to the Hebrew root ברא; note the convergence of final א and final ה verbs in Aramaic.

ביני שימשתא — "twilight"; according to rabbinic tradition, God created several important things just before sunset during the week of creation (e.g., *Mishna Avot* 5:6).

(14) ואודי וצלי אברהם תמן באתרא ההוא ואמר: בבעו ברחמין מן קדמך ייי גלי קדמך דלא הוה בלבבי עוקמא ובעית למיעבד גזירתך בחדווא. כדין כד יהון בנוי דיצחק ברי עליין לשעת אניקי תהוי מידכר להום ועני יתהום ופריק יתהום. ועתידין הינון כל דריא דקימון למהוי אמרין: בטוורא הדין כפת אברהם ית יצחק

ברייה ותמן איתגליית עילוי שכינתא דייי. (15) וקרא מלאכא דייי לאברהם
תניינות מן שמיא (16) ואמר: במימרי קיימית אמר ייי חולף דעבדת ית פיתגמא
הדין ולא מנעת ית ברך ית יחידך (17) ארום ברכא אברכינך ואסגא אסגי ית בנך
ככוכבי שמיא והי כחלא דעל כיף ימא. ויירתון בנך ית קורי שנאיהון. (18)
ויתברכון בגין זכוות בנך כל עממי ארעא חולף דקבילתא במימרי. (19) ודברו
מלאכי מרומא ית יצחק ואובלוהי לבי מדרשא דשם רבא והוה תמן תלת שנין.
ובההוא יומא תב אברהם לות עולימוי וקמו ואזלו כחדא לבירא דשבע. ויתיב
אברהם בבירא דשבע. (20) והוה בתר פתגמיא האילין מן בתר דיכפת אברהם
ית יצחק ואזל סטנא ותני לות שרה דאברהם נכס ית יצחק. וקמת שרה ופגנת
ואשתנקת ומיתת מן אניקא.

Vocabulary

word	מימרא		anguish	אניקה
angel	מלאך		behold	ארום
withhold	מנע		on account of	בגין
multiply (H)	סגי		son	* בן
Satan	סטנה		school house	בי מדרש
youth	עולימו		petition	בעו
trickery	עוקמא		blessing	ברכה
cry out	פגן		decree	גזירה
save	פרק		innocence	זכו
city	קורא		joy	חדווא
swear	קיים		sand	חל
hate	שנא		praise (H/ʾafʿel)	ידה
Divine Presence	שכינתא		sea	ים
choke (Gt)	שנק		dwell	יתב
tell	תני		now	כדון
second	תניינות		star	כוכב
			shore	כיף

Use the biblical vowel system to vocalize the passage above.

Translate it into English:

סֹנִי — This word is consistently spelled שַׂגִּיא in the Bible, but סֹנִי at Ein Gedi (p. 173). The letter שׁ came to be written ס in post-biblical Aramaic. Two examples of this which can be found already in the Bible are the spelling of the name אַרְתַּחְשַׁסְתְּא in Ezra 7:21 and of כַּסְדָּי in Ezra 5:12 (see p. 38).

שכינה — is a hypostasis of God's presence, as is God's מימרא (cf. the end of verse 1; the term is used more literally in verse 18).

בי — from בית

בירא דשבע — "the well of seven," a literal translation of the name Beer-sheba in accordance with the explanation of it given in Genesis 21:25–31.

AFTERWORD

The biblical readings in this book have covered the substance of the entire Aramaic corpus in the Hebrew Bible; however, these passages have been abridged and simplified to fit the levels appropriate to the individual chapters in which they are found. Now that you are familiar with the language's grammar, you can read all of these texts in the original. The vocabulary is readily available in most standard biblical dictionaries, including:

> *A Hebrew and English Lexicon of the Old Testament* by Francis Brown, S. R. Driver, and Charles A. Briggs (Oxford: Clarendon Press, 1907).

> *Lexicon in Veteris Testamenti Libros* by Ludwig Koehler and Walter Baumgartner (Leiden: E. J. Brill, 1958).

> *Hebräisches und Aramäisches Lexikon zum alten Testament,* Aramaic section ed. Johann Jakob Stamm and Benedikt Hartmann (Leiden: E. J. Brill, 1995), translated into English under the supervision of M. E. J. Richardson as *The Hebrew and Aramaic Lexicon of the Old Testament* (vol. 5, 2000).

In addition, Ernestus Vogt's *Lexicon linguae aramaicae veteris testamenti documentis antiquis illustratum* (Rome: Pontifical Biblical Institute, 1971) is devoted solely to biblical Aramaic. The standard biblical concordances (by S. Mandelkern, G. Lisowsky, and A. Even-Shoshan) also include Aramaic sections.

There are several valuable commentaries on the biblical books which contain passages in Aramaic. The most useful ones on Ezra are by Loring Batten (International Critical Commentary), Jacob Myers (Anchor Bible), and H. G. M. Williamson (Word Biblical Commentary). For Daniel, see those by James Montgomery (International Critical Commentary), John Collins (Hermeneia), and Louis Hartman and Alexander Di Lella (Anchor Bible).

The following tools will prove helpful for grammatical questions that may arise as you read selections from the Bible or investigate specific problems:

> Franz Rosenthal, *A Grammar of Biblical Aramaic* (Wiesbaden: Otto Harrassowitz, 1963).

Hans Bauer and Pontus Leander, *Grammatik des Biblisch-Aramäischen* (Halle/Saale: Max Niemayer Verlag, 1927).

Several other bodies of literature are written in Aramaic. The best sources for ancient Aramaic inscriptions are:

Herbert Donner and Wolfgang Röllig, *Kanaanäische und Aramäische Inschriften* (Wiesbaden: Otto Harrassowitz, 1971–76).

John C. L. Gibson, *Textbook of Syrian Semitic Inscriptions,* vol. 2, "Aramaic Inscriptions" (Oxford: Clarendon Press, 1975).

Joseph A. Fitzmyer and Daniel J. Harrington, *A Manual of Palestinian Aramaic Texts* (Rome: Biblical Institute Press, 1978).

Arthur E. Cowley, *Aramaic Papyri of the Fifth Century B.C.* (Oxford: Clarendon Press, 1923).

Emil G. Kraeling, *The Brooklyn Museum Aramaic Papyri* (New Haven: Yale University Press, 1953).

G. R. Driver, *Aramaic Documents of the Fifth Century B.C.* (Oxford: Clarendon Press, rev. ed., 1965).

Bezalel Porten and Ada Yardeni, *Textbook of Aramaic Documents from Ancient Egypt* (Jerusalem: Hebrew University, 1986–99).

In addition to the glossaries in these works, the following dictionaries may prove helpful:

Charles-F. Jean and Jacob Hoftijzer, *Dictionnaire des inscriptions sémitiques de l'ouest* (Leiden: E. J. Brill, 1965).

Jacob Hoftijzer and Karel Jongeling, *Dictionary of the North-West Semitic Inscriptions* (Leiden: E. J. Brill, 1995).

Several of the Dead Sea Scrolls are in Aramaic. Many of these texts are collected in:

Florentino García Martínez and Eilbert J. C. Tigchelaar, *The Dead Sea Scrolls Study Edition* (Leiden: E. J. Brill, 1997).

B. Jongeling, C. J. Labuschagne, and A. S. van der Woude, *Aramaic Texts from Qumran* (Leiden: E. J. Brill, 1976–).

Klaus Beyer, *Die Aramäischen Texte vom Toten Meer* (Göttingen: Vandenhoeck & Ruprecht, 1994-2004).

The diversity of rabbinic literature, much of which is written in a mixture of Aramaic and Hebrew, and the targumim makes it impossible to provide a definitive list of the material available. Most of the targumim are published in:

Alexander Sperber, *The Bible in Aramaic* (Leiden: E. J. Brill, 1959–73).

E. G. Clarke, *Targum Pseudo-Jonathan of the Pentateuch* (Hoboken, NJ: Ktav Publishing House, 1984).

Michael L. Klein, *The Fragment-Targums of the Pentateuch According to their Extant Sources* (Rome: Biblical Institute Press, 1980).

Alejandro Díez Macho, *Neophyti I* (Madrid: Consejo Superior de Investigaciones Científicas, 1968).

The best available tools for working with this material are:

Marcus Jastrow, *A Dictionary of the Targumim, the Talmud Babli and Jerusalmi, and the Midrashic Literature* (New York: G. P. Putnam's Sons, 1903; reprinted often).

Michael Sokoloff, *A Dictionary of Jewish Palestinian Aramaic of the Byzantine Period* (2nd ed.; Ramat Gan: Bar-Ilan University Press; Baltimore: Johns Hopkins University Press, 2002).

Michael Sokoloff, *A Dictionary of Jewish Babylonian Aramaic of the Talmudic and Geonic Periods* (Baltimore, London: Johns Hopkins University Press, 2002).

Michael Sokoloff, *A Dictionary of Judean Palestinian Aramaic* (Ramat Gan: Bar-Ilan University Press, 2003).

The Syrian church and its adherents also produced a vast literature in the Syriac dialect. The best available dictionaries for this dialect are:

C. Brockelmann, *Lexicon Syriacum* (Hallis: Saxonum, 1928).

R. Payne Smith, *Thesaurus Syriacus* (Oxford: Clarendon Press, 1879; supplement by J. P. Margoliouth, 1927).

Reference tools for other dialects of Aramaic include:

Takamitsu Muraoka and Bezalel Porten, *A Grammar of Egyptian Aramaic* (2nd ed.; Leiden: E. J. Brill, 2003).

Friedrich Schulthess, *Lexicon Syropalaestinum* (Berlin: Georg Reimer, 1903).

Ethel Drower and R. Macuch, *A Mandaic Dictionary* (Oxford: Clarendon Press, 1963).

J. A. MacLean, *A Dictionary of the Dialects of Vernacular Syriac* (Oxford: Clarendon Press, 1901).

Gotthelf Bergsträsser, *Glossar des neuaramäischen Dialekts von Maʿlūla* (1921).

Helmut Ritter, *Tūrōyo: Die Volkssprache der syrischen Christen des Tūr ʾAbdîn* (Beirut: Orient-Institut der Deutschen Morgenländischen Gesellschaft, 1976).

Rudolf Macuch, *Grammatik des samaritanischen Aramäisch* (Berlin: De Gruyter, 1982).

In recent years, scholars have begun to compile a Comprehensive Aramaic Lexicon, which will embrace the entire language. As work proceeds on this project, a variety of tools and reference works are being generated; already available is the first part of *An Aramaic Bibliography* by Joseph A. Fitzmyer, S.J., and Stephen A. Kaufman (Baltimore: The Johns Hopkins University Press, 1992). Other tools can be found on the Lexicon's Web site at http://cal1.cn.huc.edu. You may also wish to read some general descriptions of the Aramaic languages. Broad surveys of this type include:

Eduard Yechezkel Kutscher, "Aramaic" in *Current Trends in Linguistics,* ed. Thomas A. Seboek (The Hague: Mouton, 1970), vol. 6, pp. 347–412.

Eduard Yechezkel Kutscher, "Aramaic," *Encyclopedia Judaica* (Jerusalem: Keter Publishing, 1972), vol. 3, pp. 259–87.

Joseph A. Fitzmyer, S.J., "The Phases of the Aramaic Language" in *A Wandering Aramean: Collected Aramaic Essays* (Chico, CA: Scholars Press, 1979) pp. 57–84.

Klaus Beyer, *The Aramaic Language* (Göttingen: Vandenhoeck & Ruprecht, 1986).

Stephen A. Kaufman, "Languages (Aramaic)" in *The Anchor Bible Dictionary* (New York: Doubleday, 1992), vol. 4, pp. 173–78.

With these tools and the grammar you have already learned, you can begin to explore any part of the huge corpus of Aramaic literature. Good luck!

PARADIGMS

Nouns and Adjectives

		Masculine	Feminine
Singular	Absolute	מֶלֶךְ	מַלְכָּה
	Construct	מֶלֶךְ	מַלְכַּת
	Determined	מַלְכָּא	מַלְכְּתָא
Plural	Absolute	מַלְכִין	מַלְכָן
	Construct	מַלְכֵי	מַלְכָת
	Determined	מַלְכַיָּא	מַלְכָתָא

Pronouns

Independent Pronouns	Possessive Suffixes			
	Singular Nouns		Plural Nouns	
Singular	Masculine	Feminine	Masculine	Feminine
אֲנָה	פִּשְׁרִי	מַלְכוּתִי	פִּשְׁרִי	מַלְכְוָתִי
אַנְתְּ (or אַנְתָּה)	פִּשְׁרָךְ	מַלְכוּתָךְ	פִּשְׁרָיךְ	מַלְכְוָתָךְ
אַנְתִּי	פִּשְׁרֵכִי	מַלְכוּתֵכִי	פִּשְׁרֵיכִי	מַלְכְוָתֵכִי
הוּא	פִּשְׁרֵהּ	מַלְכוּתֵהּ	פִּשְׁרוֹהִי	מַלְכְוָתֵהּ
הִיא	פִּשְׁרֵהּ	מַלְכוּתַהּ	פִּשְׁרַיהּ	מַלְכְוָתַהּ
Plural				
אֲנַחְנָה	פִּשְׁרַנָא	מַלְכוּתַנָא	פִּשְׁרַינָא	מַלְכְוָתַנָא
אַנְתּוּן (אַנְתֹּם)	פִּשְׁרְכֹם	מַלְכוּתְכֹם	פִּשְׁרֵיכֹם	מַלְכְוָתְכֹם
אַנְתֵּן	פִּשְׁרְכֵן	מַלְכוּתְכֵן	פִּשְׁרֵיכֵן	מַלְכְוָתְכֵן
הִמּוֹ (אִנּוּן or הִמּוֹן)	פִּשְׁרְהֹם	מַלְכוּתְהֹם	פִּשְׁרֵיהֹם	מַלְכְוָתְהֹם
אִנִּין	פִּשְׁרְהֵן	מַלְכוּתְהֵן	פִּשְׁרֵיהֵן	מַלְכְוָתְהֵן

Demonstratives

		Singular	Plural
Near (this, these)	*Masculine*	דְּנָה }	אֵלֶּה *also*) אֵלֶּין אֵל *and* אֵלֶּין
	Feminine	דָּא }	
Far (that, those)	*Masculine*	דֵּךְ }	אִלֵּךְ
	Feminine	דָּךְ }	
Masculine and Feminine		דִּכֵּן	

Numerals

	CARDINAL		ORDINAL
	Masculine	*Feminine*	
1	חַד	חֲדָה	קַדְמָי
2	תְּרֵין (תְּרֵי)	תַּרְתֵּין (תַּרְתֵּי)	תִּנְיָן
3	תְּלָתָה	תְּלָת	תְּלִיתָי
4	אַרְבְּעָה	אַרְבַּע	רְבִיעָי
5	חַמְשָׁא	חֲמֵשׁ	
6	שִׁתָּה	שֵׁת	
7	שִׁבְעָה	שְׁבַע	
8	תְּמָנְיָה	תְּמָנֶה	
9	תִּשְׁעָה	תְּשַׁע	
10	עֲשַׂרְה	עֲשַׂר	
20	עֶשְׂרִין		
30	תְּלָתִין		
100	מְאָה		
200	מָאתַיִן		
1,000	אֲלַף		
10,000	רִבּוֹ		

Verbs

	G	D	H
PERFECT			
Singular			
1	כִּתְבֵת	קַבְּלֵת	הַשְׁלְטֵת
2 masculine	כְּתַבְתְּ (or כְּתַבְתָּ)	קַבֵּלְתְּ	הַשְׁלֵטְתְּ
feminine	כְּתַבְתִּי	קַבֵּלְתִּי	הַשְׁלֵטְתִּי
3 masculine	כְּתַב	קַבֵּל	הַשְׁלֵט
feminine	כִּתְבַת	קַבְּלַת	הַשְׁלְטַת
Plural			
1	כְּתַבְנָא	קַבֵּלְנָא	הַשְׁלֵטְנָא
2 masculine	כְּתַבְתּוּן	קַבֵּלְתּוּן	הַשְׁלֵטְתּוּן
feminine	כְּתַבְתֵּן	קַבֵּלְתֵּן	הַשְׁלֵטְתֵּן
3 masculine	כְּתַבוּ	קַבִּלוּ	הַשְׁלִטוּ
feminine	כְּתַבָה	קַבִּלָה	הַשְׁלִטָה
IMPERFECT			
Singular			
1	אֶכְתֻּב	אֲקַבֵּל	אֲהַשְׁלֵט
2 masculine	תִּכְתֻּב	תְּקַבֵּל	תְּהַשְׁלֵט
feminine	תִּכְתְּבִין	תְּקַבְּלִין	תְּהַשְׁלְטִין
3 masculine	יִכְתֻּב	יְקַבֵּל	יְהַשְׁלֵט
feminine	תִּכְתֻּב	תְּקַבֵּל	תְּהַשְׁלֵט
Plural			
1	נִכְתֻּב	נְקַבֵּל	נְהַשְׁלֵט
2 masculine	תִּכְתְּבוּן	תְּקַבְּלוּן	תְּהַשְׁלְטוּן
feminine	תִּכְתְּבָן	תְּקַבְּלָן	תְּהַשְׁלְטָן
3 masculine	יִכְתְּבוּן	יְקַבְּלוּן	יְהַשְׁלְטוּן
feminine	יִכְתְּבָן	יְקַבְּלָן	יְהַשְׁלְטָן

	G	D	H
PARTICIPLE			
Singular			
masculine	כָּתֵב	מְקַבֵּל	מְהַשְׁלֵט
feminine	כָּתְבָה	מְקַבְּלָה	מְהַשְׁלְטָה
Plural			
masculine	כָּתְבִין	מְקַבְּלִין	מְהַשְׁלְטִין
feminine	כָּתְבָן	מְקַבְּלָן	מְהַשְׁלְטָן
IMPERATIVE			
Singular			
masculine	כְּתֻב	קַבֵּל	הַשְׁלֵט
feminine	כְּתֻבִי	קַבְּלִי	הַשְׁלִטִי
Plural			
masculine	כְּתֻבוּ	קַבִּלוּ	הַשְׁלִטוּ
feminine	כְּתֻבָה	קַבִּלָה	הַשְׁלִטָה
INFINITIVE	מִכְתַּב	קַבָּלָה	הַשְׁלָטָה

Passives

	G	D	H
PERFECT			
Singular			
1	כְּתִיבֵת	קַבְּלֵת	הֻשְׁלְטֵת
2 masculine	כְּתִיבְתָּ	קַבַּלְתָּ	הֻשְׁלַטְתָּ
feminine	כְּתִיבְתִּי	קַבֵּלְתִּי	הֻשְׁלַטְתִּי
3 masculine	כְּתִיב	קַבַּל	הֻשְׁלַט
feminine	כְּתִיבַת	קַבְּלַת	הֻשְׁלְטַת
Plural			
1	כְּתִיבְנָא	קַבֵּלְנָא	הֻשְׁלַטְנָא
2 masculine	כְּתִיבְתּוּן	קַבֵּלְתּוּן	הֻשְׁלַטְתּוּן
feminine	כְּתִיבְתֵּן	קַבֵּלְתֵּן	הֻשְׁלַטְתֵּן
3 masculine	כְּתִיבוּ	קַבְּלוּ	הֻשְׁלַטוּ
feminine	כְּתִיבָה	קַבְּלָה	הֻשְׁלַטָה
PARTICIPLE			
Singular			
masculine	כְּתִיב	מְקַבַּל	מְהֻשְׁלַט
feminine	כְּתִיבָה	מְקַבְּלָה	מְהֻשְׁלַטָה
Plural			
masculine	כְּתִיבִין	מְקַבְּלִין	מְהֻשְׁלַטִין
feminine	כְּתִיבָן	מְקַבְּלָן	מְהֻשְׁלַטָן

Prefix-t Conjugations

	Gt	Dt
PERFECT		
Singular		
1	הִתְקְטֵלֵת	הִתְחַבְּלֵת
2 masculine	הִתְקְטֵלְתְּ	הִתְחַבַּלְתְּ
feminine	הִתְקְטֵלְתִּי	הִתְחַבַּלְתִּי
3 masculine	הִתְקְטֵל	הִתְחַבַּל
feminine	הִתְקַטְלַת	הִתְחַבְּלַת
Plural		
1	הִתְקְטֵלְנָא	הִתְחַבַּלְנָא
2 masculine	הִתְקְטֵלְתּוּן	הִתְחַבַּלְתּוּן
feminine	הִתְקְטֵלְתֵּן	הִתְחַבַּלְתֵּן
3 masculine	הִתְקְטִלוּ	הִתְחַבַּלוּ
feminine	הִתְקְטִלָה	הִתְחַבַּלָה
IMPERFECT		
Singular		
1	אֶתְקְטֵל	אֶתְחַבַּל
2 masculine	תִּתְקְטֵל	תִּתְחַבַּל
feminine	תִּתְקַטְלִין	תִּתְחַבְּלִין
3 masculine	יִתְקְטֵל	יִתְחַבַּל
feminine	תִּתְקְטֵל	תִּתְחַבַּל
Plural		
1	נִתְקְטֵל	נִתְחַבַּל
2 masculine	תִּתְקַטְלוּן	תִּתְחַבְּלוּן
feminine	תִּתְקַטְלָן	תִּתְחַבְּלָן
3 masculine	יִתְקַטְלוּן	יִתְחַבְּלוּן
feminine	יִתְקַטְלָן	יִתְחַבְּלָן

	Gt	Dt
PARTICIPLES		
Singular		
masculine	מִתְקְטֵל	מִתְחַבַּל
feminine	מִתְקַטְלָה	מִתְחַבְּלָה
Plural		
masculine	מִתְקַטְלִין	מִתְחַבְּלִין
feminine	מִתְקַטְלָן	מִתְחַבְּלָן
INFINITIVE	הִתְקַטָלָה	הִתְחַבָּלָה

Irregular Verbs

Hollow Roots

	Perfect	Imperfect		Participles Active	Passive	Imperative
Singular						
1	שָׂמֶת	אֲשִׂים	ms	שָׂאֵם	שִׂים	שִׂים
2 masculine	שָׂמְתָ	תְּשִׂים	fs	שִׂימָה	שִׂימָה	שִׂימִי
feminine	שָׂמְתִּי	תְּשִׂימִין	mp	שָׂימִין	שִׂימִין	שִׂימוּ
3 masculine	שָׂם	יְשִׂים	fp	שָׂימָן	שִׂימָן	שִׂימָה
feminine	שָׂמַת	תְּשִׂים				
Plural						
1	שָׂמְנָא	נְשִׂים				
2 masculine	שָׂמְתּוּן	תְּשִׂימוּן				
feminine	שָׂמְתֵּן	תְּשִׂימָן		*Infinitive*	מְשָׂם	
3 masculine	שָׂמוּ	יְשִׂימוּן				
feminine	שָׂמָה	יְשִׂימָן				

Final-ה
G

	Perfect	Imperfect		Participles Active	Passive
Singular					
1	בְּנֵית	אֶבְנֵא	ms	בָּנֵה	בְּנֵה
2 masculine	בְּנַיְתָ	תִּבְנֵא	fs	בָּנְיָה	בַּנְיָה
feminine	בְּנַיְתִי	תִּבְנַיִן	mp	בָּנַיִן	בְּנַיִן
3 masculine	בְּנָה	יִבְנֵא	fp	בָּנְיָן	בַּנְיָן
feminine	בְּנָת	תִּבְנֵא			

	Perfect	Imperfect		Imperative		Passive Perfect
Plural						
1	בְּנֵינָא	נִבְנֵא				
2 masculine	בְּנֵיתוּן	תִּבְנוֹן	ms	בְּנִי/בְּנֵא	3 ms	בְּנִי
feminine	בְּנֵיתֵן	תִּבְנְיָן	mp	בְּנוֹ	3 mp	בְּנִיו
3 masculine	בְּנוֹ	יִבְנוֹן				
feminine	בְּנָה	יִבְנְיָן	*Infinitive*	מִבְנֵא		

Final-ה

	היה	D	H
PERFECT			
Singular			
1	הֲוֵית	——	——
2 masculine	הֲוֵיתָ	מַנִּיתָ	——
3 masculine	הֲוָה	מַנִּי	הַגְלִי
3 feminine	הֲוָת	——	——
Plural			
3 masculine	הֲווֹ	מַנִּיו	הַגְלִיו
IMPERFECT			
Singular			
1	——	אֲמַנֵּה	——
2 masculine	תֶּהֱוֵה	תְּמַנֵּה	——
3 masculine	לֶהֱוֵא	יְמַנֵּה	יְהַגְלִי
Plural			
1	——	נְמַנֵּה	נְהַגְלִי
2 masculine	——	——	תְּהַגְלוֹן
3 masculine	לֶהֱוֹן	יְמַנּוֹן	יְהַגְלוֹן
3 feminine	לֶהֱוְיָן	——	——
PARTICIPLE (active)			
masculine singular	——	מְמַנֵּא	——
feminine singular	——	מְמַנְיָה	——
IMPERATIVE			
masculine singular	——	מַנִּי	——
plural	הֱווֹ	——	הַגְלוֹ
INFINITIVE	——	——	הַגְלָיָה

NOTE that 3d person forms of היה begin with ל in the imperfect.

GLOSSARY

Numbers in parentheses are the chapters in which these words are first assigned to be learned. Hebrew words which appear in the texts presented in this book are also listed here (marked with an asterisk).

א

אַב	father (14; *plural* אֲבָהָת)
אבד	perish, be lost
	H—destroy, kill (14)
אבה	desire (Htn)
אֶבֶן	stone (15)
אגורא	temple
אִגְּרָה	letter (3)
אֱדַיִן	then (5)
אונס	force
אור	flame
אזה	heat (18)
אזל	go (7)
אֹזֶן *	ear
אַח	brother (28)
אחד	grasp
אֲחַז *	grasp
אַחֲרֵי	after (12)
אָחֳרִי	another (16)
אָחֲרֵין	last
אָחֳרָן	another (13)
אֲחַשְׁדַּרְפַּן	satrap (25)
איבר	organ
אִילוּ	if
אִילָן	tree (20)
אימר	lamb
אֵימְתָן	frightful

אִין	if
אִיקְרָא	glory
אִיתַי	there is (9)
אִיתְתָא	woman (*see* אנתה)
אכל	eat
אֶלָא	except
אֵלֶה	these (14)
אֱלָה	god (3)
אֲלוּ	behold (20)
אלוהים *	god
אִלֵּין	these (14)
אִלֵּך	those (7)
אֲלַף	thousand
אֵם	mother
אֻמָּה	nation
אמן	be faithful (H) (24)
	passive participle—מְהֵימַן
אמן	amen
אמר	say (6)
אַמְתָא	handmaid
אֲנָה	I (10)
אֲנוּן	they (11)
אֱנוֹשׁ	human
אֲנַחְנָה	we (4)
אִנִּין	they, those (*f*) (11)
אניקה	anguish
אנס	trouble (G)

220

אֲנַף	face, nose (30)
אֱנָשׁ	man (10)
אַנְתְּ (אַנְתָּה)	you (*m s*) (11)
אנתה	wife (30)
אַנְתִּי	you (*f s*) (11)
אַנְתּוּן (אַנְתֹּם)	you (*m p*) (11)
אַנְתֵּן	you (*f p*) (11)
אָסְפַּרְנָא	exactly, diligently (11)
אֱסָר	prohibition (26)
אָע	wood
אַף	nose, anger
אַף	also
אֶצְבַּע	finger (23)
אַרְבַּע	four (17)
אַרְגְּוָן	purple
אֲרוּ	behold
ארום	behold
ארז	cedar
אַרְיֵה	lion (25)
אריך	long
ארך	wait (ʾafʿel—אוֹרִיךְ)
אַרְכָה	duration
ארמלה	widow
אֲרַע	earth (8)
אַרְעִית	bottom
אַרְקָא	earth
אֶשָּׁ(א)	fire (29)
אֻשִּׁין	foundations
אשרן	beams
אשתמודע	recognize
אָת	sign
אתה	come (G) (6); (H/A—bring, 18)
אַתּוּן	furnace (17)
אֲתַר	place (31)
בָּאתַר (בתר)	after (12; *see*)
אתרג	citron

ב

	בְּ-	in (4)
	באש	be evil
	בְּגִין	on account of
	בהל	disturb (D) (20)
	בּוּכְרִיא	senior
	בּוּקְלְסָא	club
*	בוש	embarrass (Dt)
	בחן	examine
	בחר	choose
	בטל	stop (5)
		G—*intransitive*
		D—*transitive*
	בֵּי	*dialect form of* בַּיִת
	בֵּי מדרש	school house
	בֵּין	between (12)
	בִּירָה	fortress
	בִּישׁ	evil (28)
	בַּיִת	house (5)
	בכה	cry
	בלא	wear out (D)
	בְּלוֹ	tax
*	בֵּן	son
	בנה	build (4)
	בעה	seek, pray (14)
	בָּעוּ	petition
	בְּעֵל	master (5)
	בקר	search (9—D)
	בַּר	son (6; בְּנֵי—*p cstr*)
	בַּר	field (16)
	ברי	create
	ברך	bless, kneel (D) (22)
	ברכה	blessing
	בְּרַם	but
	בשר	announce (Gt)
	בְּשַׂר	flesh

בְּתוּלָה	virgin		דִּי	which, of (3)
בָּתַר	after (*from* בְּאָתַר) (32)		כְּדִי	when (26)
			דִּיכְרָא	ram
ג			דִּיל-	*possessive* (*cf.* זִיל-)
			דִּילְמָא	perhaps
גַּב	side		דֵּין	this
גְּבוּרָה	power		דִּין	judgment, court (12)
גְּבַר	man (6)		דַּיָּן	judge (12)
גדד	cut down (21)		דֵּךְ	that (*m*) (14)
גַּו	interior (7)		דָּךְ	that (*f*) (4)
בְּגוֹא	in the midst of (12)		דִּכֵּן	that (4)
גּוֹב	pit (25)		דכר	remember (28)
גוח	stir up (H)		דְּכַר	ram
גזר	cut, break off (15)		דָּכְרָן	memorandum
גְּזֵירָה	decree		דלק	burn
גַּלְגַּל	wheel		דמה	resemble
גלה	reveal (14)		דמי	price
H—take exile			דְּנָא/דְּנָה	this (3)
גָּלוּ	exile (26)		דִּקְלָא	palm (*also spelled* דִּיקְלָא)
גנב	steal		דקק	be crushed (15; H—smash)
גנון	bridal chamber		דָּר	generation (19)
גְּנַז	treasure (9)		דרג	stair
גַּף	wing		דְּרָע	arm
גְּשֵׁם	body (19)		דש	door
			דָּת	law (12)
ד			**ה**	
דְּ-	which, that, of		הָא	behold
דָּא	this (*f*) (14)		הָאנָא	behold, how (32)
דֹּב	bear		הַדָּם	limb
דבח	sacrifice (*verb*)		הדס	myrtle
דְּבַח	sacrifice (*noun*)		הוּא	he (11)
דבר	lead (away), take		הַהוּא*	that
דְּהַב	gold (9)		הוה	be (8)
דּוּר	dwell (16)		הִי	or
דּוּשׁ	trample on		הִיא	she (11)
דחה	thrust		הֵיכַל	palace, temple (8)
דחל	fear (20)		הכא	here

הֲלֹא is it not (*inter. particle*)
הלך go (12)
הֵמּוֹ they, them (5)
המונית עם in agreement with
הֵן if (9)
הרי * behold

ו

וְ and
ווי woe!

ז

זבן buy
זהב gold
זִי who, which, of
זִיו splendor (23)
זילן our
זית olive
זך who, which
זכּאי worthy
זְכוּ innocence
זכי that
זְמַן time (14)
זְמָר music (17)
זַן type (17)
זנה this
זְעֵיר small
זקף lift (32)
זרז saddle
זֶרַע seed

ח

חֲבוּלָה damage
חבל destroy (D) (10)
חֲבַל damage (19)
חֲבַר companion (30)
(חַבְרָה—*f*)

חַד one (8)
חֲדֵה breast
חדה happiness
הֶדְוָה joy
חוד singly (לְחוֹד)
חוה tell (13) (D/H)
חוה prostrate self (מִשְׁתַּחֲוֶה—Št)
חוֹלָף instead of (32)
חִוָּר white
חזה see (15)
(*pass ptc*—proper)
חֶזוּ vision
חַי living (26)
חיה live
חֵיוָה animal (16)
חַיִּין life
חַיִל strength, army (22)
חַכִּים wise (13)
חָכְמָה wisdom (14)
חל sand
חלֵם dream (G)
חֵלֶם dream (*noun*—13)
חלף pass by
חֲלָק portion
חמה see (28)
(*pass ptc*—proper)
חֲמִיד attractive
חמר parch
חֲמַר donkey (29)
חֲמַר wine (23)
חֲמֵשׁ five (17)
חמשין fifty
חֲנֻכָּה dedication
חַסִּיר lacking
חסן possess (H)
חֲסַף clay (15)
חַרְטֹם magician (20)

חרי	noble
חרישׁותא	thicket
חרך	scorch (D)
חֲשַׁח	need (18)
חַשְׁחָה	needed thing

ט

טָב	good (9)
טׁבה	goodness
טוּבען	flood
טוּר	mountain (15)
טַל	dew (21)
טליה	young servant (32)
טלל	seek shade (H)
טלל	shadow
טם	bone
טְעֵם	decree, taste (5; *see* שׂים)
טען	carry
טפה	extinguish (ʾafˁel)
טְפַר	claw
טרד	drive out (22)

י

יא	lovely (30)
יאות	well
יבל	bring (H) (31)
יַד	hand (18)
ידה	praise (H/A)
ידע	know (4; H—inform)
יהב	give (8)
יום, יומת	day (22)
יומנא	today
יחיד	only
יטב	be pleasing
יכל	be able, prevail (16)
יַם	sea
יסף	add (H)

יעט	advise (Dt—take counsel)
יצא	go out
יצב	make certain (D)
יַצִּיב	surely (19)
יקד	burn (17)
יַקִּיר	difficult
יְקָר	glory (24)
ירד	descend
יְרַח	month (29)
יַרְכָה	thigh
ירת	inherit (32)
ישׁב	dwell (H—set)
ישׁט	stretch forth (H)
יָת	*direct object marker* (12)
יתב	dwell, sit
יַתִּיר	very, excellent (18)

כ

כ־	like, as (12)
כא	here
כבל	chain
כבשׁן	furnace
כדון	now
כְּדִי	when (26; *see* דִי)
כָּה	here
כהל	be able (21)
כָּהֵן	priest (11)
כוכב	star
כזי	when (*cf.* כְּדִי)
כיון	when (31)
כיף	shore
כַיִן	summer, cf. קַיט
כל	all (10)
	כֹּלָא everything
כלא	protest (ʾafˁel)
כלב	dog
כלה	bride

כְּלִיל	perfect
כְּמָה	how (many) (19)
כמר	priest
כֵּן	thus (28)
כְּנָת	colleague (7)
כנכר	*coin*
כְּנֵמָא	thus (11)
כנש	gather
כסס	slaughter
כְּסַף	silver (9)
כְּעַן	now (4)
כַף	hand
כפר	deny
כפת	bind (D) (18)
כרה	become distressed (Gt)
כָּרוֹז	herald
כרז	proclaim (H)
כָּרְסֵא	throne (24)
כתב	write (3)
כְּתָב	writing (11)
כְּתַל	wall

ל

לְ-	to, for, *direct obj. marker* (3)
לָא	not (4)
לְבַב	heart (21)
לבונא	incense
לְבוּשׁ	garment
לבן	whiteness
לבש	wear (23)
לָהֵן	except, therefore (13)
לְוָת	to, with (29)
לחוד	*see* חוד
לחיא	evil
לְחֶם	meal (23)
לֵילִי	night (25)

לַיְשָׁה	is not (28)
לֵית	there is not
ללב	palm
לם	surely
לקח	take
לִשָׁן	language

מ

מ-	from
מְאָה	hundred
מָאן	vessel (8)
מְגִלָּה	scroll
מגר	overthrow, throw down (D)
מַדְבַּח	altar (29)
מְדוֹר	dwelling (22)
מְדִינָה	province (7)
מָה	what(ever) (10)
מה	how
מוי	water
מות	die (31)
מָזוֹן	food
מזרק	basin
מחא	hit
מחזה	appearance
מחנה	camp
מַחְצְפָה	urgent
מחתא	grain offering (*cf.* מִנְחָה)
מטא	reach (21), bring (H)
מטלל	roof
מידעם	anything (*cf.* מנדעם)
מייא	water
מימרא	word
מכר	sell
מַלְאַךְ	angel
מִלָּה	word, thing (13)
מֶלֶךְ	king (3)

מַלְכוּ reign (11)

מלל speak (D) (26)

מַן who(ever) (6)

מִן from (9)

    מִן דִּי after, because

    מִן יַד immediately

מַנְדַּע understanding

מנדעם anything (*cf.* מִידַעם)

מנה count (G; D—appoint)

מִנְחָה grain offering

מנע withhold

מסר deliver (31)

מְעֵה belly

מצעת middle

מָרֵא master (24)

מְרַד rebellion

מָרָד rebellious (4)

מרום height (32)

מרט tear off

מֹשַׁח oil (*noun*)

מֹשַׁח anoint (*verb*)

מִשְׁכַּב bed

מִשְׁתֵּא banquet

נ

נבא prophesy (Dt)

נְבוּאָה prophecy

נְבִיא prophet

נגד flow

נדב be willing (Dt) (12)

נדד flee

נדח banish

נִדְנֶה sheath

נדש destroy

נַהִירוּ illumination

נְהַר river

נוד flee

נְוָלוּ/נְוָלִי dunghill (10)

נוּר fire (17)

נזק suffer damage

נְחָשׁ copper (15)

נחת descend (21)

    ʾafʿel (אֲחֵת) deposit

נטל lift (22)

נטר guard

נכס slaughter (32)

נְכַס property

נְמַר panther

נסב take (30)

נסה lift

נסי test

נפל fall (16)

נפק go out (8)

נִפְקָה expenses

נפֹשׁ self (29), will

נִץ radiance, bloom

נצה quarrel

נצח win (D—distinguish self)

נציח splendid

נצל save (H)

נְקֵא pure

נֹשׁ human (31)

נְשִׁין women (29)

נְשַׁר eagle

נִשְׁתְּוָן letter

נתן give (4)

ס

סבל endure

סבר intend

סגד bow down (16)

סגי multiply (H)

סְגַן	prefect	עִלִּי	Most High (21)
סגר	close (26)	עֶלְיוֹן	Most High
סדר	arrange	עלל	enter (14)
סוֹף	end	עָלַם	eternity (5)
סטנה	Satan	עֶלַע	rib
סַכִּין	knife	עלתא	burnt offering (29)
סכל	look (Dt)	עִם	with (12)
סלה	*liturgical term*	עַם	people, nation (12)
סלק	go up (26)	עמוד	pillar
הסיק (H) sacrifice		עַמִּיק	deep
סֹלֶת	flour	עמל	exert oneself, toil
סֵפֶר	book (11)	עמר	load·
סָפַר	scribe (3)	עֲמַר	wool
סָרַךְ	chief	ענה	answer (13)
סתירה	hidden thing	עֲנָן	cloud
סתר	tear down (G)	עֲנַף	branch
		עֳפִי	foliage (20)
ע		עק	wood
עֶבֶד	servant	עקר	uproot (Gt—be uprooted)
עֲבִידָה	work, service (5)	עָר	enemy
עבד	do, make (5)	ערבא	willow
עַד	until (12)	עֲשַׂר	ten (17)
עדה	pass away (22; H—remove)	עֶשְׂרִין	twenty
עִדָּן	time (13)	עשׁת	intend
עובע	haste	אתעשׁת (Gt) be thought	
עולימו	youth	עֲתִיד	ready (18)
עוֹף	bird	עַתִּיק	old
עוקמא	trickery		
עִילִּיִּ	on, above (32)	**פ**	
עַיִן	eye (30)		
עכב	refuse	פּ־	and
עַל	on, concerning, to, against (3)	פגן	cry out
		פה *	mouth
עִלָּה	pretext (25)	פֶּחָה	governor (6)
עֵלָּה	above	פִּינך	plate
עֲלָוָה	burnt offering (29)	פכר	destroy
		פלא	trick

פְּלַג	half
פלג	discord
פְלוּגְתָּא	division (= Babel)
פלח	worship, serve (17)
פָּלְחָן	worship
פְּלִיג	divided, undecided
פֻּם	mouth (22)
פַּס	palm (of hand)
פְּסוּלָא	blemish
פְּסִיל	cut stone
פַּרְזֶל	iron (15)
פרכס	struggle
פרס	divide
פרק	save
פַּרְתָּרֵךְ	commander
פשׁט	extend
פשׁר	interpret (D) (23)
פְּשַׁר	interpretation (13)
פִּתְגָּם	message, word (10)
פתח	open (28)

צ

צבה	want (21)
צְבוּ	wish, property
צבע	be wet (Dt) (21)
צְדָא	true
צדק	righteousness
צִדְקָה	merit
צוור	neck
צוֹם	fast
ציר	pivot (of door)
צלה	pray (D) (10)
צלח	make prosper (H) (26)
צְלֵם	statue, form (15)
צער	pain
צִפַּר	bird
צִפְרָא	morning

ק

קֳבֵל	just as (11)
לְקֳבֵל	opposite, corresponding to (12)
כָּל קֳבֵל דִּ-	inasmuch as, because, although
כָּל קֳבֵל דְּנָה	thereupon (14)
קבל	receive (D) (25)
קַדִּישׁ	holy (20)
קֳדָם	before (5)
קדם	do early (H)
קַדְמָה	formerly (26)
קַדְמָי/קַדְמָאי	first (17)
קוּדְשָׁא	the Holy One
קוּם	arise, stand (G) (6)
	H—establish
קַיֵּם	D—swear
הִתְקַיַּים	Dt—be fulfilled
קוּר(א)	city
קַטִּין	delicate
קטל	kill (G/D) (18)
קטע	cut
קטר	rise in circle
קַיִט	summer
קַיָּם	enduring
קְיָם	statute (25)
קִים	standing
קִיסָא	twig
קָל	sound (17)
קנה	buy, acquire
קצף	be angry
קצץ	cut down
קְצָת	end (22)
קרא/קרה	call, read (23)
קרב	approach (26) (D/H—sacrifice)

קְרָב	war
קרבן	offering
קִרְיָה	city (4)
קֶרֶן	horn (17)
קְרָץ	piece

אֲכַל קְרָץ accuse

ר

רֵאשׁ	head (chief) (7)

רֵאשׁ מִלִּין complete
account or essential
contents

רַב	great (7)
רבה	grow (20)
רִבּוֹ	myriad, 10,000
רְבוּ	greatness (24)
רבחיל	general
רְבִיעִי	fourth (16)
רבע	quarter
רַבְרְבָנִין	chiefs
רגג	pleasant
רגז	anger (H)
רְגַז	anger
רְגַל	foot (15)
רגש	assemble (25) (H)
רוּחַ	wind (20)
רוּם	rise (24)
רוּם	height
רוּץ	run
רָז	secret (14)
רַחִיק	distant (10)
רחם	love (30)
רַחֲמִין	compassion (29)
רחמן	Merciful One
רמה	throw, impose (17)
רְעוּ	wish
רַעְיוֹן	thought (23)

רפס	trample on
רְקִיק	soft
רשׁם	write (24)

שׂ

שָׂב	elder
שׂגא	grow great (19)
שַׂגִּיא	many, large (8)
שְׂטַר	side
שִׂים	issue, give (lit. "place") (6)

שִׂים טְעֵם issue decree or
pay attention

שׂכל	consider (Dt)
שׂנא	hate
שְׂעַר	hair (19)
שׂקק	sackcloth (sing. שׂק)
שׂרף	burn
שׂתו	winter

שׁ

שׁאל	ask (12)
שְׁאָר	remnant (11)
שׁבח	praise (D) (14)
שְׁבִיב	flame
שְׁבַע/שִׁבְעָה	seven (17)
שׁבק	leave alone, abandon (10)

Gt—be transferred

שׁוה	be like (G) (24)
שׁוה	place (32)
שׁוּפַר	beauty
שׁטט	wander
שֵׁיזִב	save (18)
שֵׁיצִיא	finish
שׁירי	remainder
שׁכח	find (H) (23)
שְׁכִינְתָּא	Divine Presence
שׁכלול	completion

שׁכלל	complete (11)		שֵׁת	six (11)
שְׁלָה	blasphemy		שׁתה (אֶשְׁתִּיו)	drink (23)
שָׁלוּ	negligence			
שׁלח	send (3)			**ת**
שׁלט	rule (16)			
שָׁלְטָן	dominion (19)		תֵּאנָה	fig
שַׁלִּיט	authorized, mighty (12)		תְּבִיר	breakable
שׁלים	perfect		תבר	break (29)
שׁלך	throw (H) (31)		תּוב	return (*intrans*) (22)
שׁלם	perfect			H—return (*trans*), reply
שׁלם	be finished (24) (H—deliver)		תּוֹר	ox
שְׁלָם	peace (5)		תְּחוֹת	underneath (12)
שֵׁם	name (6) (*pl* שְׁמָהָת)		תחת *	instead of
שׁמד	exterminate (H)		תְּלַג	snow
שְׁמַיָּא	heavens (8)		תלי	weapon
שׁמם	be appalled		תְּלִיתָי	third (16)
	אִשְׁתּוֹמֵם *itpolʿel*		תלסירי	thirteen
שׁמע	hear, obey (17)		תְּלָת	three (17)
שׁמשׁ	serve (D)		תַּלְתִּי/תַּלְתָּא	ruler (24)
שׁמשׁ	sun		תְּלָתִין	thirty
	בֵּין שִׁימְשָׁתָא twilight		תמה	wonder (H)
שֵׁן	tooth		תַּמָּה	there (9)
שׁנה	change (13)		תְּמָנֶה	eight (17)
שְׁנָה	year (8)		תמר	palm
שְׁנָה	sleep		תנה	here (29)
שׁנק	choke (Gt)		תני	tell
שׁעה	talk (Gt)		תִּנְיָן/תִּנְיָנוּת	second (17)
שָׁעָה	hour (18)		תַּקִּיף	strong (5)
שַׁפִּיר	beautiful		תקל	weigh
שׁפל	be low (24)		תקן	prepare (H—restore)
שׁפר	please, be beautiful (25)		תְּרֵין/תַּרְתֵּין	two (28)
שָׁק	leg (29)		תְּרֵי־עֲשַׂר	twelve (17)
שׁרב	family		תְּרַע	gate
שׁרה	loosen (19)		תְּשַׁע	nine (17)
שָׁרִיר	prosperous			
שֹׁרֶשׁ	root			

ANSWER KEY

Note: English translations are rather literal in order to facilitate comparison with the original. Translations into Aramaic have generally been made in the most straightforward way possible; however, other renderings may be equally correct. In lessons 28–32 the vocalization of some words and names that do not exist in the Bible is uncertain.

Chapter 3

P. 11   Ezra 4:8–11

Rehum and Shimshai, the scribe, wrote a letter concerning Jerusalem to King Artaxerxes. This is the letter which they sent to King Artaxerxes.

(1) The scribe wrote the letter to them.
(2) God made heaven.
(3) The king said concerning Jerusalem.

P. 12   (4) The king sent the letter to the scribe.
(5) God said from heaven . . .
(6) This scribe perished under the earth.
(7) God said that the earth is the king's.

Chapter 4

P. 16   Ezra 4:12–16

Let it be known to the king that the Jews are building Jerusalem, the rebellious city. Now, let it be known to the king that if that city will be built, they will not give tax [i.e., the tax will not be paid]. We have sent and informed the king concerning this, that he search in the book of memoranda and [where] you will find that that city is a rebellious city. We are informing the king that if that city will be rebuilt, you will not have a portion in Trans-Euphrates.

231

P. 17

	Aramaic	Hebrew		Aramaic	Hebrew
(guard)	נטר	נצר	(there is)	אִיתַי	יֵשׁ
(three)	תְּלָת	שָׁלוֹשׁ	(snow)	תְּלַג	שֶׁלֶג
(lie)	כדבה	כָּזָב	(summer)	קַיִט	קַיִץ
(advise)	יעט	יעץ	(unit of weight)	תְּקֵל	שֶׁקֶל
(arm)	אֶדְרָע	אֶזְרֹעַ	(memorandum)	דָּכְרָן	זִכָּרוֹן
(sit, dwell)	יתב	ישב	(ox)	תּוֹר	שׁוֹר
(gold)	דְּהַב	זָהָב	(riddle)	אֲחִידָה	חִדָה
(land)	אֲרַע	אֶרֶץ	(new)	חֲדַת	חָדָשׁ
(sacrifice)	דְּבַח	זֶבַח	(return)	תּוֹב	שׁוּב
			(six)	שֵׁת	שֵׁשׁ

P. 18 (1) We are building the city.

(2) The scribe sent that letter.

(3) You will find God in the rebellious Jerusalem.

(4) They have no portion in Trans-Euphrates.

(5) Now it is known that the Judeans will give tax to the king.

(6) Rehum wrote this memorandum.

Chapter 5

P. 22   Ezra 4:17-24

The king sent the message to Rehum, the chief official, and Shimshai, the scribe, who dwell in Samaria and the remnant of Trans-Euphrates: Peace! The letter which you sent has been read before me. Rebellion has been made in that city from eternity, and strong kings have been over Jerusalem. Now issue a decree to stop the building of that city.   Then, after the letter of King Artaxerxes was read before Rehum and Shimshai, the scribe, they went to Jerusalem to the Jews, and stopped them. Then the work on the house of God which is in Jerusalem stopped.

לֹא   There is no Canaanite shift in Aramaic, so it preserves *ā* where Hebrew has *ō*.

עֲמַר   Semitic *ḍ* becomes צ in Hebrew, but ע in Aramaic; also words that are segholates in Hebrew often have only a single vowel under their second consonant in Aramaic.

דָּא — There is no Canaanite shift in Aramaic, which represents Semitic _d_ with ד rather than ז as in Hebrew.

אֶדְרָע — Aramaic represents Semitic _d_ with ד rather than ז as in Hebrew, in which _ā_ often shifts to _ō_.

תְּלַג — Semitic _t_ is represented as ת in Aramaic rather than שׁ as in Hebrew, where words with one vowel become segholates rather than having a vowel under the second consonant as in Aramaic.

שָׁפְטִין — There is no Canaanite shift in Aramaic (for the plural ending ין_ where Hebrew has ים_, see chapter 6).

נְהַר — Pretonic _a_ reduces in Aramaic rather than lengthening as in Hebrew.

תּוּב — Aramaic uses ת for Semitic _t_, where Hebrew uses שׁ.

P. 23 שֵׁת — Semitic _t_ is represented with ת in Aramaic but with שׁ in Hebrew.

סְפַר — There is no Canaanite shift in Aramaic, so _ā_ corresponds to Hebrew _ō_; the _a_ where Hebrew has _ē_ is due to the consonant ר.

נְשִׁין — Pretonic _a_ reduces in Aramaic, but lengthens in Hebrew (for the plural ending ין_ rather than Hebrew ים_, see chapter 6).

חֲדַת — Semitic _t_ is represented as ת in Aramaic rather than as שׁ as in Hebrew; note also the reduction of pretonic _a_, which is lengthened in Hebrew.

שְׂעַר — Pretonic _a_ is reduced in Aramaic but lengthened in Hebrew.

חֲבַר — Pretonic _a_ is reduced in Aramaic but lengthened in Hebrew (the presence of _a_ where Hebrew has _ē_ is due to the consonant ר).

דְּהַב — Aramaic represents Semitic _d_ with ד rather than ז as in Hebrew and reduces pretonic _a_, which is lengthened in Hebrew.

עֲשַׂר — Words that are segolates in Hebrew typically have one full vowel under their second consonant in Aramaic.

אָת — _ā_ does not shift to _ō_ in Aramaic as it does in the Canaanite languages.

תבר — Semitic _t_ is represented as ת in Aramaic rather than שׁ as in Hebrew.

עֲלַם — _ā_ does not shift to _ō_ in Aramaic as it does in Hebrew.

(1) The Master of Eternity wrote a letter to strong kings.
(2) We are building a house in the rebellious city.
(3) Then they stopped (the) building in Jerusalem.

P. 24 (4) Issue a decree before the scribe after the letter has been read.

(5) Now they will not give (i.e. assign) work over the Jews.

(6) The strong kings went to the city.

(7) God's decree is read before the master.

(8) Then Shimshai said to stop building this house.

(9) They made rebellion in Jerusalem.

(10) Issue peace for them from eternity.

(11) We are informing the scribe that work on the house of the king has stopped.

Chapter 6

P. 27   Ezra 5:1–5

Then the prophets Haggai and Zechariah, the son of Iddo, prophesied to the Jews who were in Judah and in Jerusalem with the name of the God of Israel over them. Then Zerubbabel, the son of Shealtiel, and Jeshua, the son of Jozadak, arose to build the house of God which is in Jerusalem. Tattenai, the governor of Trans-Euphrates, and Shetar-Bozenai came to them and said (lit. saying) thus to them: "Who issued a decree to build this house? What (lit. who) are the names of the men who are building this?" But their God's eye was over the Jews, and they didn't stop them.

P. 28 (1) מֶלֶךְ

(2) סָפְרָא

(3) שְׁמָהָת

	SINGULAR			PLURAL		
	Absolute	*Construct*	*Determined*	*Absolute*	*Construct*	*Determined*
P. 29	רֵאשׁ	רֵאשׁ	רֵאשָׁא	רֵאשִׁין	רֵאשֵׁי	רֵאשַׁיָּא
	נְבִיא	נְבִיא	נְבִיאָא	נְבִיאִין	נְבִיאֵי	נְבִיאַיָּא
	סְפַר	סְפַר	סָפְרָא	סִפְרִין	סִפְרֵי	סִפְרַיָּא
	עֲבִידָה	עֲבִידַת	עֲבִידְתָּא	עֲבִידָן	עֲבִידָת	עֲבִידָתָא
	קִרְיָה	קִרְיַת	קִרְיְתָא	קִרְיָן	קִרְיָת	קִרְיָתָא
P. 30	אֱלָהּ	אֱלָהּ	אֱלָהָא	אֱלָהִין	אֱלָהֵי	אֱלָהַיָּא
	סְפַר	סְפַר	סָפְרָא	סִפְרִין	סִפְרֵי	סִפְרַיָּא

(1) סָפְרָא כְּתַב שְׁמָהָת גֻּבְרַיָּא.

(2) קָמוּ נְבִיאֵי יִשְׂרָאֵל קֳדָם מַלְכַיָּא.

(3) שְׁלַחוּ אִגַּרְתָּא עַל עֲבַר־נַהֲרָא.

(4) אֲתָא אֱלָהָא עַל יִשְׂרָאֵל.

P. 31

(5) הִמּוֹ בָּנַיִן יְרוּשְׁלֶם קִרְיְתָא.

(6) בְּעֵל שָׁם טְעֵם.

(7) הוֹדַעְנָא גֻּבְרֵי קִרְיְתָא.

(8) מַן פֶּחֲוָת יְהוּד וְשָׁמְרָיִן?

Chapter 7

P. 34   Ezra 5:6–10

The letter which Tattenai, governor of Trans-Euphrates, and Shetar-Bozenai and his colleagues who were in Trans-Euphrates sent to King Darius, and this was written in it: "To King Darius, peace (over) everything. Let it be known to the king that we went to Judah, the province, to the house of the great God. Then we asked these elders, we said to them, 'Who issued the decree to you to build this house?' And we also asked them their names so that we would write the name of the men who are at their heads."

G	הִתְקְטָלָה	D	נְחַוֵּא	G	אֲכַלָה
H	מְהֵימַן	G	סָגְדִין	D	הַדְּרֶת
D	מִתְכַּנְּשִׁין	G	בְּנַס	H	הוּבַד
D	מִתְנַשְּׂאָה	H	הַרְגִּזוּ	H	הָחָרְבַת
D	יְבַקַּר	H	הֶעְלוּ	G	יִשְׁאֲלֶנְכוֹן
G	תִּקְנָא	H	הַשְׁכַּחַת	G	בְּטֵלַת
G	רְשַׁמְתָּ	G	תִּתְרְמוֹן	H	הַשְׁפֵּלְתְּ
G	הִתְרְחִצוּ	G	נְפַלוּ	D	מַלִּל
D	מְהַלְּכִין	D	הִתְנַבִּי	D	שַׁבַּחַת
D	אִתְעֲקַרוּ	D	בַּטִלוּ	G	חֲשִׁיבִין
D	מְצַבְּעִין	H	מְהַעְדֵּה	G	אֲבֵעֵה
		G	הִתְגְּזֶרֶת		

P. 35

(1) אֲזַלְנָא לִמְדִינְתָּא רַבְּתָא.

(2) שְׁלַחוּ אִגְּרָה לְבַיְתָא וּלְגֻבְרַיָּא בְּגַוֵּהּ.

(3) כְּעַן דָּרְיָוֶשׁ רֵאשׁ שָׁבַיָּא אֲלֵךְ.

(4) שָׁבַיָּא אָמְרִין דִּי טַעֲמָא יְדִיעַ לְהֹם.

(5) לֶהֱוֵא שְׁלָמָא עַל יְרוּשְׁלֶם.

(6) כֹּלָא כְּתִיבָא.

Chapter 8

P. 38   Ezra 5:11–15

They replied, "We are the servants of the God of heaven and earth and are building the house which was built many years before this. Our ancestors angered the God of heaven, and He gave them to Nebuchadnezzar, king of Babylon, the Chaldean; and he tore down this house and exiled the people to Babylon. In the first year of Cyrus, the king of Babylon, Cyrus the king issued a decree to build this house of God; and the vessels of the house of God which Nebuchadnezzar removed from the temple which is in Jerusalem to the temple of Babylon—Cyrus the king took them out from the temple of Babylon and they were given to Sheshbazzar, and he said, 'These vessels—deposit them in the temple which is in Jerusalem and let the house of God be rebuilt.'"

P. 39

עֲבְדֵת	נְטְלֵת	רְשְׁמֵת	שְׁלַחַת
עֲבַדְתְּ	נְטַלְתְּ	רְשַׁמְתְּ	שְׁלַחְתְּ
עֲבַדְתִּי	נְטַלְתִּי	רְשַׁמְתִּי	שְׁלַחְתִּי
עֲבַד	נְטַל	רְשַׁם	שְׁלַח
עֲבַדַת	נְטַלַת	רְשְׁמַת	שְׁלַחַת
עֲבַדְנָא	נְטַלְנָא	רְשַׁמְנָא	שְׁלַחְנָא
עֲבַדְתּוּן	נְטַלְתּוּן	רְשַׁמְתּוּן	שְׁלַחְתּוּן
עֲבַדְתֵּן	נְטַלְתֵּן	רְשַׁמְתֵּן	שְׁלַחְתֵּן
עֲבַדוּ	נְטַלוּ	רְשַׁמוּ	שְׁלַחוּ
עֲבַדָה	נְטַלָה	רְשְׁמָה	שְׁלַחָה

P. 40

יְדַעְתָּ	ידע	2 masculine singular
יְדְעֵת	ידע	1 common singular
יְהַב	יהב	3 masculine singular
כְּתַבְנָא	כתב	1 common plural
כְּתַבוּ	כתב	3 masculine plural
מְלַחְנָה	מלח	1 common plural
נְטְרֵת	נטר	1 common singular
נְפַל	נפל	3 masculine singular
סְלְקֵת	סלק	1 common singular
עֲבַד	עבד	3 masculine singular

P. 41   (1) The king went before the city.

(2) We knew that the Master of Eternity was in Jerusalem.

(3) I wrote a letter to the king's house.

P. 41 (*cont.*)

 (4) Then God sent a decree to that province.

 (5) You gave many servants to the governor of the Jews.

 (6) Our fathers gave those vessels to Cyrus.

 (7) The head of the palace was in heaven.

 (8) Nebuchadnezzar did not take the men out to the land.

 (9) That great house will be built in one year.

Chapter 9

P. 44 Ezra 5:16–6:5

Then Sheshbazzar came; he gave (i.e. laid) the foundations of the house of God which is in Jerusalem, and from then until now it was being built, but was not completed. And now if it is good to the king, let it be searched in the king's treasure house that is there in Babylon if a decree was issued by King Cyrus to build the house of God in Jerusalem; and let him send the king's wish concerning this to us. Then King Darius issued a decree, and they searched there in Babylon, and a scroll was found and thus was written in it: "In the first year of King Cyrus, King Cyrus issued a decree (that) the house of God in Jerusalem be built, and the expenses will be given (i.e. paid) from the king's house, and they will return the gold and silver vessels of the house of God which Nebuchadnezzar brought out from the temple which is in Jerusalem."

נְטֵל	רְשֵׁם	טְרֵד	קְטֵל
נְטֵל	רְשֵׁם	טְרֵד	קְטֵל
נְטִלָא	רְשִׁמָא	טְרִדָא	קְטִילָא
נְטִילָה	רְשִׁמָה	טְרִידָה	קְטִילָה
נְטִילַת	רְשִׁמַת	טְרִידַת	קְטִילַת
נְטִילְתָא	רְשִׁמְתָא	טְרִידְתָא	קְטִילְתָא
נְטִילִין	רְשִׁמִין	טְרִידִין	קְטִילִין
נְטִילֵי	רְשִׁמֵי	טְרִידֵי	קְטִילֵי
נְטִילַיָּא	רְשִׁמַיָּא	טְרִידַיָּא	קְטִילַיָּא
נְטִלָן	רְשִׁמָן	טְרִדָן	קְטִלָן
נְטִלַת	רְשִׁמַת	טְרִדַת	קְטִלַת
נְטִלְתָא	רְשִׁמְתָא	טְרִדְתָא	קְטִלְתָא

P. 45

קְטִיל   טְרִיד   רְשִׁים   נְטִיל
קְטִיל   טְרִיד   רְשִׁים   נְטִיל
קְטִילָא   טְרִידָא   רְשִׁימָא   נְטִילָא

קְטִילָה   טְרִידָה   רְשִׁימָה   נְטִילָה
קְטִילַת   טְרִידַת   רְשִׁימַת   נְטִילַת
קְטִילְתָּא   טְרִידְתָּא   רְשִׁימְתָא   נְטִילְתָּא

קְטִילִין   טְרִידִין   רְשִׁימִין   נְטִילִין
קְטִילֵי   טְרִידֵי   רְשִׁימֵי   נְטִילֵי
קְטִילַיָּא   טְרִידַיָּא   רְשִׁימַיָּא   נְטִילַיָּא

קְטִילָן   טְרִידָן   רְשִׁימָן   נְטִילָן
קְטִילָת   טְרִידָת   רְשִׁימָת   נְטִילָת
קְטִילָתָא   טְרִידָתָא   רְשִׁימָתָא   נְטִילָתָא

(1) Nebuchadnezzar says that the city will be given to Jews.

(2) A big scroll is sent to the governor of the province.

(3) The king knew that (the) work stopped.

P. 46 (4) We know (how) to build this house.

(5) There is gold in the treasure house there in Babylon.

(6) The men searched if good silver was given to the scribe.

(1) גֻּבְרַיָּא קָמוּ עֲלֵיהוֹן.

(2) מַן שְׁלַח כַּסְפָּא וְדַהֲבָא מִן עֲבַר־נַהֲרָא?

(3) אִיתַי פֶּחָה בְּגוֹ יְרוּשְׁלֶם.

(4) יַהַבְנָא בַּיְתָא לְהֹם.

(5) אֲתָה סָפְרָא לְקִרְיְתָא.

Chapter 10

P. 50 Ezra 6:6–12

Now Tattenai, governor of Trans-Euphrates, Shetar-Bozenai, and their colleagues, be (i.e. stay) far from there. Leave the work of the house of God, and from me a decree is issued for the Jews to build the house of God, and the expenses will be given (paid) from the king's property to those men that it not stop. And whatever they need for the God of heaven is to be given to them so that they will sacrifice to the God of heaven and pray for the king's life. And from me a decree is issued that any person who changes this message—his house will be made a dunghill concerning this, and may God overthrow any king or nation which extends its hand to destroy the house of God which is in Jerusalem. I, Darius, have issued (the) decree."

	Aramaic	*Hebrew*	*English*
P. 50	אֲזַל	הָלַךְ	go
	אִיתַי	יֵשׁ	there is
	אֱלָהַיָּא	אֱלֹהִים	god
P. 51	אֲנַחְנָה	אֲנַחְנוּ	we
	אָע	עֵץ	tree
	אַרְעָא	אֶרֶץ	land
	אתה	בוא	come
	בַּר	בֵּן	son
	דְּבַח	זֶבַח	sacrifice
	דְּהַב	זָהָב	gold
	דִּכְרָן	זִכָּרוֹן	memorandum
	דְּנָה	זֶה	this
	דְּרָע	זְרוֹעַ	arm
	חַד	אֶחָד	one
	יְדִיעַ	יָדוּעַ	known
	יהב	נתן	give
	יתב	ישב	dwell
	כִּדְבָה	כָּזָב	lie
	לֶהֱוֵא	יִהְיֶה	it will be
	לְהֹם	לָהֶם	to them
	נחת	ירד	go down

	Aramaic	Hebrew	English
P. 51 (*cont.*)	נְפַק	יצא	go out
	סְלֵק	עלה	go up
	סְפַר	סֵפֶר	document
	סָפְרָא	הַסוֹפֵר	(the) scribe
P. 52	עֲבַד	עשׂה	do
	פְּלַח	עבד	work
	קַיִט	קַיִץ	summer
	רַב	גָּדוֹל	big
	שַׂגִּיא	רַב	many
	שְׁלָם	שָׁלוֹם	peace
	שְׁמַיָּא	שָׁמַיִם	heaven
	שֵׁת	שֵׁשׁ	six
	תּוּב	שׁוּב	return
	תּוֹר	שׁוֹר	ox
	תְּלַג	שֶׁלֶג	snow
	תְּלָת	שָׁלוֹשׁ	three
	תְּקֵל	שֶׁקֶל	weight
	תְּרֵי	שְׁנֵי	two

(1) גִּנְזַיָּא רַחִיקִין מִן נְוָלוּ.

(2) כִּתְבֵת אִגְּרָה לְסָפְרַיָּא.

(3) שְׁלַח פִּתְגָם אֱלָהָא לְקִרְיְתָא.

(4) רֵאשׁ מְדִינְתָּא אֱנָשׁ (גְּבַר).

(5) שְׁבַקוּ כֹּלָא תַּמָּה!

(6) מְצַלִּין הִמּוֹ לֵאלָהַיָּא לְחַבָּלָה אַרְעָא.

Chapter 11

P. 56   Ezra 6:13–18

Then Tattenai, governor of Trans-Euphrates, Shetar-Bozenai, and their colleagues did exactly as King Darius sent. The Jews are building and succeeding according to the prophecy of Haggai and Zechariah, the son of Iddo; and they completed (it) at the command of the God of Israel and the command of Cyrus and Darius and Artaxerxes, king of Persia. And he finished this house on the third day of the month Adar, which is the sixth year of King Darius' reign. And the children of Israel, the priests, and the Levites and the rest of the exiles made a dedication of this house of God with joy. And they established the priests and the Levites over the service of God, who is in Jerusalem, according to the writing of Moses' book.

P. 57   (1)   אַנְתְּ   You sacrificed an ox to God.

         (2)   הוּא   He knew that the elders are in the province.

         (3)   אַנְתָּן   You gave the book to a governor.

         (4)   אַנְתּוּן   You wrote a letter.

         (5)   הִמּוֹ   They fell to the earth.

P. 58   (6)   אֲנַחְנָה   We went out from the house.

         (7)   אֲנָה or הִיא   I (or she) worship(ed) in Jerusalem.

         (8)   הוּא   He issued a decree.

         (9)   אַנְתִּי   You sent a message to Babylon.

         (10)   אֲנָה   I knew (how) to build a house.

         (11)   הִמּוֹ   They went up to heaven.

         (12)   אֲנַחְנָה   We sent a scroll to the treasure house.

P. 59   (1)   There is a palace in the large city.
         (2)   You are priests of the God of heaven.
         (3)   The house of God is in Jerusalem.
         (4)   The man does not have a head.
         (5)   Zerubbabel is governor of the Jews.
         (6)   Thus is it written in the book of Darius: We are praying to the earth.
         (7)   You are a king of peace.
         (8)   Then they finished the work of a strong house.

P. 60

(1) דִּי אָמַר מַלְכָּא כְּנֵמָא אַסְפַּרְנָה עֲבַדוּ גֻּבְרַיָּא שְׁתָּה.

(2) שְׁאָר מַלְכוּתָא לְדָרְיָוֶשׁ יְהַבְנָא.

(3) טַעְמָא אִיתַי בִּכְתָב.

(4) הֵיכַל לָא אִיתַי בִּיהוּד.

(5) סְפַר שְׁלַחַת לְכָהֲנָה תַּמָּה.

Chapter 12

P. 64   Ezra 7:12–26

Artaxerxes, king of kings, to Ezra the priest, scribe of the law of God of heaven: From me a decree is issued that anyone in my kingdom from the people of Israel and their priests and Levites who is willing to go to Jerusalem with you may go. It is sent from before the king to search concerning Judah and Jerusalem according to the law of your God and to bring the king's silver and gold to the God of Israel who is in Jerusalem along with all the silver and gold in the entire province of Babylon to the house of their God which is in Jerusalem. You will diligently buy rams with this silver and sacrifice them in Jerusalem. And whatever is pleasing to you to do with the rest of the silver and gold you may do in accordance with the wish of your God. And deliver the vessels which are given to you for your God's house before the God of Jerusalem. And from me, King Artaxerxes, a decree is issued that everything that Ezra, the priest, the scribe of the law of the God of heaven, requests shall be done exactly. Everything which is from the decree of the God of heaven will be done for the house of the God of heaven. And (we) inform you that (you) are not authorized to impose a tax on all the priests and Levites. And you, Ezra, in accordance with the wisdom of your God, appoint judges for the whole people that is in Trans-Euphrates, for all who know the laws of your God, and you shall inform those who do not know. And judgement will be diligently done to all who will not do the law of your God and the law of the king.

(1) He asked about the king's law.

(2) This people is authorized to bring vessels from the palace.

P. 65   (3) Nebuchadnezzar was king of Babylon from eternity.

(4) Who is willing to make a dunghill on the earth?

(5) You will inform the judge that there will be a rebellion in the province.

P. 65 (*cont.*)

(1) נְהָךְ לִירוּשְׁלֶם עִם עֶזְרָא.

(2) קִרְיְתָא תִּתְבְּנֵה בַּנְיָה אַחֲרֵי דִּי יְהַבִין הִמּוֹ בְּלוֹ לְמַלְכָּא.

(3) הֲוָה דִינָא בֵּין מַלְכָּא לְעַמָּא.

(4) הִמּוֹ אֲמַרוּ שְׁבַקוּ סָפְרָא בְּבָבֶל.

(5) רֵאשָׁא הֲוָה בִּשְׁמַיָּא.

Chapter 13

P. 70   Daniel 2:4–13

"King, say the dream to your servants and we will tell its interpretation." The king answered and said to the Chaldeans, "If you will not tell me the dream and its interpretation, you will be made into limbs and your houses will be made a dunghill; but if you do tell the dream and its interpretation, you will receive much glory from before me. Therefore, tell me the dream and its interpretation." They answered and said, "Let the king say the dream to his servants, and we will tell the interpretation." The king answered and said, "I know that you are buying time until the time changes." The Chaldeans answered before the king and said, "There is no man who will be able to tell the king's thing. No great king has asked a thing like this of any Chaldean, and the thing which the king asks is difficult; and there is no other except the gods who will tell it before the king." The king became very angry and said to kill all the wise men of Babylon.

P. 71

כָּהֲנוֹהִי	his priests	אֲבוּךְ	your father
עַבְדָּיךְ	your servants	אַחֲרֵיהוֹן	after them
עֲלַי	on me	אִיתֵיכוֹן	you are
עֲלָיךְ	on you	אִיתוֹהִי	he is
עִמֵּהּ	with him	אֱלָהִי	my God
לְקָבְלָךְ	opposite you	אֱלָהֵהּ	his God
קֳדָמוֹהִי	before him	בַּתְרָךְ	after you
רֵאשְׁהוֹן	their head	בֵּינֵיהוֹן	between them
שָׂמֵהּ	he placed him	בַּיְתֵהּ	his house
שְׁמָהָתְהֹם	their names	בְּרֵהּ	his son
תְּחוֹתוֹהִי	instead of him	בְּגַוַּהּ	in the midst of her
תְּלָתְהוֹן	the three of them	הֵיכְלִי	my palace
		יָתְהוֹן	them

P. 72

(1) לֶהֱוֵה מַלְכָּא עֲבֵד בְּעִדָּן אָחֳרָן.

(2) עֲנוֹ גֻבְרַיָּא חַכִּימַיָּא לְרֵאשׁ מְדִינְתָּא.

(3) פִּשְׁרָא יִשְׁתַּנֵּה הֵן סָפְרָא יִנְפַּק מִן קִרְיְתָא.

(4) אִיתַי מִלָּה דִּי לָא יִדְעֵת בְּחֶלְמִי.

(5) נְחַוֵּה כֹלָּא לָהֵן שֵׁם אֱלָהָנָא.

(6) בַּיְתֵהּ עַל נְוָלוּ.

Chapter 14

P. 75   Daniel 2:14–24

Then Daniel sought from the king that he would give him time in order to tell the meaning to the king. Then Daniel went to his house and informed Hannaniah, Mishael, and Azariah, his companions, of the thing and to seek compassion from before the God of heaven concerning this secret that they not kill Daniel and his companions along with the wise men of Babylon.

P. 76   Then the secret was revealed to Daniel. Then Daniel blessed the God of heaven. Daniel answered and said, "Let the name of God be blessed from eternity to eternity, for wisdom and power are His, and He changes the seasons and the times, establishes kings, gives wisdom to the wise. He reveals deep things. I praise You, God of my fathers, for You have given me wisdom and power, and now You have informed me of that which I sought from You so that I could make the king's matter known." Thereupon Daniel went in to Arioch, whom the king had appointed to kill the wise men of Babylon. He went and said thus to him: "Do not kill the wise men of Babylon. Bring me before the king, and I will tell the interpretation to the king."

(1) We knew these secrets.

(2) Who built that palace?

(3) The scribe wrote that wisdom is lost from Babylon in the time of Nebuchadnezzar.

P. 77   (4) Daniel entered heaven.

(5) Thereupon it was revealed that the king established the governor's head over this city.

(6) There is a man who seeks compassion.

P. 77 (*cont.*)

(1) אַבָּא דְנָה מְשַׁבַּח דָּתָא דִּי אֱלָהָא.

(2) שַׁלִּיט אֲנָה לְמִבְעֵה סִפְרָא דֵּךְ בְּבֵית גִּנְזַיָּא.

(3) מְדִינָתָא אִלֵּין תְּחוֹת מֶלֶךְ תַּקִּיף.

(4) שְׁבַקוּ אִגַּרְתָּא דָךְ תַּמָּה.

(5) אֲנַחְנָה יָהֲבִין מָאנִין שַׂגִּיאִין בְּגוֹא אַרְעָא.

Chapter 15
P. 80 Daniel 2:25–36

Then Arioch brought Daniel in before the king, and thus he said to him, "I found a man from among the exiles of Judah who will inform the king of the interpretation." The king answered and said to Daniel, whose name was Belteshazzar, "Are you able to inform me of the dream which I saw and its interpretation?" Daniel answered before the king and said, "Wise men are not able to tell the king the secret which the king asks, but there is a God in heaven (who) reveals secrets, and He has informed King Nebuchadnezzar what will be. And it is not by wisdom that is in me that this secret is revealed to me, but that the interpretation be made known to the king. You, O King, saw a large statue; that statue was big. That statue—its head was of good gold, its breasts and its arms were of silver, its belly and its thighs were of copper, its legs were of iron, its feet partly of iron and partly of clay. You saw until a stone broke off, which was not by hands, and hit the statue on its iron and clay feet and crushed them. Then the iron, clay, copper, silver, and gold were crushed together, and the stone which hit the statue became a big mountain. This was the dream, and we will say its interpretation before the king."

P. 81

אֶפֵּל	אֶשְׁלֵט	אֶשְׁבֵּק	אֶסְגֵּד
תְּפֵּל	תִּשְׁלֵט	תִּשְׁבֵּק	תִּסְגֵּד
תִּפְּלִין	תִּשְׁלְטִין	תִּשְׁבְּקִין	תִּסְגְּדִין
יִפֵּל	יִשְׁלַט	יִשְׁבֵּק	יִסְגֵּד
תִּפֵּל	תִּשְׁלֵט	תִּשְׁבֵּק	תִּסְגֵּד
נִפֵּל	נִשְׁלֵט	נִשְׁבֵּק	נִסְגֵּד
תִּפְּלוּן	תִּשְׁלְטוּן	תִּשְׁבְּקוּן	תִּסְגְּדוּן
תִּפְּלָן	תִּשְׁלְטָן	תִּשְׁבְּקָן	תִּסְגְּדָן
יִפְּלוּן	יִשְׁלְטוּן	יִשְׁבְּקוּן	יִסְגְּדוּן
יִפְּלָן	יִשְׁלְטָן	יִשְׁבְּקָן	יִסְגְּדָן

P. 82

תֵּאכֻל	אכל	2 masculine singular or 3 feminine singular
נֵאמַר	אמר	1 common plural
אֶבְעֵה	בעה	1 common singular
תֶּחֱוֵה	הוה	2 masculine singular or 3 feminine singular
לֶהֱוֹן	הוה	3 masculine plural
נִכְתֻּב	כתב	1 common plural
תַּעַבְדוּן	עבד	2 masculine plural
יִפְלְחוּן	פלח	3 masculine plural
אֶקְרֵא	קרא	1 common singular

P. 83

(1) אֶכְתֻּב אִגְּרָה עַל אֶבֶן מִן טוּרָא.

(2) תִּשְׁלַח פִּתְגָּם לְסָפְרָא.

(3) גְּזַר רֵאשָׁא וְרַגְלָא מִן צַלְמָא.

(4) גַּבְרָא דֵּךְ חֲזָה מָאנֵי חַסְפָּא דִּי הַדֵּק דָּנִיֵּאל.

(5) אִיתַי פַּרְזֶל תְּחוֹת אַרְעָא.

(6) נִשְׁאַל לְמִבְנֵה הֵיכַל תַּמָּה.

(7) יְהוּדָיֵא שְׁבַקוּ נְחָשׁ בְּבָבֶל.

Chapter 16

P. 87 Daniel 2:37–49

"You are the king, the king of kings, to whom the God of heaven gave the king-dom, and into your hand He has given human beings, animals of the field, and birds of the sky—wherever they dwell—and made you rule over all of them; you are the head of gold. And after you there will arise another kingdom, lower (lit. more earthly) than you, and afterwards a third kingdom of copper which will rule the whole earth. And a fourth kingdom will be as strong as iron, smashing everything. And the feet and toes which you saw, partly of clay and partly of iron, will be a divided kingdom, and the toes of the feet will be part-ly iron and partly clay—part of the kingdom will be strong and part of it will be breakable. And in the days of those kings, the God of heaven will establish a kingdom that will not ever be destroyed; and the kingdom will not be aban-doned to another people, but it will stand forever, inasmuch as you saw that a stone was broken off from the mountain not by hands, and it smashed the iron, the copper, the clay, the silver, and the gold. The great God has informed the king what will be after this." Then King Nebuchadnezzar fell on his face and bowed down to Daniel. The king answered Daniel and said, "Your God is the God of gods and revealer of secrets, since you were able to reveal this secret." Then the king made him rule over the entire province of Babylon and over all the wise men of Babylon.

(1) We dwell in a house of gold.
(2) The king will rule over the province of Trans-Euphrates.
(3) Haggai smashed a strong animal.
P. 88   (4) A fourth man came.
(5) They will bow to the head of the statue.
(6) There are many fingers on Darius' hand.

(1) פְּשַׁר טַעֲמָא רְבִיעָיָא כְּתִיב בְּבֵית אֱלָהּ.
(2) הִמּוֹ נָפְלִין מִן רַגְלֵיהֹם וּמְצַלַּין לֵאלָהּ.
(3) אֲזַלְנָא לִבְרָא רַחִיקָא.
(4) סָפְרָא חַכִּימָא אֲתָא עִם פִּתְגָּם תְּלִיתָי.
(5) יָכֵלְנָא לְמִבְנֵה בַּיְת אָחֳרִי.

Chapter 17
P. 92   Daniel 3:1–12

King Nebuchadnezzar made a statue of gold and sent to gather the prefects and the governors for the dedication of the statue which King Nebuchadnezzar had erected. Then the prefects and the governors gathered for the dedication of the statue which King Nebuchadnezzar had erected and stood before the statue which Nebuchadnezzar had erected, and the herald called out strongly, "Say to you, O peoples, 'At the time that you hear the sound of the horn and all kinds of music, you will fall and bow down to the statue of gold, which King Nebuchadnezzar has erected; and whoever will not fall down and bow will be thrown into the midst of a furnace of burning fire.'" Thereupon, at that time, when all the peoples heard the sound of the horn and all kinds of music, all the peoples fell down, bowing to the statue of gold which King Nebuchadnezzar had erected. Thereupon, at that time, Chaldean men drew near. They answered and said to King Nebuchadnezzar, "O king, live forever. You, O king, issued a decree that every person who hears the sound of the horn and all kinds of music should fall down and bow to the statue of gold, and whoever does not fall down and bow will be thrown into the midst of a furnace of burning fire. There are Judean men, Shadrach, Meshach, and Abed-nego—those men have not paid attention to you, O king. They do not worship your god, and they do not bow down to the statue of gold which you erected."

P. 93   חֲמֵשׁ + חֲמֵשׁ   שֵׁת + אַרְבַּע   שְׁבַע + תְּלָת   תְּמָנֶה + תַּרְתֵּין   תְּשַׁע + חַד

תְּשַׁע = $4 + 5$	אֶלֶף = 10^3
6 = חַד – 7	תְּלָת = $5 + 2$
תַּרְתֵּין = $4 \div 8$	מָאתַיִן = 10×20
2 = עֲשַׂר $\div 20$	שֵׁת = $2 + 4$
חֲמֵשׁ = $3 - 8$	תְּשַׁע = 3^2
תְּלָת = $2 + 1$	שְׁבַע = $8 \div 56$
שֵׁת = 3×2	תְּמָנֶה = $2 - 10$
אַרְבַּע = $2 \div 8$	מְאָה = $40 + 60$
6 = 1 + חֲמֵשׁ	חַד= $17 \div 17$
תַּרְתֵּין = $9 - 11$	16 = תְּמָנֶה – 24
שְׁבַע = $0 + 7$	$29{,}286$ = רִבּוֹ + $19{,}286$
2 = שֵׁת – 4	עֶשְׂרִין = 2×10
13 = אַרְבַּע – 17	תְּרֵי־עֲשַׂר = $6 + 6$

P. 94

(1) גַּבְרָא קַדְמָיָא (הוּא) רֵאשׁ מְדִינְתָּא.
(2) אֲנַחְנָא מְצַלַּיִן לֶאֱלָהָא שְׁמַיָּא.
(3) הֲווֹ חַמְשָׁה רָזִין בְּחֶלְמָא.
(4) נְפַק קָלָא מִבָּבֶל כְּאֶשָּׁא.
(5) יִפְלְחוּן לִצְלֵם פַּרְזֶל.
(6) אִיתַי רִבּוֹ סָפְרִין יָקְדִין בְּהֵיכְלָא.
(7) קֶרֶן חַד מִתְרַמֵה לְאַתּוּנָא.
(8) הִמּוֹ שְׁמַעוּ אַרְבַּע זְנֵי זְמָרָא.

Chapter 18
P. 96   Daniel 3:13–23

Then Nebuchadnezzar said in anger to bring Shadrach, Meshach, and Abed-nego. Then they brought those men before the king. Nebuchadnezzar answered and said to them, "Is it true, Shadrach, Meshach and Abed-nego, that you are not worshipping my god and not bowing to the statue of gold which I erected? Now if you are ready to fall down and bow to the statue which I made at the time that you hear the sound of the horn and all kinds of music, you will; and if you do not bow down at that hour, you will be thrown into the midst of the furnace of burning fire. And who is the god that will save you from my hands?" Shadrach, Meshach, and Abed-nego answered and said to the king, "Nebuchadnezzar, we do not need to reply to you concerning this matter. If our God, whom we worship, is able to save us from the furnace of burning fire and from your hand, O king, he will save; and if not, let it be known to you, O king, that we are not worshipping your god and not bowing down to the statue of gold which you erected." Then Nebuchadnezzar answered and said to heat the furnace seven times more than is proper to heat it and to bind Shadrach, Meshach, and Abed-nego to throw into the furnace of burning fire. Inasmuch as the king's word was urgent and the fire was heated very much, the fire killed those men who brought up Shadrach, Meshach, and Abed-nego. And those three men—Shadrach, Meshach, and Abed-nego—fell bound into the midst of the furnace of burning fire.

P. 97

Perfect	*Imperfect*	*Participles*		*Imperative*
		Active	*Passive*	
כִּתְבֵת	אֶכְתֻּב	כָּתֵב	כְּתִיב	כְּתֻב
כְּתַבְתְּ	תִּכְתֻּב	כָּתְבָה	כְּתִיבָה	כְּתֻבִי
כִּתְבֵתִי	תִּכְתְּבִין			
כְּתַב	יִכְתֻּב	כָּתְבִין	כְּתִיבִין	כְּתֻבוּ
כִּתְבַת	תִּכְתֻּב	כָּתְבָן	כְּתִיבָן	כְּתֻבָה
כְּתַבְנָא	נִכְתֻּב			
כְּתַבְתּוּן	תִּכְתְּבוּן			
כְּתַבְתֵּן	תִּכְתְּבָן		*Infinitive*	מִכְתַּב
כְּתַבוּ	יִכְתְּבוּן			
כְּתַבָה	יִכְתְּבָן			

P. 98

מֶעְבַּד	עבד	G infinitive "to make"
שְׁבֻקוּ	שבק	G imperative 2 masculine plural "leave!"
מֶחֱזָא	חזה	G infinitive "to see"
אֻכֻלִי	אכל	G imperative 2 feminine singular "eat!"

P. 98 (*cont.*)   מִגְלֵא   גלה   G infinitive "to reveal"

אֱמַר   אמר   G imperative masculine singular "say!"

מִבְנֵא   בנה   G infinitive "to build"

מִכְנַשׁ   כנש   G infinitive "to gather"

מִבְעֵא   בעה   G infinitive "to seek"

מִקְרֵא   קרא   G infinitive "to call"

מִפְשַׁר   פשר   G infinitive "to interpret"

P. 99

(1) אַל תְּקַטֵּל גֻּבְרַיָּא תַּקִּיפִין אִלֵּין.

(2) עֲתִיד אֱלָהָא לְמֶעְבַּד אֲתַר בִּשְׁמַיָּא.

(3) יְדָא תִכְתָּב אִגְּרָה טָבָה יַתִּירָה.

(4) חֲשַׁח מַלְכָּא קִרְיְתָא דָא לְמֶזָא בְּנוּרָא.

(5) שְׁמַע קָל זְמָרָא בְּבָרָא רַחִיקָא.

(6) הֵיתָיוּ סָפְרָא מְכַפְּתָא לְנָוָלוּ.

(7) עַמָּא יְשֵׁיזִיב גִּנְזַיָּא שַׂגִּיָּא.

Chapter 19
P. 102 Daniel 3:24–33

Then King Nebuchadnezzar arose, answered and said, "Did we not throw three men bound into the midst of the fire?" They answered and said to the king, "Surely, O king." He answered and said, "Behold, I see four men free, walking in the midst of the fire, and there is no damage on them. And the fourth resembles a divine being (lit. son of God)." Then Nebuchadnezzar approached the furnace of burning fire. He answered and said, "Shadrach, Meshach, and Abed-nego, servants of God, leave and come (i.e. come out)." Then Shadrach, Meshach, and Abed-nego came out from the midst of the fire. The fire had not ruled their body, nor was the hair of their head scorched. Nebuchadnezzar answered and said, "Blessed is the God of Shadrach, Meshach, and Abed-nego, who sent His angel and saved his servants, who gave their body that they not worship nor bow to any god except their God. And from me let a decree be issued that any people that will say blasphemy concerning the God of

Shadrach, Meshach, and Abed-nego—his house will be made a dunghill inasmuch as there is no other god like this." Then the king made Shadrach, Meshach, and Abed-nego prosper in the province of Babylon. King Nebuchadnezzar to all peoples who live in the entire land: May your peace grow great. The signs which God did with me—how powerful; His kingdom is an eternal kingdom and His dominion is with every generation.

P. 103	מְמַלִּל	מלל	active participle masculine singular
	בַּטִּלוּ	בטל	imperative or perfect 3 masculine plural
	יִטְעֲמוּן	טעם	imperfect 3 masculine plural
	שַׁבְּחֵת	שבח	perfect 1 common singular
	מְהַדַּר	הדר	participle masculine singular
	חַבִּלוּ	חבל	imperative or perfect 3 masculine plural
	לְנַסָּכָה	נסך	infinitive
	הַדְרֵת	הדר	perfect 1 common singular
	חַבָּלָה	חבל	infinitive
	יְבַקַּר	בקר	imperfect 3 masculine singular
	מְמַלְלָא	מלל	active participle feminine singular
	מְהַלֵּךְ	הלך	active participle masculine singular
	מַנִּיתָ	מנה	perfect 2 masculine singular
	מְפַשַּׁר	פשר	active participle masculine singular
	תְקַבְּלוּן	קבל	imperfect 2 masculine plural
	קַטֵּל	קטל	imperative or perfect 3 masculine singular
P. 104	יְשַׁמְשׁוּן	שמש	imperfect 3 masculine plural
	שַׁבַּחְתָּ	שבח	perfect 2 masculine singular
	מְצַבְּעִין	צבע	active participle masculine plural
	לְקַטָּלָה	קטל	infinitive
	יְמַלִּל	מלל	imperfect 3 masculine singular
	מְשָׁרֵא	שרה	active participle masculine singular
	יְבַהֲלוּ	בהל	imperfect 3 masculine plural
	בַּדִּרוּ	בדר	imperative or perfect 3 masculine plural
	מְשַׁבַּח	שבח	active participle masculine singular

P. 104 (*cont.*)

Perfect	Imperfect	Participle	Imperative
חַבְּלֵת	אֲחַבֵּל	מְחַבֵּל	חַבֵּל
חַבֵּלְתְּ	תְּחַבֵּל	מְחַבְּלָה	חַבְּלִי
חַבֵּלְתִּי	תְּחַבְּלִין		
חַבֵּל	יְחַבֵּל	מְחַבְּלִין	חַבִּלוּ
חַבְּלַת	תְּחַבֵּל	מְחַבְּלָן	חַבִּלָה
חַבֵּלְנָא	נְחַבֵּל		
חַבֵּלְתּוּן	תְּחַבְּלוּן		
חַבֵּלְתֵּן	תְּחַבְּלָן	*Infinitive* חַבָּלָה	
חַבִּלוּ	יְחַבְּלוּן		
חַבִּלָה	יְחַבְּלָן		

P. 105

(1) כַּפְתוּ גֶשְׁמֵהּ מֵרֵאשָׁא לְרַגְלָא.

(2) יַצִּיב דִּי נְחַבֵּל אַרְבַּע מְדִינָן.

(3) יְהַב מַלְכָּא שָׁלְטָן לִבְרֵהּ לְעָלְמִין.

(4) כְּמָה חַכִּים אַנְתְּ לְמִשְׁבַּק קִרְיְתָא מָרְדְתָּא בִּשְׁלָם.

(5) הִיא מְשַׁבְּחָא לְשָׁפְטָא דִּי שְׂנָא בְּדָרָא דְּנָה.

(6) בִּקְּרֵת בְּבֵית גִּנְזַיָּא וְאִיתַי חֲבָל תַּמָּה.

(7) יְחַוֵּה לַנָא פְּשַׁר חֶלְמָךְ.

(8) גֻּבְרַיָּא חַכִּימַיָּא אֲמַרוּ לְמִשְׁרֵהּ שְׂעָרָא מִן רֵאשִׁי.

Chapter 20

P. 108 Daniel 4:1–9

I, Nebuchadnezzar, was in my house. I saw a vision and it scared me. The visions of my head disturbed me. A decree was issued from me to bring all the wise men of Babylon before me in order to inform me the interpretation of the dream. Then the magicians and Chaldeans entered, and I said the dream before them, but they did not inform me of its interpretation. At last Daniel, whose name is Belteshazzar like the name of my god and in whom is the spirit of the holy God, entered before me, and I said the dream before him: "Belteshazzar, chief magician, in whom I know is the spirit of the holy God and no secret troubles you, tell the visions of my dream which I saw and its intepretation. I saw visions of my head, and behold a tree in the midst of the earth, and its height was great. The tree grew and its height reached heaven. Its foliage was beautiful, and in it was food for everything. Animal(s) of the field sought shade under it, and birds of the sky dwelt in its branches."

P. 109

מְהַלְכִין	הלך	active participle masculine plural
לְהַחֲוָיָה	חוה	infinitive
נְהַחֲוֵה	חוה	imperfect 1 common plural
הַשְׁפָּלָה	שפל	infinitive
הֶחֱסֵנוּ	חסן	imperative or perfect 3 masculine plural
לְהַשְׁנָיָה	שנה	infinitive
הוֹדַעְנָה	ידע	perfect 1 common plural
מְהוֹדְעִין	ידע	active participle masculine plural
מְהַנְזְקַת	נזק	active participle feminine singular
תְּהַנְזִק	נזק	imperfect 2 masculine singular or 3 feminine singular
הַצְלַח	צלח	perfect 3 masculine singular
מְהַחְצְפָה	חצף	active participle feminine singular
יְהַשְׁפֵּל	שפל	imperfect 3 masculine singular
הַרְגִּזוּ	רגז	imperative or perfect 3 masculine plural
הַרְגִּשׁוּ	רגש	imperative or perfect 3 masculine plural
הַשְׁכַּחַת	שכח	perfect 1 common singular
לְהַשְׁכָּחָה	שכח	infinitive
מְהַשְׁנֵא	שנה	active participle masculine singular

P. 110

Perfect	Imperfect	Participle	Imperative
הַקְרְבֵת	אֲהַקְרֵב	מְהַקְרֵב	הַקְרֵב
הַקְרְבְתְּ	תְּהַקְרֵב	מְהַקְרְבָה	הַקְרִבִי
הַקְרְבְתִּי	תְּהַקְרְבִין		
הַקְרֵב	יְהַקְרֵב	מְהַקְרְבִין	הַקְרִבוּ
הַקְרְבַת	תְּהַקְרֵב	מְהַקְרְבָן	הַקְרִבָה
הַקְרֵבְנָא	נְהַקְרֵב		
הַקְרֵבְתּוּן	תְּהַקְרְבוּן		
הַקְרֵבְתֵּן	תְּהַקְרְבָן	Infinitive הַקְרָבָה	
הַקְרִבוּ	יְהַקְרְבוּן		
הַקְרִבָה	יְהַקְרְבָן		

P. 110 (*cont.*)

(1) קָל קַרְנָא מָטֵא לִשְׁמַיָּא.

(2) אֲלוּ רוּחָא מְהַדֶּקֶת מָאנַיָּא תְּחוֹת הֵיכְלָא.

P. 111

(3) יִרְבֵּא שַׂעֲרָא כְּעָפִי.

(4) צִפְּרָא הַיְתִיו דִּהֲב מִן אִילָנָא.

(5) מִלַּת מַלְכָּא תְּדַחַל קַדִּישֵׁי בָּבֶל.

(6) חַרְטֻמַּיָּא דָּחֲלִין דִּי אֱלָהָא יְהַשְׁלֵט דָּנִיֵּאל עֲלֵיהֶם.

(7) אֲמַרוּ סָפְרַיָּא לְהַיְתָיָא פִּתְגָּמַיָּא קֳדָם אֱלָהָא.

Chapter 21

P. 115   Daniel 4:10–19

I saw in visions of my head, and behold a holy one was descending from heaven. It called and said thus, "Cut down the tree; the animal(s) will flee from under it; but leave its roots in the ground, and it will be watered with dew of heaven. Its heart will be changed (lit. "they will change") from (that of) men, and an animal's heart will be given to it until the living things will know that the Most High is mighty (i.e. rules) over the kingdom of man and gives it to whomever He wants." This is the dream King Nebuchadnezzar saw, and you,

P. 116   Belteshazzar, say the interpretation inasmuch as all the wise men of my kingdom are not able to inform me of the interpretation, but you are able since the spirit of the holy God is in you." Then Daniel, whose name is Belteshazzar, was appalled for an hour. The king answered and said, "Belteshazzar, do not let the dream and its interpretation disturb you." Belteshazzar answered and said, "The dream and its interpretation are for your enemies. The tree which you saw, which grew and reached heaven with food for everything in it, under it dwelling animal(s) of the field—you are it, O king, for you grew and your greatness grew and reached heaven."

טְאֵב	טוב	G perfect 3 masculine singular
דַּע	ידע	G imperative 2 masculine singular
מִנְתַּן	נתן	G infinitive
יִקְרוֹן	קרא	G imperfect 3 masculine plural
יְהוֹבְדוּן	אבד	H imperfect 3 masculine plural
יָדַע	ידע	G active participle masculine singular
יַחְלְפוּן	חלף	G imperfect 3 masculine plural
תִּפְּלוּן	נפל	G imperfect 2 masculine plural

הַדְּקֶת	דקק	H perfect 3 feminine singular
הוֹתֵב	יתב	H perfect 3 masculine singular
שָׂם	שׂים	G perfect 3 masculine singular
מְהָקֵים	קום	H participle masculine singular
אֶבְעֵא	בעה	G imperfect 1 common singular
פֻּקוּ	נפק	G imperative masculine plural
אֱתוֹ	אתה	G perfect 3 masculine plural
הֵיבֵל	יבל	H perfect 3 masculine singular
נֵאמַר	אמר	G imperfect 1 common plural
הוֹבָדָה	אבד	H infinitive
יִנְדְּעוּן	ידע	G imperfect 3 masculine plural
יִפֵּל	נפל	G imperfect 3 masculine singular

P. 117

P. 118

(1) אֱדַיִן יְדַעוּ חַרְטֻמַיָּא דִּי שְׁמַע מַלְכָּא חֶלְמָא.

(2) אֲנָה כָּהֵל לְכַפָּתָה גֻּשְׁמָא עַל רֵאשׁ טוּרָא.

(3) חָכְמָה דָמְיָה לְנוּרָא יָקֶדְתָּא.

(4) פִּשְׁרָא חַבַּלַת כָּל דִּי שְׁמַעוּ לֵהּ.

(5) בְּנָה גְבַר חַד בַּיִת וּמְהַדֵּק לֵהּ גְּבַר אָחֳרָן.

(6) שַׂעֲרִי מִצְטַבַּע בְּטַל.

(7) פְּשַׁר חֶלְמָא שַׁנִּי לְבַב מַלְכָּא.

(8) נְחַת קַדִּישׁ דִּי שְׁמַע מִלַּת עֶלְיָא.

(9) גָּדּוּ אִילָנָא דִּי מְטָה לִשְׁמַיָּא.

(10) אֲזַלְנָא לְשַׁבָּחָה לְהֹם.

Chapter 22

P. 120 Daniel 4:20–34

"And that which the king saw, a holy one descending from heaven and saying, 'Cut down the tree and destroy it, but leave its roots in the earth, and let it be watered with dew of heaven'"—this is the interpretation which reached the king: They will drive you out from mankind, and your dwelling will be with the animal(s) of the field, and they will wet you with dew from the sky. And seven times will pass by you until you will know that the Most High rules over the kingdom of man and He gives it to whomever He wishes. And what they said to leave the roots of the tree—your kingdom is enduring for you because you will know that heaven reigns." Everything reached (i.e. happened to) King

Nebuchadnezzar. At the end of twelve months he was walking at Babylon's royal palace. The king answered and said, "Is this not the great Babylon which I built as a royal house?" The word was in the king's mouth when a voice fell from heaven, "To you they say, O King Nebuchadnezzar: 'The kingdom has passed away from you, and they are driving you out from men. And your dwelling will be with the animal(s) of the field, and seven times will pass over you until you know that the Most High is ruler over the kingdom of man, and He will give it to whomever He wishes." At that time he was driven from men, and his flesh was watered from heavenly dew. And at the end of the days, I, Nebuchadnezzar—I lifted my eyes to heaven, and my knowledge returned to me. And I blessed the Most High, and I praised the Ever-living, whose dominion is an eternal dominion and whose kingdom is forever. And He does as He wishes with the host of heaven and those who dwell on earth. And there is none who says to Him, "What did you do?" At that time my knowledge returned to me and I was restored to my kingdom, and much greatness was added to me.

P. 121

הַנְעֵל	עלל	H perfect 3 masculine singular
הֻעַל	עלל	H passive perfect 3 masculine singular
לֶהֱוֵא	הוה	G imperfect 3 masculine singular
הֲווֹ	הוה	G perfect 3 masculine plural
הַסִּקוּ	סלק	H perfect 3 masculine plural
הַנְסָקָה	סלק	H infinitive
מַהְלְכִין	הלך	H active participle masculine plural
מְהַלֵּךְ	הלך	D active participle masculine singular
יְהָךְ	הלך	G imperfect 3 masculine singular
יְכֵלְתָּ	יכל	G perfect 2 masculine singular
יָכֵל	יכל	G participle masculine singular
תֻּכַל	יכל	G imperfect 2 masculine singular or 3 feminine singular
יוּכַל	יכל	G imperfect 3 masculine singular
כָּהֲלִין	(יכל) כהל	G active participle masculine plural

P. 122

(1) כָּהֲנַיָּא טְרַדוּ פָּחֲתָא מִן קִרְיְתָא.

(2) מְדוֹר חֵיוָתָא בְּאִילָן.

(3) בְּסוֹפָא דִּי יוֹמָא עֲדָה חֵילֵהּ.

(4) נְטַל חַרְטֻמַּא יְדוֹהִי וּבָרֵךְ צַלְמָא דִּי כְסַף.

(5) תָּבֵת לְהַנְסָקָה אִגַּרְתָּא לְרֵאשׁ טוּרָא.

Chapter 23

P. 125 Daniel 5:1–12

King Belshazar made a big meal and drank wine. Under the influence of the wine Belshazar said to bring the gold and silver vessels which Nebuchadnezzar, his father, had brought out from the temple which was in Jerusalem and they would drink from them. Then they brought the gold vessels which they had brought out from the temple of the house of God which is in Jerusalem, and they praised the gods of gold and silver, copper, iron, wood, and stone. At that time, fingers of a human hand came out and wrote on the wall of the king's palace, and the king saw the palm of the hand which was writing. Then the king—his splendor changed and his thoughts disturbed him. The king called with strength to bring the Chaldeans. The king answered and said to the wise men of Babylon that, "Any man who will read this writing and tell me its interpretation will wear purple and rule third in the kingdom. Then all the wise men of the king entered, but they were not able to read the writing and make its interpretation known to the king. Then King Belshazar was greatly disturbed, and his splendor changed. On account of the king's words, the queen entered

P. 126 the drinking house. The queen answered and said, "O king, live forever. Do not let your thoughts disturb you nor your splendor be changed. There is a man in your kingdom in whom is the spirit of the holy God, and illumination and wisdom like the wisdom of the gods was found in him in the days of your father. And King Nebuchadnezzar, your father—your father, the king, established him as chief of the magicians and Chaldeans inasmuch as great spirit and knowledge of interpreting dreams was found in him, in Daniel, whom the king named Belteshazzar. Now let Daniel be called, and he will tell the interpretation."

P. 126 *Rewrite* *Direct Object*	P. 127 *Rearrange* *Sentence*	*Translate*
1. לְחַרְטֻמַיָּא יָת חַרְטֻמַיָּא	כְּפַת מַלְכָּא חַרְטֻמַיָּא. חַרְטֻמַיָּא כְּפַת מַלְכָּא.	The king bound the magicians.
2. לְחֶלְמָא חֶלְמָא	פְּשַׁר דָּנִיֵּאל יָת חֶלְמָא. דָּנִיֵּאל פְּשַׁר יָת חֶלְמָא.	Daniel interpreted the dream.
3. יָת כָּהֲנַיָּא כָּהֲנַיָּא	גֻּבְרַיָּא קְטַלוּ לְכָהֲנַיָּא. לְכָהֲנַיָּא קְטַלוּ גֻּבְרַיָּא.	The men killed the priests.

P. 128

שְׁתוֹ חֲמַר עִם לַחְמָא. (1)

אֶצְבְּעָא רַבְּתָא כָּתְבַת פִּתְגָּם. (2)

מָאנֵי דַּהֲבָא הִשְׁתְּכַחוּ בְּבֵית אֱלָהּ. (3)

קְרָא כָּהֲנָא לְעַמְמָא לְצַלָּיָה. (4)

לִבְשַׁת מַלְכְּתָא דְּהַב עַל רֵאשַׁהּ. (5)

בַּהֲלוּ רַעְיוֹנַיָא תַּקִּיפַיָא לִי. (6)

כְּתַל בַּיְתָא אָע. (7)

זִיו חָכְמְתֵהּ נְפַק לְכֹל אַרְעָא. (8)

Chapter 24

P. 131 Daniel 5:13–29

Then Daniel was brought in before the king. The king answered and said to Daniel, "You are Daniel from the Jews that the king, my father, brought from Judah. And I have heard concerning you that the spirit of God is in you and much wisdom is found in you. And now the wise men have been brought in before me in order that they read this writing and to inform me of its interpretation, but they are not able to tell the interpretation of the thing. And I have heard concerning you that you are able to give interpretations. Now if you are able to read the writing and to tell me its interpretation, you will wear purple and rule third in the kingdom." Then Daniel answered and said before the king, "I will read the writing to the king, and I will tell him the meaning. You, O King—God Most High gave the kingdom and greatness and glory to Nebuchadnezzar, your father. And on account of the greatness which He gave him, all the peoples were afraid before him. He would kill whomever he wanted, and he would raise up whomever he wanted, and he would lower whomever he

P. 132 wanted. And when his heart and his spirit were elevated, he was brought down from the throne of his kingdom and they removed the glory from him. He was driven out from men, and his heart was like (that) with (the) animal(s); and his body was watered by the dew of heaven until he knew that God Most High was ruler over the kingdom of man and he would raise over it whomever He wished. And you, his son, Belshazzar, did not lower your heart although you knew all of this. You raised yourself up over the Master of Heaven, and they brought the vessels of His house before you, and you and your chiefs drink wine in them and you praised the gods of silver and gold, copper, iron, wood, and stone who do not see nor hear nor know. Then a hand was sent from before him and this writing inscribed. And this is the writing which was inscribed: *meney meney teqel ufarsin.* This is the interpretation of the thing: *meney*—God has counted your kingdom and completed it; *teqel*—you have been weighed and found lacking; *peres*—your kingdom has been divided and given to Media and Persia." Then Belshazaar said, and they clothed Daniel in purple and proclaimed concerning him that he would be third ruler in the kingdom.

	שְׁלִיחַ	שלח	G participle or perfect 3 masculine singular
	יְהִיב	יהב	G participle or perfect 3 masculine singular
	קְטִילַת	קטל	G perfect 3 feminine singular
	מְפָרַשׁ	פרשׁ	D participle masculine singular
	עֲשִׁית	עשׁת	G participle or perfect 3 masculine singular
P. 133	מְעָרַב	ערב	D participle masculine singular
	שִׂים	שׂים	G participle or perfect 3 masculine singular
	הֻסֲפַת	יסף	H perfect 3 feminine singular
	יְהִיבַת	יהב	G perfect 3 feminine singular
	חֲשִׁיבִין	חשׁב	G participle masculine plural
	זְקִיף	זקף	G participle or perfect 3 masculine singular
	זְהִירִין	זהר	G participle masculine plural
	שֻׂמַת	שׂים	G perfect 3 feminine singular
	דְּחִיל	דחל	G participle or perfect 3 masculine singular
	גְּמִיר	גמר	G participle or perfect 3 masculine singular
	יְהִיבוּ	יהב	G perfect 3 masculine plural
	פְּרִיסַת	פרס	G perfect 3 feminine singular
	מְכַפְּתִין	כפת	D participle masculine plural
	שְׁלִם	שׁלם	G participle or perfect 3 masculine singular

P. 134

(1) אִגַּרְתָּה כְּתִיבַת בִּירוּשְׁלֶם.

(2) הוּא מְהָקֵים הֵיכְלָא עַל טוּרָא.

(3) כַּרְסָא הָנְחַת מִן שְׁמַיָּא.

(4) חֵלֶם מָרֵא פֻּשַׁר תַּמָּה.

(5) אֱלָהַיָּה רַבַּיָּא מְשַׁבְּחִין עַל אַרְעָא.

(6) שְׁאַלוּ לֵהּ כַּסְפָּא לְהַיְתָיָה לְהֵיכְלָא רַבָּא.

(7) דָּנִיֵּאל הֲוָה שַׁלִּיט וִיקָרֵהּ שְׁוִי עִם מֶלֶךְ.

(8) יְהַב אֱלָהּ רְבוּ לִמְדִינְתָּא וּלְפֶחָתֵהּ.

(9) שְׁלִים אַרְעָא בְּיוֹמִין שִׁת.

Chapter 25

P. 137 Daniel 5:30–6:10

In that night, Belshazzar, king of the Chaldeans, was killed; and Darius the Mede received the kingdom at the age of 62. It was pleasing before Darius to establish 120 satraps over the kingdom who would be in the whole kingdom, and above them were 3 chiefs, of whom Daniel was one, that these satraps report to them so that the king not suffer damage. Then this Daniel was distinguishing himself over the chiefs and the satraps inasmuch as an excellent spirit was in him, and the king intended to establish him over the entire kingdom. Then the chiefs and the satraps sought to find a pretext against Daniel, but they were not able to find any pretext, since he was faithful and no negligence was found concerning him. Then those men said that, "We will not find any pretext in Daniel except if we find a pretext concerning him in his God's law." Then these chiefs and satraps assembled before the king and said thus, "Darius, O king, live forever! All the chiefs of the kingdom and the satraps and the governors have taken counsel to establish a royal statute that anyone who seeks a petition from any God or man except from you, O king, for 30 days will be thrown into the pit of lions. Now, O king, write a decree (lit. writing) that can not be changed like the law of Media and Persia which will not pass away." Thereupon Darius wrote the decree.

P. 138	מִתְיְהֵב	יהב	G active participle masculine singular
	הִתְמְלִי	מלא	G perfect 3 masculine singular
	יְצַטַּבַּע	צבע	D imperfect 3 masculine singular
	הִתְחָרַךְ	חרך	D perfect 3 masculine singular
	מִתְנַשְּׂא	נשא	D active participle feminine singular
	הָזְדְּמִנְתּוּן	זמן	G perfect 2 masculine plural
	מִשְׂתַּכַּל	שכל	D active participle masculine singular
	יִתְקְרֵי	קרא	G imperfect 3 masculine singular
	תִּשְׁתְּבִק	שבק	G imperfect 2 masculine or 3 feminine singular
	תִּתְעַבְדוּן	עבד	G imperfect 2 masculine plural
	הִשְׁתְּכַחַת	שכח	G perfect 3 feminine singular
	יִתְעֲבֵד	עבד	G imperfect 3 masculine singular
	יִשְׁתַּמְעוּן	שמע	G imperfect 3 masculine plural
	הִתְנַדַּבוּ	נדב	D perfect 3 masculine plural
	יִתְבַּקַּר	בקר	D imperfect 3 masculine singular

P. 139	מִתְכַּנְּשִׁין	כנש	D active participle masculine plural
	יִשְׁתַּנֵּא	שנה	D imperfect 3 masculine singular
	הִתְגְּזֶרֶת	גזר	G perfect 3 feminine singular
	יִתְבְּנֵא	בנה	G imperfect 3 masculine singular
	תִּתְחַבַּל	חבל	D imperfect 2 masculine singular or 3 feminine singular
	הִתְרְחִצוּ	רחץ	G perfect 3 masculine plural

(1) אַבָּא חַכִּימָא כְּתַב קְיָם בְּלֵילְיָא.

(2) אַרְיֵא תַּקִּיף נְפַל לְגֻבָּא רַבָּא.

(3) אֲחַשְׁדַּרְפְּנַיָּא הִתְכַּנַּשׁוּ קֳדָם כָּרְסָאָא.

(4) פִּתְגָמָא קַבֵּל בְּקִרְיְתָא מָרְדְתָּא.

(5) יַצִּיבָא כָּהֲנָא מְהֵימְנָא יְשַׁפַּר לְעַמְמַיָּא.

(6) בְּעָה פֶּחֲתָא עִלָּה לְקַטָּלָה לְגֻבְרַיָּא.

P. 140

Chapter 26

P. 144 Daniel 6:11–29

And when Daniel knew that the decree had been written, he went into his house and he knelt, praying before his God three times a day, just as he had done previously. Then those men assembled and found Daniel praying before his God. Then they approached and said before the king concerning the royal prohibition, "Did you not write a prohibition that any man who seeks from any god or man except from you, O king, for 30 days will be thrown into the lions' pit?" The king answered and said, "The thing is certain, like the law of Media and Persia that will not pass away." Then they answered and said before the king that, "Daniel, who is from the children of the exiles of Judah, has not paid attention to you, O king, and to the prohibition that you wrote; and he prays 3 times a day." Then when the king heard the thing, it was very distressing to him. Then those men gathered before the king and said to the king, "Know, O king, that it is a law of Media and Persia not to change any prohibition or statute which the king establishes." Then the king said and they brought Daniel and threw into the pit of lions. The king answered and said to Daniel, "Your God, whom you serve, He will save you." And a stone was brought and put over the mouth of the pit. Then the king went to his palace and his sleep fled (over) him. Then the king arose and in his distress he went to the pit of the lions, and as he approached the pit, the king answered Daniel and said to

Daniel, "Daniel, servant of the living God: your God, whom you serve — was He able to save you from the lions?" Then Daniel spoke with the king, "O king, live forever. My God sent His angel, and he closed the lions' mouth, and they did not harm me inasmuch as I was found innocent (lit. innocence was found to me) before Him; and even before you, O king, I have not done damage." Then the king was very pleased (lit. it was very good over the king), and he said to bring Daniel up from the pit. And Daniel was brought up from the pit, and no harm was found on him since he had faith in his God. And the king said and they brought those men who had accused Daniel and threw them, their sons, and their wives into the pit of the lions; and they had not reached the bottom of the pit when the lions overpowered them. Then King Darius wrote to all the peoples who dwelt in all the land, "May your peace be great. A decree is issued before me that in every dominion of my kingdom they will fear the God of Daniel, since He is the living God and enduring forever; and He saves His kingdom which will not be damaged. And he makes signs in heaven and on earth, as He saved Daniel from the lions." And this Daniel prospered in the kingdom of Darius and in the kingdom of Cyrus, the Persian.

נִפְקָה	נפק	G	הַב	יהב	G
הֵיבֵל	יבל	H	מֶעְבַּד	עבד	G
קָאֵם	קום	G	תְּקַבְּלוּן	קבל	D
מְשֵׁיזֵב	עזב	Š	הֻסַּק	סלק	H
יִפֵּל	נפל	G	דָּאֲנִין	דין	G
יְדִיעַ	ידע	G	מְכַפְּתִין	כפת	D
אַחֲוָיֵה	חוה	A	תּוּכַל	יכל	G
יִשְׁתַּנֵּא	שנה	Dt	מַנִּיתָ	מנה	D
הִתְחָרַךְ	חרך	Dt	פֵּקוּ	נפק	G
הַנְעֵל	עלל	H	חֲזֵיתוּן	חזה	G
אֶשְׁתַּנִּי	שנה	At	אֲקִימֵה	קום	A
שֵׁיצִיא	יצא	Š	מְבָרַךְ	ברך	D
הֲוָת	הוה	G	יִשְׁתַּכְלְלוּן	כלל	Št
פְּתִיחוּ	פתח	G	בְּעֵינָא	בעה	G
אַנְדַּע	ידע	G	הוֹתֵב	יתב	H
תְּהַשְׁכַּח	שכח	H	מֵמַר	אמר	G
תְּהוֹבַר	אבד	H	יְשֵׁיזִב	עזב	Š

P. 145

P. 146

הוה	לֶהֱוֺן	G	אתה	הַיְתִי	H
קרא	יִתְקְרִי	Gt	קרב	מְהַקְרְבִין	H
קום	יְהָקֵים	H	רעע	תְּרֹעַ	G
שׂים	שָׂמֵת	G	ידע	יְהוֹדַע	H
עדה	תֶּעְדֵּא	G	ענה	עֲנוֹ	G
בנה	תִּתְבְּנֵא	Gt	דקק	הַדֶּקֶת	H
חוה	נְחַוֵּא	D	הלך	יְהָךְ	G
שנה	יְשַׁנּוֹן	D	רום	הִתְרוֹמַמְתָּ	polel-t

יְהָקֵים is H, יְקוּם is G; both are imperfect 3 masculine singular.

לְהַנְעָלָה and לְהֶעָלָה are both H infinitives of עלל; the נ in לְהַנְעָלָה is a result of nasalization.

מִתְבָּהַל is a Dt active participle (there is no dagesh because ה is guttural), whereas הִתְבְּהָלָה is Gt (infinitive).

P. 147 אָמַר is an active participle; אֲמַר is perfect (3 masculine singular)

תִּתְיְהִב is Gt, תִּתְחַבַּל is Dt (both are imperfect 2 masculine singular)

מִתְנַשְּׂאָה is Dt, מִתְעֲבֵד is Gt (both are active participles, though מִתְנַשְּׂאָה is feminine and מִתְעֲבֵד masculine).

מִתְקַטְּלִין is Dt (active participle mp); לְהִתְקְטָלָה is Gt (infinitive).

הִתְגְּזֶרֶת is Ht; אִתְגְּזֶרֶת is At.

P. 148

(1) אַבָּא שֵׁיזִיב בְּרֵהּ מִן חֵיוַת בָּרָא.

(2) סָפְרָא שַׁכְלֵל עֲבִידְתָּא עַל מַלְכוּתָא רְבִיעָיְתָא.

(3) מַלְכָּא הַרְגֵּשׁ עַמָּא לְשַׁבָּחָא לֶאֱלָהָא בְּלֵילְיָא.

(4) בְּעֵית לְמִנְפַּק מִן קִרְיְתָא כְּדִי מַלְכָּא שָׂם אֶסְרָא דֵּךְ.

(5) סִלְקֵת עַל טוּרָא כְּדִי קְרִיב אַרְיֵהּ.

(6) אֲנַחְנָא סָגְרִין פֻּם צַלְמָא.

(7) יְהוּדָיֵא הַצְלַחוּ כְּדִי טְרִידוּ לְגָלוּ.

(8) אֱלָהָא חַיָּא מַלֵּל מִקַּדְמַת דְּנָה.

Chapter 27
P. 149 Daniel 7:1

> In the first year of Belshazzar, king of Babylon, Daniel saw a dream and visions of his head on his bed. Then he wrote (down) the dream, a complete account; he said:

P. 150

חֲזָה	חזה	G perfect 3 masculine singular
כְּתַב	כתב	G perfect 3 masculine singular
אֲמַר	אמר	G perfect 3 masculine singular

חֲדָה   אַחַת (or רִאשׁוֹנָה)

רֵאשֵׁה   רֹאשׁוֹ

חֶלְמָא   הַחֲלוֹם

מִלִּין   מִלִּים

> (2) Daniel answered and said, "I saw in a night vision, and behold 4 winds of the heaven were stirring up the great sea. (3) And 4 great animals, each different from the other, were coming up from the sea.

P. 151

עָנֵה	ענה	G active participle masculine singular
חָזֵה	חזה	G active participle masculine singular
הֲוֵית	הוה	G perfect 1 common singular
סָלְקָן	סלק	G active participle feminine plural
שָׁנְיָן	שנה	G active participle feminine plural
מְגִיחָן	גוח	A active participle feminine plural

the subject of מְגִיחָן is רוּחֵי

אֹמֵר Hebrew = אֲמַר

חָזֵה הֲוֵית means "was seeing" (i.e., saw)

P. 152 (4) The first was like a lion, and it had wings like an eagle. I saw until its wings were torn out and it was lifted from the earth and set up on feet like a man, and a human heart was given to it. (5) And behold, another, second animal, resembling a bear; and it was raised up on one side, and there were 3 ribs in its mouth between its teeth. And thus they said to it, "Arise, eat much flesh." (6) After this I saw and, behold, another like a panther, and it had 4 bird wings on its back; and the animal had 4 heads, and dominion was given it.

P. 152 (*cont.*)

עִלָּעוֹת	עִלְעִין
אוֹמְרִים	אָמְרִין
לְחֵיוָה	לְחֵיוָתָא
נֶשֶׁר	נְשַׁר

P. 153

מְרִיטוּ	מרט	G passive perfect 3 masculine plural
נְטִילַת	נטל	G passive perfect 3 feminine singular
הֳקִימַת	קום	H passive perfect 3 feminine singular
דָּמְיָה	דמה	G active participle feminine singular
יְהִיב	יהב	G passive participle perfect 3 masculine singular

subject — חֵיוָה

P. 154 (7) After this I saw in night visions, and behold a fourth animal, frightening and frightful and very strong; and it had big iron teeth, eating and smashing and trampling on the remnant with its feet. And it was different from any of the animals that were before it, and it had 10 horns. (8) I looked at its horns and, behold, another, small horn went up among them, and three of the first horns were uprooted from before it; and behold, there were eyes like human eyes on this horn and a mouth speaking great things.

רַבְרְבָן	plural feminine
חֵיוָתָא	plural feminine

P. 155

מִשְׂתַּכַּל הֲוֵית	I was looking
פֻם	subject
מְמַלִּל	predicate (or verb)
רַבְרְבָן	object

דְּחִילָה	דחל	G passive participle feminine singular
רָפְסָה	רפס	G active participle feminine singular
מְשַׁנְּיָה	שנה	D active participle feminine singular
מִשְׂתַּכַּל	שכל	Dt active participle masculine singular
סִלְקַת	סלק	G perfect 3 feminine singular
אֶתְעֲקַרָה	עקר	Gt perfect 3 feminine plural

subject — תְּלָת קַרְנַיָּא

G   אָכְלָה
A   מַדְּקָה   } both are feminine singular active participles

P. 156

גַּפִּין דִּי נְשַׁר לַהּ   it had wings of an eagle

לַהּ גַּפִּין אַרְבַּע דִּי עוֹף   it had 4 wings of a bird

שִׁנַּיִן דִּי פַרְזֶל לַהּ רַבְרְבָן   it had large iron teeth

(9) I saw until thrones were put in place, and one old of days sat, his dress like white snow and the hair of his head like pure wool. His throne was flames of fire, its wheels burning fire. (10) A river of fire was flowing and going out from before Him; a thousand thousands served Him, and a myriad of myriads rose before Him, the judgment sat and books were open.

Passive verbs: פְּתִיחוּ, רְמִיו

P. 157 Active participles: נָפֵק, נָגֵד, דָּלִק, חָזֵה

Verbs   הֲוֵית   הוה   G perfect 1 common singular

יְתִב   יתב   G perfect 3 masculine singular

יְשַׁמְּשׁוּנֵהּ   שמש   D imperfect 3 masculine plural

+ 3 masculine singular pronominal suffix

יְקוּמוּן   קום   G imperfect 3 masculine plural

Suffixes   כָּרְסָוָן   feminine plural

לְבוּשֵׁהּ   3 masculine singular

גַּלְגִּלּוֹהִי   3 masculine singular

שְׁבִיבִין   masculine plural

דִּינָא   masculine singular determined

P. 158 (11) I saw, then, because of the sound of the great words which the horn was speaking; I saw until the animal was killed and its body destroyed and given over to the burning fire. (12) And the rest of the animals—they removed their dominion, but length of life was given to them until a time and a season.

קָל = Hebrew קוֹל

P. 158 (*cont.*)

קְטִילַת	קטל	G
הוּבַד	אבד	H

מְמַלְלָה	מלל	D active participle feminine singular
הֶעְדִּיו	עדה	H perfect 3 masculine plural

P. 159

מִלַּיָּא	masculine plural determined
אֶשָּׁא	masculine singular determined
גִּשְׁמַהּ	feminine singular possessive
רַבְרְבָתָא	feminine plural determined

חֵיוְתָא is singular, חֵיוָתָא is plural (both are feminine determined)

(13) I saw in night visions and behold (one) like a son of man (i.e. human being) was coming with the clouds of the sky; and he reached the Ancient of Days, and they brought him near before Him. (14) And dominion was given to him, and glory and kingship and all the peoples, the nations and the languages served Him. His dominion is an eternal dominion which will not pass, and His kingdom one which will not be destroyed.

לֵילְיָא has a masculine singular determined suffix

אָתֵה הֲוָה — "was coming"

מַלְכוּתֵהּ is מַלְכוּ with a 3 masculine singular possessive suffix

P. 160

אָתֵה	אתה	G active participle masculine singular
מְטָה	מטה	G perfect 3 masculine singular
יֶעְדֵּה	עדה	G imperfect 3 masculine singular
תִּתְחַבַּל	חבל	Dt imperfect 3 feminine singular
יִפְלְחוּן	פלח	G imperfect 3 masculine plural
הַקְרְבוּהִי	קרב	H perfect 3 masculine plural + 3 masculine singular

הַקְרְבוּהִי — the subject is indefinite

כֹּל עַמְמַיָּא אֻמַיָּא וְלִשָּׁנַיָּא — יִפְלְחוּן

(15) My spirit—I, Daniel—became distressed in the midst of a sheath (i.e. my body), and the visons of my head disturbed me. (16) I approached one of those standing before me, and I sought certainty from him concerning all this. And he said to me and informed me of the thing's interpretation: (17) "These great animals which are 4—4 kings will arise from the earth; (18) and holy ones of the Most High will receive the kingdom, and they will possess the kingdom forever and forever."

קְרֵבֵת	קרב	G perfect 1 common singular
אֶבְעֵה	בעה	G imperfect 1 common singular
יְהוֹדְעַנַּנִי	ידע	H imperfect 3 masculine singular + 1 common singular
יְקַבְּלוּן	קבל	D imperfect 3 masculine plural
קָאֲמַיָּא	קום	G active participle masculine plural determined

P. 162   אִנִּין — they (feminine plural)

(19) Then I wanted to make certain concerning the fourth animal, which was different from all of them, more frightening with teeth of iron and claws of copper, eating, smashing, and trampling the rest with its feet. (20) And on the ten horns which were on its head and the other one which went up and before which three fell—that horn had eyes and a mouth speaking great things, and its appearance was bigger than its companions. (21) I saw, and that horn made war with the holy ones and prevailed over them. (22) Until the Ancient of Days came and judgment was given to the holy ones of the Most High, for the time had arrived and the holy ones possessed the kingdom.

P. 163   דִּכֵּן   demonstrative pronoun feminine singular (it can also be masculine)

צְבִית	—	צבה	G perfect 1 common singular
שָׁנְיָה	—	שנה	G active participle feminine singular
דְּחִילָה	—	דחל	G passive participle feminine singular
מַדֲּקָה	—	דקק	A active participle feminine singular
סִלְקַת	—	סלק	G perfect 3 feminine singular
נְפַלָה	—	נפל	G perfect 3 feminine plural
מְטָה	—	מטה	G perfect 3 masculine singular

P. 164   תְּלָת קַרְנַיָּא

(23) Thus he said: The fourth animal—there will be a fourth kingdom on the earth which will be different form all the kingdoms, and it will devour the entire earth and trample it and smash it. (24) And the 10 horns—from the kingdom will arise ten kings, and after them will arise another, and he will be different from the earlier ones and will lower three kings. (25) And he will speak words against the Most High and will wear out the holy ones of the Most High, and he will intend to change times and law. And they will be given into his hand for a time and times and half a time. (26) And he will sit in judgment and they will remove his dominion to be destroyed and killed until the end. (27) And the kingdom and dominion and greatness of the kingdoms under all heaven is given to the people of the holy ones of the Most High. His kingdom is an eternal kingdom, and all dominions will worship and be obedient to Him.

P. 165	הוה	תֶּחֱוֵה	G imperfect 3 feminine singular
	יהב	יִתְיַהֲבוּן	Gt imperfect 3 masculine plural
	יהב	יְהִיבַת	G passive perfect 3 feminine singular
	שפל	יְהַשְׁפִּל	H imperfect 3 masculine singular

	יְמַלִּל	D
	יְבַלֵּא	D
	יִסְבַּר	G

	שנה	לְהַשְׁנָיָה	
	שמד	לְהַשְׁמָדָה	all are H infinitives
	אבד	לְהוֹבָדָה	

P. 166	פלח	יִפְלְחוּן	G
	שמע	יִשְׁתַּמְּעוּן	Dt
	עדה	יְהַעְדּוּן	H

(28) Here is the end of the word. I, Daniel, my ideas disturbed me very much, and my spendor changed over me. And I guarded the thing in my heart.

בהל	יְבַהֲלֻנַּנִי	D imperfect 3 masculine plural + 1 common singular
שנה	יִשְׁתַּנּוֹן	Dt imperfect 3 masculine plural
נטר	נִטְרֵת	G perfect 1 common singular

Chapter 28

Pp. 168–69

אֲנָה בַּר רָכָב בַּר פַּנַמֻו מֶלֶךְ שַׁמְאָל עֶבֶד תִּגְלַתְפְּלֵיסֶר מָרֵא רַבְעֵי אַרְקָא.
בְּצֶדֶק אֲבִי וּבְצֶדְקִי הוֹשַׁבַנִי מָרֵאִי רַכְבְּאֵל וּמָרֵאִי תִּגְלַתְפְּלֵיסֶר עַל כָּרְסֵא אֲבִי.
וּבֵית אֲבִי עֲמַל מִן כָּל. וְרָצֶת בְּגַלְגֻל מָרֵאִי מֶלֶךְ אַשּׁוּר בְּמִצְעַת מַלְכִן
רַבְרְבִן בַּעֲלֵי כְסַף וּבַעֲלֵי זְהַב. וְאַחֲזֶת בֵּית אֲבִי וְהֵיטִבְתֵּהּ מִן בֵּית חַד
מַלְכִן רַבְרְבִן. וְהִתְנָאֲבוּ אַחַי מַלְכַיָּא לְכָל מַה טָבַת בַּיְתִי. וּבֵי טָב
לִישֵׁהּ לַאֲבָהַי מַלְכֵי שַׁמְאָל. הָא בֵית כַּלַמֻו לְהֹם פָּהָא בֵית שִׁתְוָא לְהֹם
וְהָא בֵית כֵּיצָא. וַאֲנָה בְּנֵית בַּיְתָא זְנָה.

I am Bar Rakib, son of Panamuwa, king of Sam'al, servant of Tiglath-Pileser, the master of the four quarters of the earth. Because of my father's righteousness and my (own) righteousness, my master Rakib-el and my master Tiglath-Pileser seated me on my father's throne. And my father's house toiled more than all others, and I ran in the wheel of my master, the king of Assyria, in the midst of many kings, owners of silver and owners of gold. And I grasped my father's house and made it better than the house of any of the great kings. And my brothers, the kings, envied all the goodness of my house. And there was no good house for my fathers, the kings of Sam'al. Behold, the house of Kilamuwa was theirs, and behold, the winter house was theirs and the summer house. But I built this house.

P. 172

לְכָה הֶתָיַת טַמֵי עֻזִּיָּה מֶלֶךְ יְהוּדָה וְלָא לְמִפְתַּח.

Hither were brought the bones of Uzziah, king of Judah. Do not open.

Pp. 173–174

דְּכִירִין לְטָב יוֹסֵה וְעִירוֹן וְחִזְקִיוֹ בְּנוֹהִ דְּחַלְפִי. כָּל מַן דְּיָהֵב פְּלֹגוּ בֵּן גְּבַר לְחַבְרֵיהּ
הִי אָמַר לִשָּׁן בִּישׁ עַל חַבְרֵיהּ לְעַמְמַיָּה הִי גָּנֵיב צְבוּתֵיהּ דְּחַבְרֵיהּ הִי מַן דְּגָלֵי רָזָא
דְּקַרְתָּא לְעַמְמַיָּה דִּין דְּעֵינוֹהִ מְשׁוֹטְטָן בְּכָל אַרְעָה וְחָמֵי סְתִירָתָה הוּא יִתֵּן אַפּוֹהּ
בְּגַבְרָה הַהוּ וּבְזַרְעֵיהּ וַיַעֲקוֹר יָתֵיהּ מִן תְּחוֹת שׁוּמַיָּה. וְיֵמְרוּן כָּל עַמָּה אָמֵן וְאָמֵן
סֶלָה. רַבִּי יוֹסֵה בֵּן חַלְפִי חִזְקִיוֹ בֵּן חַלְפִי דְּכִירִין לְטָב. דַּרְגֵּי סַגִּי
אִנּוּן עֲבַדוּ לִשְׁמֵהּ דְּרַחֲמָנָה שָׁלוֹם.

May Yose and Iron and Hezekiah, the sons of Halpy, be remembered for good. Whoever gives (i.e. makes) discord between a man and his comrade, speaking (with an) evil tongue concerning his comrade to the peoples (i.e. foreigners) or stealing his comrade's property, or whoever reveals the city's secret to the peoples—the Judge whose eyes wander over the whole earth and sees hidden things will direct His anger against that man and against his seed (descendants), and He will uproot him from under heaven. And let all the people say, "Amen, amen, selah." May Rabbi Yose, son of Halpy, (and) Hezekiah, son of Halpy, be remembered for good. They made many stairs for the name of the Merciful One. Peace.

Chapter 29
Pp. 176–77 (lines 1–3)

אֶל מָרְאַן בָּגוֹהִי פַּחַת יְהוּד. עַבְדָיךְ יְדַנְיָה וּכְנָוָתֵהּ כָּהֲנַיָּא זִי בְּיֵב בִּירְתָא.
שְׁלָם מָרְאַן אֱלָה שְׁמַיָּא יִשְׁאַל שַׂגִּיא בְּכָל עִדָּן וּלְרַחֲמִן יְשִׂימִנָּךְ קֳדָם דָּרְיָוֶהוּשׁ מַלְכָּא
וּבְנֵי בִיתָא יַתִּיר מִן זִי כְּעַן חַד חַד אֲלַף. וְחַיִּן אֲרִיכִן יִנְתֶּן לָךְ וַחֲדֵה וְשָׁרִיר הֲוִי
בְּכָל עִדָּן.

To our master Bagohi, governor of Judah. Your servants Yedaniah and his colleagues, the priests who are in Yeb, the fortress: May the God of heaven seek our master's peace abundantly at every time, and may He give you compassion before King Darius and the members of (his) household, a thousand times more than now. And may He give you long life and may (you) be happy and prosperous at all times.

Pp. 178–79 (lines 4–13)

כְּעַן עַבְדָךְ יְדַנְיָה וּכְנָוָתֵהּ כֵּן אָמְרִן: בְּיֶרַח תַּמּוּז שְׁנַת 14 דָּרְיָוֶהוּשׁ מַלְכָּא כְּזִי אַרְשָׁם
נְפַק וַאֲזַל עַל מַלְכָּא כֻּמְרַיָּא זִי אֱלָהָא חְנוּב זִי בְּיֵב בִּירְתָא הַמוּנִית עִם וִידְרַנְג
זִי פְּרָתְרָךְ תְּנָה הֲוָה: לָם אֲגוּרָא זִי יְהוּ אֱלָהָא זִי בְּיֵב בִּירְתָא יְהַעְדּוּ מִן תַּמָּה.
אַחַר וִידְרַנְג זֶךְ לַחְיָא אִגֶּרֶת שְׁלַח עַל נְפָיִן בְּרֵהּ זִי רַבְחַיִל הֲוָה בְּסָוָן בִּירְתָא לֵאמַר:
אֲגוּרָא זִי בְּיֵב בִּירְתָא יְנְדְּשׁוּ. אַחַר נְפָיִן דְּבַר מִצְרָיֵא עִם חַיְלָא אָחֳרָנָן אֲתוֹ לְבִירַת
יֵב עִם תְּלֵיהֹם עַלּוּ בַּאֲגוּרָא זֶךְ נְדְשׁוּהִי עַד אַרְעָא וְעַמּוּדַיָּא זִי אַבְנָא זִי הֲווֹ תַּמָּה
תְּבַרוּ הִמּוֹ. אַף הֲוָה תַרְעֵן זִי אֶבֶן 5 בְּנָיִן פְּסִילָה זִי אֶבֶן זִי הֲווֹ בַּאֲגוּרָא זֶךְ נְדַשׁוּ
וְדַשֵׁיהֹם קַיְמָן וְצִירֵיהֹם זִי דַשַּׁיָּא אִלֵּךְ נְחָשׁ וּמַטְלַל עֲקָהֶן זִי אֶרֶז כֹּלָּא זִי עִם שֵׁירִית
אַשַׁרְנָא וְאָחֳרָן זִי תַּמָּה הֲוָה כֹּלָּא בְּאֶשָּׁה שְׂרָפוּ. וּמִזְרָקַיָּא זִי זַהֲבָא וּכְסַף וּמִנְדַּעַמְתָּא
זִי הֲוָה בַּאֲגוּרָא זֶךְ כֹּלָּא לְקַחוּ וּלְנַפְשְׁהוֹם עֲבַדוּ.

Now your servant Yedaniah and his colleagues say thus: In the month of Tammuz, year 14 of King Darius, when Arsham went out and came to the king, the priests of the god Khnub, the god who is in Yeb the fortress, were in agreement with Vidranga, who is the commander here. "Surely, they will remove the temple of YHW, the God which is in Yeb the fortress, from there." After that, the evil Vidranga sent a letter to Naphaina, his son, who is military chief in Syene, the fortress, saying, "They will destroy the temple which is in Yeb, the fortress." After Naphaina led the Egyptians with the other forces, they came to the fortress of Yeb with their weapons. They entered that temple, destroyed it to the ground, and smashed its stone pillars which were there. Also, there were five stone gates, built out of cut stone, which were in that temple—they destroyed; and their standing doors and the copper pivots of those doors, and their wooden roof which was entirely of cedar with the rest of the beams and the other things which were there they burned entirely with fire. And the gold and silver basins and anything which was in that temple—all of it they took and made it for themselves.

P. 180 (lines 13–17)

וּמִן יוֹמֵי מֶלֶךְ מִצְרַיִן אֲבָהִין בְּנוֹ אֲגוּרָא זֵךְ בְּיֵב בִּירְתָא. וּכְזִי כַּנְבּוּזִי עַל לְמִצְרַיִן אֲגוּרָא זֵךְ בְּנֵה הַשְׁכַּחַה. וַאֲגוּרֵי אֱלָהֵי מִצְרַיִן כָּל מְגָרוּ וְאִישׁ מִנְדַּעַם בַּאֲגוּרָא זֵךְ לָא חַבֵּל וּכְזִי כּוֹנָה עֲבִיד אֲנַחְנָה עִם נְשִׁין וּבְנִין שַׂקְקָן לָבְשִׁן הֲוֵין וְצָיְמִין וּמְצַלַּין לִיהוּ מָרֵא שְׁמַיָּא זִי הַחֲוִין בְּוִידְרַנְג זֵךְ. כַּלְבַּיָּא הַנְפִּקוּ כְּבָלָא מִן רַגְלוֹהִי וְכָל נִכְסִין זִי קְנָה אֲבַדוּ וְכָל גֻּבְרִין זִי בְעוֹ בְּאִישׁ לַאֲגוּרָא זֵךְ כָּל קְטִילוּ וַחֲזַיִן בְּהוֹם.

And from the days of the king of Egypt, our ancestors had built that temple in Yeb, the fortress. And when Cambyses entered Egypt, he found that temple built. And they overthrew all the temples of the Egyptian gods, but no one destroyed anything in that temple. And when this was done, we were wearing sack-cloth and with our wives and children fasting and praying to YHW, the Lord of Heaven, who let us see (vengeance upon) that Vidranga. The dogs removed the chain from his feet, and all the property which he had bought was lost, and all the men who sought evil for that temple were all killed, and we saw them.

P. 181–82 (lines 17–22)

אַף קַדְמַת זְנָה בְּעִדָּן זִי זָא בְּאִישְׁתָּא עֲבִיד לַן אִגְּרָה שְׁלַחֲןְ עַל מָרְאַן וְעַל יְהוֹחָנָן כָּהֲנָא רַבָּא וּכְנָוָתֵהּ כָּהֲנַיָּא זִי בִּירוּשְׁלֶם וְעַל אוֹסְתָּן אֲחוּהִי זִי עֲנָנִי וְחֹרֵי יְהוּדָיֵא. אִגְּרָא חֲדָה לָא שְׁלַחוּ עֲלַיְן. אַף מִן יְרַח תַּמּוּז שְׁנַת 14 דָּרְיַהוֹשׁ מַלְכָּא וְעַד זְנָה יוֹמָא אֲנַחְנָה שַׂקְקִן לָבְשִׁן וְצָיְמִין. נְשַׁיָּא זִילַן כְּאַרְמְלָה עֲבִידָן. מְשַׁח לָא מָשְׁחִין וַחֲמַר לָא שָׁתַיִן. אַף מִן זָכִי וְעַד יוֹם שְׁנַת 17 דָּרְיַהוֹשׁ מַלְכָּא מִנְחָה וּלְבוֹנָה וַעֲלָוָה לָא עֲבַדוּ בַּאֲגוּרָא זֵךְ.

Even before this, at the time that this evil was done to us, we sent a letter to our master and to Yehohanan, the high priest, and his colleagues, the priests who are in Jerusalem, and to Ostanes, Anani's brother, and the Judean nobles. They did not send us a single letter. Even from the month of Tammuz in the 14th year of King Darius and to this day we wear sackcloth and fast. Our wives are made like widows; we do not anoint (with) oil and do not drink wine. Even from that (time) and to the day of King Darius' 17th year they have not made a grain offering or incense or burnt offering in that temple.

P. 182–83 (lines 22–30)

כְּעַן עַבְדָּיְךָ יְדַנְיָה וּכְנָוָתֵהּ וִיהוּדָיֵא כָּל בַּעֲלֵי יֵב כֵּן אָמְרִין. הֵן עַל מָרְאַן טָב אִתְעֲשֵׁת עַל אֲגוּרָא זֵךְ לְמִבְנֵה בְּוִי לָא שָׁבְקִן לַן לְמִבְנְיֵהּ. חֲזִי בַּעֲלֵי טָבָתָךְ וְרַחֲמָיךָ זִי תְּנָה בְּמִצְרָיִן. אִגְּרָה מִנָּךְ יִשְׁתְּלַח עֲלֵיהוֹם עַל אֲגוּרָא זִי יְהוּ אֱלָהָא לְמִבְנְיֵהּ בְּיֵב בִּירְתָּא לָקֳבֵל זִי בְּנֵה הֲוָה קַדְמִין. וּמִנְחָתָא וּלְבוֹנְתָּא וַעֲלָוָתָא יְקַרְבוּן עַל מַדְבְּחָא זִי יְהוּ אֱלָהָא בְּשְׁמָךְ וּנְצַלֵּה עֲלַיְךָ בְּכָל עִדָּן אֲנַחְנָה וּנְשִׁין וּבְנִין וִיהוּדָיֵא כָּל זִי תְּנָה. הֵן כֵּן עֲבַדוּ עַד זִי אֲגוּרָא זֵךְ יִתְבְּנֵה וּצְדָקָה יֶהֱוֵה לָךְ קֳדָם יְהוּ אֱלָהּ שְׁמַיָּא מִן גְּבַר זִי יְקַרְב לֵהּ עֲלָוָה וְדִבְחָן דְּמִן כְּדְמֵי כְּסַף כִּנְכְּרִין אֶלֶף וְעַל זְהַב. עַל זְנָה שְׁלַחְןְ הוֹדַעְןָ. אַף כֹּלָּא מִלַּיָּא בְּאִגְּרָה חֲדָה שְׁלַחְןְ בִּשְׁמַן עַל דְּלָיָה וְשֶׁלֶמְיָה בְּנֵי סַנְאַבַלַּט פַּחַת שָׁמְרָיִן. אַף בְּזְנָה זִי עֲבִיד לַן כֹּלָּא אַרְשָׁם לָא יְדַע בְּ־20 לְמַרְחֶשְׁוָן שְׁנַת 17 דָּרְיַהוֹשׁ מַלְכָּא.

Now your servants, Yedaniah and his colleagues and the Judeans, all citizens of Yeb, say thus: "If it is good to our master, take thought to build that temple, since they do not let us build it. See to your well-wishers and your friends who are here in Egypt. Let a letter be sent to them from you concerning this temple of YHW, the God—to build it in Yeb, the fortress, as it was built before. And they will offer grain offerings and incense and burnt offerings on the altar of YHW, the God, in your name; and we will pray for you at all times—we and our wives and our children and the Judeans, everyone who is here. If they do this until that temple is built, there will be merit for you before YHW, the God of Heaven, more than for a person who offers Him a burnt offering and sacrifices whose price is 1000 silver coins and gold. Concerning this we sent, we informed. We also sent all the words in a letter in our name to Delaiah and Shelemiah, the sons of Sanballat, governor of Samaria. Also, Arsham did not know about this which was done to us at all. On the 20th of Marheshvan, the 17th year of King Darius.

P. 184

שִׁמְעוֹן לִיהוּדָה בַּר מְנַשֶּׁה לִקְרָיַת עַרְבָּיָה: שְׁלַחֵת לָךְ תְּרֵי חֲמָרִין דִּי תִּשְׁלַח עִמְּהֹן
תְּרֵי גֻבְרִין לְוָת יְהוֹנָתָן בַּר בַּעְיָן וּלְוָת מַסַבְּלָה דִּי יַעַמְרָן וְיִשְׁלְחָן לְמַחֲנֵיה לְוָתָךְ
לְלָבִין וְאֶתְרֹגִין. וְאַתְּ שְׁלַח אָחֲרָנִין מִלְוָתָךְ וְיַמְטוֹן לָךְ הֲדַסִּין וְעֲרָבִין. וְתַקֵּן יָתְהֹן
וּשְׁלַח יָתְהֹן לְמַחֲנֵיה הוּא שְׁלָם.

Pp. 184–85

Simon to Judah, son of Manasseh, of Kiryat Arbaya. I sent you two donkeys with which you will send two men—Jonathan, son of Ba'yan, and Masabala—who will load (them). And they will send palms and citrons to his camp, to you. And you—send others from you, and they will bring the myrtle and willow (branch) to you. And prepare them and send them to his camp. Peace!

Chapter 30
P. 186 (19:14–17)

וְחַלְמֵת אֲנָה אַבְרָם חֵלֶם בְּלֵילְיָה מֵעָלִי לְאַרַע מִצְרָיִן. וַחֲזֵית בְּחֶלְמִי וְהָא אֶרֶז חַד
וְתַמְרָא חֲדָא יָאְיָא שַׂגִּיא. וּבְנֵי אֱנוֹשׁ אֲתוֹ וּבְעוֹן לְמִקַץ וּלְמֶעְקַר לְאַרְזָא וּלְמִשְׁבּוּק
תַּמְרְתָא בִּלְחוֹדֵיהָ. וְאַכְלִיאַת תַּמְרְתָא וְאָמְרַת אַל תִּקוֹצוּ לְאַרְזָא אֲרֵי תְּרֵינָא
מִן שַׁרְבָּא חֲדָא. וּשְׁבִיק אַרְזָא בְּטַלַל תַּמְרְתָא וְלָא אִתְקְץ.

Pp. 186–87

And I, Abram, dreamed a dream on the night of my entering into the land of Egypt. And in my dream I saw, and behold a cedar and a very lovely palm.

And people (lit. sons of men) came and sought to cut down and uproot the
cedar and to leave the palm alone. But the palm tree protested and said, "Do
not cut down the cedar, the two of us are from one family." So the cedar was
left in the shadow (i.e. with the help) of the palm tree and not cut down.

P. 188 (20:2–8)

כְּמָה נְצִיחַ וְשַׁפִּיר לַהּ צֶלֶם צַלֶם לַהּ אַנְפֵּיהָא . . . וּכְמָא רְקִיק לַהּ שְׂעַר רֵאישַׁהּ כְּמָא יָאֵין לְהֵין
לַהּ עֵינֵיהָא וּמָא רַגֵּג הוּא לַהּ אַנְפְּהָא וְכֹל נֵץ אַנְפֵּיהָא . . . כְּמָא יָאֵא לַהּ חֲדִיהּ וּכְמָא
שַׁפִּיר לַהּ כֹּל לְבֶנְהָא דְּרָעֵיהָא מָא שַׁפִּירָן וִידֵיהָא כְּמָא כְּלִילָן וַחֲמִיד כֹּל מַחְזֵה
יְדֵיהָא כְּמָא יָאֵין כַּפֵּיה וּמָא אֲרִיכָן וּקְטִינָן כֹּל אֶצְבְּעָת יְדֵיהָא. רַגְלֵיהָא כְּמָא
שַׁפִּירָן וּכְמָא שְׁלָמָא לְהֵן לַהּ שָׁקֵיהָא. וְכָל בְּתוּלָן וְכַלָּאן דִּי יַעֲלָן לְגַנּוּן לָא יִשְׁפְּרָן
מִנָּהָא. וְעַל כֹּל נָשִׁין שׁוּפְּר שַׁפְּרָה וְעֶלְיָא שַׁפְרָהָא לְעֵלָּא מִן כּוֹלְהֵן וְעִם כֹּל
שֻׁפְרָא דֵּן חָכְמָה שַׂגִּיא עִמָּהָא וְדִלְיְדֵיהָא יָאָא.

Pp. 188–89

How splendid and beautiful the form of her face, and how soft the hair of her
head. How lovely are her eyes, and how pleasant is her nose and all the radiance of her face. How lovely are her breasts, and how beautiful all her white-
ness. Her arms, how beautiful, and her hands, how perfect; how attactive all
the appearance of her hands. How lovely her hands (palms), and how long and
delicate all the fingers of her hands. Her feet, how beautiful, and how perfect
her legs. And no virgins nor brides who go into the bridal chamber are more
beautiful than she. And her beauty is more beautiful than all women; her beauty is above all of theirs. And with all this beauty she has great wisdom. And
everything she has is lovely.

P. 189 (20:8–11)

וּכְדִי שְׁמַע מַלְכָּא מִלֵּי חִרְקָנוֹשׁ וּמִלֵּי תְּרֵין חַבְרוֹהִי דִּי בְּפֻם חַד תְּלָתְהוֹן מְמַלְּלִין שַׂגִּי
רַחֲמָהּ וּשְׁלַח לְעוֹבַע דְּבָרְהָא וְחֶזְיָהָא וְאִתְמַהּ עַל כֹּל שַׁפְרָהָא וּנְסַבְהָא לַהּ לְאִנְתָּא
וּבְעָא לְמִקְטַלְנִי וְאָמְרַת שָׂרֵי לְמַלְכָּא דְּאָחִי הוּא כְּדִי הֲוֵית מִתְגַּר עַל דִּילָהָא.
וּשְׁבִיקֵת אֲנָה אַבְרָם בְּדִילָהָא וְלָא קְטִילֵת. וּבְכֵית אֲנָה אַבְרָם בְּכִי תַּקִּיף אֲנָה וְלוֹט
בַּר אָחִי עִמִּי בְּלֵילְיָא כְּדִי דְּבִירַת מִנִּי שָׂרֵי בְּאוֹנֶס.

Pp. 189–90

And when the king heard the words of Hirkenos and the words of his two com-
rades, since the three of them spoke in harmony (lit. with one mouth), he loved
her and sent in haste. He led her away and saw her and was surprised at all her

beauty. So he took her for his wife and sought to kill me, but Sarai said to the king, "He is my brother," that I benefit on her account. So I, Abraham, was left (alone) on her account and not killed. And I, Abram, cried powerfully—I and Lot, my brother's son with me—on the night when Sarai was led away from me by force.

Chapter 31
P. 191

תֶּרַח עוֹבֵד צְלָמִים הֲוָה. חַד זְמַן נְפַק לַאֲתַר הוֹשִׁיב אַבְרָהָם מוֹכֵר תַּחְתָּיו. הֲוָה אָתֵי בַּר נָשׁ בָּעֵי דְּיִזְבּוּן. אֲמַר לֵיהּ: בַּר כְּמָה שְׁנִין אַתְּ? אֲמַר לֵיהּ: בַּר חַמְשִׁין. אֲמַר לֵיהּ: וַוי לְהָהוּא גַּבְרָא דְּאַתְּ בַּר חַמְשִׁין וְתִסְגּוֹד לְבַר יוֹמָא. וַהֲוָה מִתְבַּיֵּישׁ וְהוֹלֵךְ לוֹ.

Pp. 191–92

Terah was a statue maker. One time he went out someplace, placing Abraham as a seller in his place. A person came wanting to buy. [Abraham] said to him, "How old are you?" [The buyer] said to him, "Fifty years old." [Abraham] said to him, "Woe to that man, for you are fifty years old and you bow down to a one day old!" And [the buyer] was embarrassed and walked on.

P. 192

חַד זְמַן אֲתָת אִיתְּתָא טְעִינָא חַד פִּינָךְ דְּסֹלֶת. אָמְרַת לֵיהּ: הָא לָךְ קָרֵב קֳדָמֵיהוֹן. קָם נָסִיב בּוּקְלָסָה וּתְבַרְהוֹן וִיהַב בּוּקְלָסָה בִּידוֹי דְּרַבָּה דִּבְהוֹן. כֵּיוָן דַּאֲתָא אֲבוּהּ אֲמַר לֵיהּ: מַה עֲבַד לְהוֹן כָּדֵין? אֲמַר לֵיהּ: מָה נְכַפּוֹר לָךְ? אֲתָת חֲדָא אִיתְּתָא טְעִינָא חַד פִּינָךְ דְּסֹלֶת וְאָמְרַת לִי: קָרֵב קֳדָמֵיהוֹן. דֵּין אֲמַר: אֲנָא אֵכֵיל קַדְמָאי וְדֵין אֲמַר: אֲנָא אֵכֵיל קַדְמָאי. קָם הָדֵין רַבָּה נָסִיב בּוּקְלָסָה וּתְבַרְהוֹן. אֲמַר לֵיהּ: מָה אַתְּ מַפְלֵה בִּי יָדְעִין אִינּוּן. אֲמַר לֵיהּ: וְלָא יִשְׁמְעוּ אָזְנָיךְ מִפִּיךְ.

Pp. 192–93

One time a woman came carrying a plate of flour. She said to him, "Behold, sacrifice before them [the statues]." He rose, took a club and broke them and gave (i.e. put) that club in the hands of the largest of them. When his father came, [the father] said to him, "Why did you do this to them?" [Abraham] said to him, "How can I deny to you? A woman came carrying a plate of flour, and she said to me, 'Sacrifice [it] before them.' This [statue] said, 'I will eat first,' and that one [statue] said, 'I will eat first.' This big one rose, took the club, and broke them [the other statues]." [His father] said to him, "Why are you trick-

ing me? Do these [statues] know?" [Abraham] said to him, "Would your ears
not listen to your mouth?"

P. 194

נְסָתֵיהּ וּמְסָרְתֵיהּ לְנִמְרוֹד. אֲמַר לֵיהּ: נִסְגּוֹד לְנוּרָא. אֲמַר לֵיהּ: נִסְגּוֹד לְמַיָּא
דְמַטְפִין לְנוּרָא. אֲמַר לֵיהּ: וְנִסְגּוֹד לְמַיָּא. אֲמַר לֵיהּ: נִסְגּוֹד לַעֲנָנֵי דְּטָעֲנֵי מַיָּא.
אֲמַר לֵיהּ: וְנִסְגּוֹד לַעֲנָנָא. אֲמַר לֵיהּ: נִסְגּוֹד לְרוּחָא דְּמוֹבְלֵי עֲנָנָא. אֲמַר לֵיהּ:
וְנִסְגּוֹד לְרוּחָא. אֲמַר לֵיהּ: נִסְגּוֹד לְבַר נָשָׁא דְּסָבֵיל רוּחָא. אֲמַר לֵיהּ: מִלִּין אַתְּ
מִשְׁתָּעֵי. לָא נִסְגּוֹד אֶלָּא לְאוֹר. הֲרֵינִי מַשְׁלִיכְךָ בּוֹ וְיָבוֹא אֱלֹהֶיךָ שֶׁאַתָּה מִשְׁתַּחֲוֶה
לוֹ וְיַצִּילְךָ מִמֶּנּוּ.

He lifted him and delivered him to Nimrod. [Nimrod] said to [Abraham], "Let
us bow down to the fire." [Abraham] said to him, "Let us bow down to the
water that extinguishes the fire." [Nimrod] said to him, "So let us bow down
to the water." [Abraham] said to him, "Let us bow down to the clouds that
carry the water." [Nimrod] said to him, "So we will bow down to the cloud."
[Abraham] said to him, "Let us bow down to the wind that brings the cloud."
[Nimrod] said to him, "So we will bow down to the wind." [Abraham] said to
him, "Let us bow down to the person who endures [i.e. withstands] the wind."
[Nimrod] said to him, "You are talking words [i.e. nonsense]. We will only
bow down to the flame. Behold, I am throwing you into it. So let your God, to
whom you prostrate yourself, come and save you from it."

P. 195

הֲוָה תַּמָּן הָרָן קָאֵים פְּלִיג. אֲמַר: מַה נַּפְשָׁךְ? אִם נָצַח אַבְרָם אֲנָא אֲמַר מִן דְּאַבְרָם
אֲנָא אִם נָצַח נִמְרוֹד אֲמַר אֲנָא מִנִּמְרוֹד אֲנָא. כֵּיוָן שֶׁיָּרַד אַבְרָם לְכִבְשַׁן הָאֵשׁ וְנוּצַל
אָמְרִין לֵיהּ מִן דְּמַן אַתְּ? אֲמַר לֵיהּ: מִן דְּאַבְרָם. נְטָלוּהוּ וְהִשְׁלִיכוּהוּ בָּאֵשׁ וְנֶחְמְרוּ
מֵעָיו וְיָצָא וָמֵת עַל פְּנֵי אָבִיו. הֲדָא הוּא דִכְתִיב וַיָּמָת הָרָן עַל פְּנֵי תֶּרַח אָבִיו.

Haran was standing there, divided [i.e. uncertain]. He said, "What is your will?
If Abram wins, I will say I am with Abram; if Nimrod wins, I will say I am
with Nimrod." When Abram went down into the furnace of fire and was saved,
they said to him [Haran], "Whose side are you on (lit. whose are you)?" He
said to them, "Abram's." They lifted him and threw him into the fire, and his
belly was parched, and he came out and died in front of his father. This is what
is written: "And Haran died עַל פְּנֵי [i.e. on account of] Terah, his father."

Chapter 32
P. 198

וַהֲוָה בָּתַר פִּתְגָמַיָּא הָאִלֵּין מִן דְּיִנְצוֹ יִצְחָק וְיִשְׁמָעֵאל. יִשְׁמָעֵאל הֲוָה אָמַר: לִי חֲמֵי לְמִירוֹת יָת אַבָּא דַּאֲנָא בְּרֵיה בּוּכְרַיָּא. וְיִצְחָק הֲוָה אָמַר: לִי חֲמֵי לְמִירוֹת יָת אַבָּא דַּאֲנָא בַר שָׂרָה אִינְתְּתֵיה וְאַנְתְּ בַּר הָגָר אַמְתָא דְאִימִּי. עֲנֵי יִשְׁמָעֵאל וְאָמַר: אֲנָא זְכָאִי יַתִּיר מִינָךְ דַּאֲנָא אִיתְגְּזָרִית לִתְלֵיסְרֵי שְׁנִין וְאִין הֲוָה צְבוּתִי לִמְעַכְּבָא לָא הֲוֵינָא מָסַר נַפְשִׁי לְאִתְגְּזָרָא. וְאַנְתְּ אִתְגְּזַרְתְּ בַּר תְּמַנְיָא יוֹמִין אִילּוּ הֲוָה בָּךְ מַנְדְּעָא דִילְמָא לָא הֲוֵיתְ מָסַר נַפְשָׁךְ לְאִתְגְּזָרָא. מָתִיב יִצְחָק וְאָמַר: הָאֲנָא בַר תְּלָתִין וּשְׁבַע שְׁנִין וְאִילּוּ בָּעֵי קוּדְשָׁא בְּרִיךְ הוּא לְכוּלֵי אִיבָרַיי לָא הֲוֵיתִי מְעַכֵּב. מִן יַד אִישְׁתְּמַעוּ פִּתְגָמַיָּא הָאִלֵּין קֳדָם מָרֵי עָלְמָא וּמִן יַד מֵימְרָא דַיָי נַסֵּי יָת אַבְרָהָם וְאָמַר לֵיה: אַבְרָהָם.

Pp. 198–99

(1) It happened after these words, after Isaac and Ishmael quarreled, Ishmael said, "It is fitting for me to inherit father, since I am his senior son," and Isaac said, "It is fitting for me to inherit father, since I am the son of Sarah his wife and you are the son of Hagar, my mother's handmaid." Ishmael answered and said, "I am more worthy than you, since I was cut (i.e. circumcised) at thirteen years; and if it had been my wish to refuse, I could have not delivered myself to be circumcised. But you were circumcised at eight days; if you had knowledge, perhaps you would not have delivered yourself to be circumcised." Isaac answered and said, "Behold, today I am thirty-seven years old, and if the Holy One, blessed be He, sought all my limbs, I would not refuse." Immediately after these words were heard before the Master of the Universe, "the Word of the Lᴏʀᴅ tested Abraham and said to him, 'Abraham.'"

P. 200

וְאָמַר לֵיה: הָאֲנָא. (2) וְאָמַר: דְּבַר כְּדוֹן יָת בְּרָךְ יָת יְחִידָךְ דְּאַתְּ רָחֵים יָת יִצְחָק וְאִיזֵל לָךְ לַאֲרַע פּוּלְחָנָא וְאַסֵּיקֵהִי תַּמָּן לַעֲלָתָא עַל חַד מִן טַוּוֹרַיָּיא דְּאֵימַר לָךְ. (3) וְאַקְדֵּים אַבְרָהָם בְּצַפְרָא וְזָרֵיז יָת חַמְרֵיה וּדְבַר יָת תְּרֵין טַלְיָיוֹי יָת אֱלִיעֶזֶר וְיָת יִשְׁמָעֵאל עִמֵּיה וְיָת יִצְחָק בְּרֵיה וְקַטַּע קֵיסִין דְּזֵיתָא וּתְאֵנָתָא וְדִיקְלָא דַּחֲזַיִין לַעֲלָתָא וְקָם וַאֲזַל לְאַתְרָא דַּאֲמַר לֵיה יְיָ. (4) בְּיוֹמָא תְּלִיתָאָה וּזְקַף אַבְרָהָם יָת עֵינוֹי וַחֲמָא עֲנַן אִיקָרָא קָטִיר עַל טַוּוֹרָא וְאִשְׁתְּמוֹדְעֵיה מִן רָחִיק (5) וְאָמַר אַבְרָהָם לְעוּלֵימוֹי: אוֹרֵיכָן לְכוֹן הָכָא עִם חַמְרָא וַאֲנָא וְעוּלֵימָא נִתְמְטֵי עַד כָּא לְבְחוֹנֵי אִין יִתְקַיַּים מַה דְּאִתְבַּשַּׂרִית כְּדֵין יְהוֹן בְּנָךְ וְנִסְגּוּד לְמָרֵי עָלְמָא וּנְתוּב לְוָותְכוֹן. (6) וּנְסֵיב אַבְרָהָם יָת קֵיסֵי דַּעֲלָתָא וְשַׁוֵּי עִילֵוִי יִצְחָק בְּרֵיה וּנְסֵיב בִּידֵיה

יָת אִישָׁתָא וְיָת סַכִּינָא וַאֲזַלוּ תַּרְוֵיהוֹם כַּחֲדָא. (7) וַאֲמַר יִצְחָק לְאַבְרָהָם אֲבוּי

וַאֲמַר: אַבָּא. וַאֲמַר: הָאֲנָא. וַאֲמַר: הָא אִישָׁתָא וְקֵיסִין וְהָאן אִימְּרָא לַעֲלָתָא?

(8) וַאֲמַר אַבְרָהָם: יְיָ יִבְחַר לֵיה אִימְּרָא לַעֲלָתָא בְּרִי: וַאֲזַלוּ תַּרְוֵיהוֹם בְּלֵב שְׁלִים כְּחַד.

Pp. 200–201

And he said to him, "Behold!" (2) And he said, "Now, take your son, your only one that you love, Isaac, and go to the land of worship and offer him up there as a burnt offering on one of the mountains which I will tell you." (3) And Abraham acted early in the morning, and he saddled his donkey and took his two young servants, Eliezer and Ishmael, with him and Isaac, his son. And he cut olive and fig and palm twigs which were fit for the offering, and arose and went to the place that the LORD said to him. (4) On the third day, Abraham lifted his eyes and saw the cloud of glory rising over the mountain, and he recognized it from afar. (5) And Abraham said to his youths, "You wait here with the donkey, and I and the youth will proceed hither to examine if what has been announced—"thus will be your son"—will be fulfilled; and we will bow down to the Master of the Universe and return to you. (6) And Abraham took twigs for the burnt offering and placed it on Isaac, his son, and he took the fire and the knife in his hand, and the two of them went together. (7) And Isaac said to Abraham, his father, "Father"; and he said, "Behold." And he said, "Here is the fire and twigs, but where is the lamb for the burnt offering?" (8) And Abraham said, "The LORD will choose the lamb for the burn offering for Himself, my son;" and the two of them went with a perfect heart (i.e. in complete harmony).

P. 202

(9) וַאֲתוֹ לְאַתְרָא דַּאֲמַר לֵיה יְיָ וּבְנָא תַמָּן אַבְרָהָם יָת מַדְבְּחָא דִּבְנָא אָדָם

וְאִיתְפְּכַר בְּמוֹי דְּטוֹבְעָנָא וְתָב נֹחַ וּבְנָיֵיה וְאִיתְפְּכַר בְּדָרָא דִּפְלוּגְתָּא וְסַדַּר עֲלוֹי יָת

קֵיסַיָּא וְכַפֵּת יָת יִצְחָק בְּרֵיה וְשַׁוִּי יָתֵיה עַל מַדְבְּחָא לְעֵיל מִן קֵיסִין. (10) וּפְשַׁט

אַבְרָהָם יָת יְדֵיה וּנְסִיבַת סַכִּינָא לְמִיכַּס יָת בְּרֵיה. עֲנֵי וַאֲמַר יִצְחָק לְאַבוֹי: כַּפֵּת יָתִי

יָאוּת דְּלָא נְפַרְכֵּס מִן צַעֲרָא דְּנַפְשִׁי וְנִדְחֵי לְגוֹבָא דְּחַבָּלָא וְיִשְׁתְּכַח פְּסוּלָא בְּקוּרְבָּנָךְ.

עַיְינוֹי דְּאַבְרָהָם מִסְתַּכְּלָן בְּעֵינוֹי דְּיִצְחָק וְעַיְינוֹי דְּיִצְחָק מִסְתַּכְּלָן לְמַלְאֲכֵי מְרוֹמָא.

יִצְחָק הֲוָה חָמֵי יָתְהוֹם וְאַבְרָהָם לָא חָמֵי יָתְהוֹם. עָנַיִין מַלְאֲכֵי מְרוֹמָא: אִיתוֹן חֲמוֹן

תְּרֵין יְחִידָאִין דְּאִית בְּעָלְמָא חַד נָכֵיס וְחַד מִתְנְכֵיס. דְּנָכֵיס לָא מְעַכֵּב וּדְמִתְנְכֵיס

פָּשֵׁיט צַוְורֵיה. (11) וּקְרָא לֵיה מַלְאֲכָא דַּיְיָ מִן שְׁמַיָּא וַאֲמַר לֵיה: אַבְרָהָם אַבְרָהָם.

וַאֲמַר: הָאֲנָא (12) וַאֲמַר: אַל תּוֹשִׁיט יְדָךְ לְטַלְיָיא וְלָא תַעֲבִיד לֵיה מִידַעַם בִּישׁ.

אֲרוּם כְּדוֹן גְּלֵי קֳדָמַי אֲרוּם דָּחֲלָא דַּיְיָ אַנְתְּ וְלָא עֲכִיבְתָּא יָת בְּרָךְ יָת יְחִידָךְ מִינִי.

(13) וּזְקַף אַבְרָהָם יָת עֵינוֹי וַחֲזָא וְהָא דִיכְרָא חַד דְּאִיתְבְּרִי בֵּינֵי שִׁימְשָׁתָא דְּשִׁכְלוּל עָלְמָא אֲחִיד בַּחֲרֵישׁוּתָא דְּאִילָנָא בְּקַרְנוֹי. וַאֲזַל אַבְרָהָם וּנְסִיב וְאַסִּיקֵהּ לַעֲלָתָא חוֹלַף בְּרֵיהּ.

Pp. 202–4

(9) And they came to the place that the Lord had said to him, and there Abraham (re)built the altar which Adam had built and had been destroyed in the waters of the flood, and Noah had returned and built it, but it was destroyed in the generation of the division. And he arranged the twigs on it and bound Isaac, his son, and placed him on the altar above the twigs. (10) And Abraham extended his hand and took the knife to slaughter his son. Isaac answered and said to his father, "Bind me well so that I will not struggle from my soul's pain and be thrust into the pit of destruction and a blemish be found in your sacrifice." Abraham's eyes were looking at Isaac's eyes, and Isaac's eyes were looking at the angels on high. Isaac saw them, but Abraham did not see them. The angels on high answered, "Come, see two unique ones in the world—one slaughters and one is slaughtered. The one that slaughters does not refuse, and the one that is being slaughtered extends his neck." (11) And the angel of the Lord called to him from heaven and said to him, "Abraham, Abraham." And he said, "Behold." (12) And he said, "Do not extend your hand to the youth, and do not do anything bad to him. Behold, now it is revealed before Me that, behold, you are a fearer of the Lord and have not refused your son, your only one, from Me." (13) And Abraham lifted his eyes, and he saw a ram, that had been created at twilight of the completion of the world, caught in the thicket of a tree by its horns. And Abraham went and took it and offered it as a burnt offering instead of his son.

Pp. 204–5

(14) וְאוֹדִי וְצַלִּי אַבְרָהָם תַּמָּן בְּאַתְרָא הַהוּא וַאֲמַר: בְּבָעוּ בְּרַחֲמִין מִן קֳדָמָךְ יְיָ גְּלֵי קֳדָמָךְ דְּלָא הֲוָה בְּלִבְּבִי עוּקְמָא וּבְעֵית לְמֶעְבַּד גְּזֵירָתָךְ בְּחֶדְוָוא. כְּדֵין כַּד יְהוֹן בְּנוֹי דְּיִצְחָק בְּרִי עֲלַיין לְשַׁעַת אֲנִיקֵי תֶּהֱוֵי מִדְּכַר לְהוֹם וַעֲנֵי יָתְהוֹם וּפָרִיק יָתְהוֹם. וַעֲתִידִין הִינּוּן כָּל דָּרַיָּא דְּקָיְמוּן לְמֶהֱוֵי אָמְרִין בְּטַוּוֹרָא הָדֵין: כְּפַת אַבְרָהָם יָת יִצְחָק בְּרֵיהּ וְתַמָּן אִיתְגְּלֵיית עֵילוֹי שְׁכִינְתָּא דַיְיָ. (15) וּקְרָא מַלְאָכָא דַיְיָ לְאַבְרָהָם תִּנְיָינוּת מִן שְׁמַיָּא (16) וַאֲמַר: בְּמֵימְרִי קַיֵּימִית אֲמַר יְיָ חוֹלַף דַּעֲבַדְתְּ יָת פִּיתְגָּמָא הָדֵין וְלָא מְנַעְתְּ יָת בְּרָךְ יָת יְחִידָךְ (17) אֲרוּם בָּרָכָא אֲבָרְכִינָךְ וְאַסְגָּא אַסְגֵּי יָת בְּנָךְ כְּכוֹכְבֵי שְׁמַיָּא וַהֲוֵי כְחָלָא דְּעַל כֵּיף יַמָּא. וְיִירְתוּן בְּנָךְ יָת קוֹרְיֵי שָׂנְאֵיהוֹן. (18)

וְיִתְבָּרְכוּן בְּגִין זַכְוָת בְּנָךְ כָּל עַמְמֵי אַרְעָא חוֹלַף דְּקַבֵּילְתָּא בְּמֵימְרִי. (19) וּדְבָרוּ
מַלְאֲכֵי מְרוֹמָא יָת יִצְחָק וְאוֹבְלוֹהִי לְבֵי מִדְרָשָׁא דְּשֵׁם רַבָּא וַהֲוָה תַּמָּן תְּלָת שְׁנִין.
וּבְהַהוּא יוֹמָא תָּב אַבְרָהָם לְוָת עוּלֵימוֹי וְקָמוּ וַאֲזַלוּ כְּחַדָא לְבֵירָא דְּשָׁבַע. וְיָתֵיב
אַבְרָהָם בְּבֵירָא דְּשָׁבַע. (20) וַהֲוָה בָּתַר פִּתְגָמַיָּא הָאִילֵּין מִן בָּתַר דִּיכַפֵת אַבְרָהָם
יָת יִצְחָק וַאֲזַל סָטָנָא וְתַנֵּי לְוָת שָׂרָה דְּאַבְרָהָם נְכַס יָת יִצְחָק. וְקָמַת שָׂרָה וּפְגֵנַת
וְאִשְׁתַּנְקַת וּמֵיתַת מִן אֲנִיקָא.

Pp. 204–6

(14) And Abraham thanked and prayed there in that place and said, "In a petition of compassion before You, O Lord, it is revealed before You that there was no trickery in my heart, and I sought to do Your decree with joy. Now when the descendants of Isaac, my son, enter into an hour of anguish, let it be remembered for them and answer them and save them. And all generations that are to be will be prepared to say, "Abraham bound Isaac, his son, on this mountain,

P. 205   and the Lord's presence was revealed to him there." (15) And the angel of the Lord called to Abraham a second time from heaven (16) and said, "By My word have I sworn, said the Lord, inasmuch as you did this thing and did not withhold your son, your only one, (17) behold, I will bless you very much and greatly multiply your son like the stars of heaven and like the sand that is on the shore of the sea. And your son will inherit the cities of those who hate them, (18) and all the people of the earth will be blessed on account of your son's merit, inasmuch as you accepted My word." (19) And the angels on high led Isaac and brought him to the school-house of Shem, the great, and he was there for three years. And on that day Abraham returned to his servants, and they rose and went together to Beersheba; and Abraham dwelt in Beersheba. (20) And after these things, after Abraham had bound Isaac, the Satan went and told Sarah that Abraham had slaughtered Isaac; and Sarah arose and cried out and choked and died of anguish.